PENGUIN BOOKS

THE KID

and The Kid Moves On

Kevin Lewis is married with two children and lives in Surrey. As well as his memoirs, *The Kid* and *The Kid Moves On*, Penguin publishes his hugely successful crime thrillers: *Kaitlyn, Frankie, Fallen Angel* and the soon to be published *Scent of a Killer*.

Praise for Kevin Lewis:

'Gripping, harrowing. A true triumph over tragedy. You may start Kevin Lewis's book in tears, but you will finish it exultant' *Mail on Sunday*

'Devastating. I can't think of a story that is more sad or a story that it feels more essential to go on reading' *Evening Standard*

'Harrowing, chilling . . . [with] passages of heartbreaking frankness. By the end, your heart is overwhelmed' *Daily Telegraph*

'Devastating . . . every parent must read' *Daily Mail*

'Incredible. A fantastic story' Fern Britton, *This Morning*

'A moving true story' *Heat*

THE KID
and
The Kid Moves On

KEVIN LEWIS

PENGUIN BOOKS

PENGUIN BOOKS

Published by the Penguin Group
Penguin Books Ltd, 80 Strand, London WC2R ORL, England
Penguin Group (USA) Inc., 375 Hudson Street, New York, New York 10014, USA
Penguin Group (Canada), 90 Eglinton Avenue East, Suite 700, Toronto, Ontario, Canada M4P 2Y3
(a division of Pearson Penguin Canada Inc.)
Penguin Ireland, 25 St Stephen's Green, Dublin 2, Ireland (a division of Penguin Books Ltd)
Penguin Group (Australia), 250 Camberwell Road,
Camberwell, Victoria 3124, Australia (a division of Pearson Australia Group Pty Ltd)
Penguin Books India Pvt Ltd, 11 Community Centre,
Panchsheel Park, New Delhi – 110 017, India
Penguin Group (NZ), 67 Apollo Drive, Rosedale, North Shore 0632, New Zealand
(a division of Pearson New Zealand Ltd)
Penguin Books (South Africa) (Pty) Ltd, 24 Sturdee Avenue,
Rosebank, Johannesburg 2196, South Africa
Penguin Books Ltd, Registered Offices: 80 Strand, London WC2R ORL, England

www.penguin.com

The Kid first published by Michael Joseph 2003
The Kid Moves On first published as *Moving On* by Michael Joseph 2005
This collected edition published in Penguin Books 2010

3

Copyright © Kevin Lewis, 2003 & 2005
Forewords copyright © Nick Moran and Ioan Gruffudd, 2010
All rights reserved

The moral right of the author has been asserted

Set in 11/14pt Garamond
Typeset by Palimpsest Book Production Limited, Grangemouth, Stirlingshire
Printed in England by Clays Ltd, St Ives plc

ISBN: 978–0–141–04859–8

www.greenpenguin.co.uk

To my dearest Jackie, my friend, my love, my life. x

Charlotte and Nathan, you are the
best kids a dad could ever have. x

Some of the names, places, and/or organizations in these works have been changed to protect the subjects' identities.

Contents

Contents

Foreword

by Nick Moran

The Kid, Kevin Lewis's brilliantly adapted screenplay based on his books The Kid *and* The Kid Moves On, *is now a major motion picture directed by Nick Moran.*

I came to *The Kid* in something of a back to front fashion. My first film, *Telstar*, had been extremely well received at the London Film Festival and I was approached by a producer to direct an adaptation of *The Kid* by Kevin Lewis, a book that I knew nothing of as I'd been living in LA at the time of the book's initial success.

I read an early screenplay of the book, met Kevin, who was not what I expected, and then finally read the book.

If only all novels came to you in this way because when I did eventually read the book I had a complete understanding of it, its origin and its true message.

You see, Kevin is not a particularly big man; he doesn't have a Sylvester Stallone thousand-yard stare or the distant intensity of a Roy Keane. He is simply a man aware of his problems and issues, who is open and honest about them at all times, and who wears his heart permanently on his sleeve.

And it is this transparent candour that powers the book. It is the book's heart and seems to me what made it so very popular, and poignant.

As we made the film and I fell into the purgatory of the editing suite, I would always fall back on the simple honesty of the story to re-focus the film's direction.

The strength of the book, and the reason it strikes a cord with all that read it, is the untold story, the part of Kevin's journey that has no narrative but is present in every paragraph. It is the story of someone who is unloved and struggles to over achieve in order to fill the hole that his past has left in him, until he makes the most basic of discoveries – in the words of Eden Ahbez, made famous by Nat King Cole – that 'The greatest gift you'll ever learn is to love and be loved in return.'

Nick Moran

Foreword

by Ioan Gruffudd

Ioan Gruffudd plays the part of Colin Smith, Kevin's beloved teacher and mentor in The Kid – *the film adaptation of* The Kid *and* The Kid Moves On.

About nine weeks ago my daughter Ella Betsi was born. As any parent will know, my life was changed in that instant. Before her arrival I dodged the platitudes, 'things will be *so* different when she's born . . . it changes everything . . . you won't even *remember* your old life . . .' I nodded politely, smiled a benign smile, but truth be told I didn't believe a word of it. It'll be me, I thought. A little more exhausted, perhaps, a little less free time, but I'll be the same person. Well . . . how wrong can a person be? Now it all makes sense. I suddenly understand, very clearly, what my own parents were going through all those years and tried valiantly (but unsuccessfully) to convey to me. It's not so much a physical change – you're still the same person, living in the same house, surrounded by the same things, going to work just as you were before – it's that all those trivial insecurities and anxieties disappear overnight. There's no room left any more for self-indulgent thought; my mind is full to the brim with my daughter. Her health, her happiness, her wants, her needs and yes – those same anxieties, now displaced: What if anything happened to her? What if she fell ill? What if she had an accident? But perhaps worst of all: *What if somebody did something to hurt her?*

What if somebody did something to hurt my child? The idea is unthinkable. Unspeakable. But it happens. For whatever reason,

Kevin Lewis was made to endure horrific abuse, mental and physical, from the people who should have been genetically programmed to take care of him, to love him and worship him, and protect him from harm. One of the most incredible personal triumphs I have ever encountered in this world is the fact that Kevin, from the depths of despair and futility, where life didn't seem worth living, somehow found the strength to claw his way back to live a happy and fulfilled (and most importantly *love*-filled) life.

I first met Kevin when I was asked to play the part of Colin Smith, Kevin's beloved teacher and mentor in his brilliantly adapted screenplay based on his books *The Kid* and *The Kid Moves On*. Colin became aware of the abuse that Kevin was suffering and persistently harassed an embarrassingly inept social service system until Kevin's circumstances were brought to light and he was eventually removed from his abusive home. I consider it one of the perks of my profession that sometimes I get to meet extraordinary people, and meeting Kevin, and then having him as a constant presence while we were filming, was a rare pleasure and a luxury, both as an artist and (more importantly) as a person. He was disarmingly open about his incredible story, and although I unfortunately didn't meet Colin, Kevin's account of him and their relationship was so vivid that I felt like I had.

Acting can be a ridiculously narcissistic business. I freely admit to a regular over-indulgent postmortem of my performance once the cameras have stopped rolling: 'Did I overdo the pathos? Should I have kept more back? Was I convincing enough?' But it didn't happen this time. I feel nothing but blessed to have been involved with this project, which has affected me so profoundly, and – I can only hope – will pave the way for more light being shed on other similar cases that tragically still occur.

I am so proud of my involvement in *The Kid* and would urge everyone to read Kevin Lewis's incredible story.

Ioan Gruffudd

The Kid

Contents

Preface

This book was originally written for my wife, Jackie. For many years I've kept my past to myself, ashamed of what happened, desperate to block it out of my memory, until I decided to explain my life to the one person I love more than anything else. I wanted her to understand who I am and what has happened to me in the past.

Once the book was written I decided to publish it in the hope that others would understand what it's like for a child to have no hope; to undergo years of physical and mental torture as well as suffering the constant ache of hunger. I hope I can give a little more insight into why some kids go so badly wrong, so that we can find ways to help them feel less frightened, abandoned and alone in the world.

It was when I was holding my baby son in my arms for the first time that I realized I had to do something about exorcizing the horrors that were locked inside my head. I had to clear them out in order to make sure he had the right start in life. It was a story that could not be allowed to fester in secrecy any longer.

Gazing down at his tiny, sleeping face was like looking at myself when I first arrived in the world. He seemed so vulnerable and helpless and I was desperate to make everything perfect for him, to give him the best start in life that any parent could, to make sure nothing from my past would ever rise up to damage him or make him unhappy. All the memories I'd dampened down and suppressed deep in my subconscious in order to survive began to smoulder and burn, making my eyes water and my chest constrict when I held him in my arms.

My son was our second child, and I had experienced similar fears before. I was so afraid when my daughter was born in 1995 that I would turn out to be a terrible father and would do her some harm. By that time I'd found out some of the secrets that had governed my own childhood and upbringing, and I had no way of knowing if the madness in my parents, which had made my own life a misery for so many years, might also be ticking inside my head, like a time bomb waiting to explode. Everything seemed so perfect in my new life, but it could so easily have gone horribly wrong again just because I didn't know if I would be a good parent. Sometimes I would lie in bed at night with my back to my wife, Jackie, and cry because of what had happened in the past and because I was so frightened the pattern might repeat itself. I still didn't dare to expose the whole story to Jackie or to the outside world. By the time my son came along, three years later, I felt brave enough to face the demons inside my head and to share them with the woman I love and the rest of the world.

I'm not the greatest person for talking about myself, or my feelings. I guess that's obvious since I haven't even been able to tell my own wife about my past, and she's always been kind enough not to ask. But I now believe I owe it to her to explain who I am and to describe some of the places that my early life took me to. I have never been able to tell her face-to-face because I've felt too ashamed, so I decided to put it down on paper instead.

The reason it makes a book, I believe, is because the life I was forced to lead for the first thirty years has been unusual as well as horrifying, and because it shows that it's possible to start with every childhood disadvantage, to travel right to the bottom of the barrel as a young man, so far down that you don't believe life is worth living any more, and still to climb back and achieve a happy and fulfilled life.

I believe readers will be shocked by the way in which a child can still be allowed to slip through the social net in modern Britain, vulnerable to predators and left believing they have no option but to turn to crime. I hope they will be uplifted by the way in which love came to my rescue and perseverance paid off. I'm not proud of everything I did in those early years, but I hope I can show how children like me are left with no other choice if they want to survive. All I wanted was to be given a chance to show what I could do. But so often the outside world is unforgiving of differences it doesn't understand. Children often behave very badly indeed, but there is always a reason, if people will just take the time and trouble to ask the right questions. Perhaps, once you've read my story, you'll have a better idea what questions should be asked and what help should be offered. I hope that you will come away as convinced as I am that small children should never, ever be beaten or abused by the people who are supposed to be their protectors.

1. The Pink Tin House

I was born on 8 September 1970, so this is not a story from the 'bad old days', this all happened at a time when British society was priding itself on becoming enlightened. We had the welfare state and child-protection laws and an army of well-meaning people dedicated to making it a fair world for children born at the bottom of the social heap. But still they couldn't save me from the fate that awaited me in my own home.

On my birth certificate it says we lived in Gypsy Hill, near Crystal Palace in South London, but I only remember living on 'The Horseshoe' – a curve of houses on King Henry's Drive in New Addington, near Croydon in Surrey – so we must have moved there when I was still too young to take in what was happening. It doesn't really matter where we were living because any house that our family occupied would soon have looked the same.

That strip of the South London suburbs was a bleak and culturally desolate area. There was row upon row of twentieth-century social housing provided for those who couldn't afford to live in the city, mixed in with street after street of dreary 'affordable' housing for those who aspired to a more genteel suburban existence. There was no cultural history for the community to feel any pride about, no sense of belonging. In New Addington there was nothing to soothe the eye or the soul. It was just a place where hundreds of thousands of people lived until they could afford to move to somewhere nicer. Many of the families, just like ours; were never going to be going anywhere, trapped in a spiral of poverty, debt and desperation.

King Henry's Drive was a long, busy, depressing road lined by row upon row of tin houses, with the Horseshoe in the middle and tower blocks at the end, and roads either side leading nowhere. The Horseshoe, as the name implies, was a curved side road allowing the houses to be set back from the main road around a large patch of grass. If a private company was building the Horseshoe today it would be called a 'crescent' and would be prettily landscaped with trees, but all we had to look at on the grass was a public phone box and the houses opposite. All the houses around it were built of corrugated tin and were owned by the council. I don't know if the architects who designed them intended these houses to last for more than a few decades, but they are still there today, although some of them have now been improved with new tiles on their roofs and wooden cladding on the outside walls. In the early seventies they were all still just tin boxes for living in, cost-effective places to put families in order to stop them ending up on the street.

Every house in the row was painted a different pastel colour, probably in the hope of lifting the spirits of those who had to live in them and giving the area some sort of character. Ours was pink on the outside, which belied the filth and misery that existed inside those flimsy walls. Behind the house was a garden, which backed on to the car park and playgrounds of Wolsey Junior School.

Some of the neighbours had managed to make their homes look quite nice, with well-tended front gardens, tubs and hanging baskets, decorative fences and pretty curtains at the windows. Their efforts to add colour and life to their houses merely drew attention to the lack of colour and life all around.

Anything like that would have been completely beyond the abilities or imaginations of Gloria and Dennis, my natural parents. Just existing was almost more than they could manage. Gloria never bothered to change out of her dressing gown unless she was leaving the house to cash her Giro and it never occurred to her that she should even clean her own house, let alone decorate it or improve it in any way. Even today I can't bring myself to call them mother and father. On the rare occasions when I'm talking to one of my brothers or sisters, I always refer to her as 'your mother'. Some wounds are just too deep to ever heal.

Gloria was a giant of a woman, over six feet tall and lean, with all the physical strength of someone constantly supercharged by a powerful bad temper. Dennis was physically strong and silent, whereas Gloria was loud – and she was violent. She never talked in a normal voice, only shouted. She was never calm, always angry. No one liked her, which made her angrier. The neighbours hated the way she was screaming at them one minute and scrounging from them the next; they hated how every other word that came from her mouth was an obscenity. It was a constant, ugly stream of the few most aggressive expletives the English language could supply, fired out by a jet of permanent spite. When she tried to be nice to people outside the family and make them her friends, which wasn't often, she was still too overpowering and they would shrink away from the onslaught of her personality.

Dennis was stocky and much shorter than her. He worked as a British Rail engineer, maintaining the tracks, one of those gangs of men you see sometimes from train windows, out in all weathers in their luminous jackets. He had jet-black hair and was naturally withdrawn. A life spent wandering the rail tracks, never having to deal with the public, must have suited him well. The passion of his life was the music of Elvis Presley. He was a desperately shy man, working every moment he could, sometimes out in the rain and snow or all through the night. But however many hours he put in, he could never make enough money to keep us at anything approaching a decent level. The pressure of it all seemed to be too much for him. The moment he got home from work he would shut himself in the kitchen with his tape machine, just playing Elvis

songs over and over again while he stood at the sink, silently drinking. The music must have provided him with an escape from
reality, something I later came to appreciate myself, but it certainly
didn't give him any joy. It never made him smile or sing along,
except when he'd had too much to drink, when he would join in
with the most soulful songs. I don't know if the rock and roll even
made him want to tap his feet. It was a sticking plaster for his
damaged soul rather than a balm. I guess the drinking provided
another means of escape, numbing the pain of failure and disappointment for at least a few hours each day.

As far as I know Gloria had never worked, certainly not in my
living memory. She was always totally dependent on the welfare
state for handouts, but who could blame her when she had so many
children to look after? Every Monday she would be queuing up
outside the Post Office in the dingy shopping precinct for her Giro
with so many others and she would immediately spend it. That
Post Office seemed to do more trade than any of the other shops
around it. Now they sell lottery tickets as well, so people can buy
a few rays of hope with their meagre handouts without even having
to leave the premises. Gloria had no budgeting abilities whatsoever.
Even if Dennis gave her money during the week, there would still
be no food in the house by Friday. She never made any plans or
harboured any dreams. She had no hopes of bettering herself or
ambitions for us; she lived from one handout to the next without
a thought to the future or even a plan to get us safely through to
the following Monday and the next Giro.

If the Giro didn't arrive when it should we knew the pressures
on us all would increase enormously. She would wait by the window
for the postman to come. Very little mail came to our house and
if the waiting became too much for her she would send me out,
even as young as five, to find the postman in the neighbouring
streets and see if he was on his way to the Horseshoe and would

be willing to let me run ahead with our mail so she would get it a few minutes earlier so that she could cash it and spend it the moment the shops opened. If the postman didn't have it and I had to return to the house empty-handed I knew I would be in big trouble, and we would have to repeat the whole process when the next post was due.

As children we were always hungry, not able to dull our appetites with drink and cigarettes, as she and Dennis did. From an early age I knew my father liked drinking and smoking and although my mother never drank anything except tea, there was always a smouldering cigarette stuck to her bottom lip.

The house was always in chaos. Anyone glancing in through an opened door or uncurtained window would have known immediately that we were a family who couldn't cope. In fact they would have known before that from the piles of junk outside the front door. Our clothes were always strewn around the living area on any surface that was free and many that were already cluttered, great limp piles of them would encircle us as we sat on the sofa, or slide to the floor if we bumped against them, where they would remain to be walked across or kicked carelessly into corners. Nothing was ever put away into a cupboard or a drawer; nothing was ever cared for or cherished. The front room always looked like the last hour of a jumble sale, just before the unsaleable items are finally consigned to the tip. In the kitchen there was always washing-up waiting to be done and frying pans would be re-used with the fat of previous meals still clinging to them. Nothing was ever washed up. Everywhere you looked there was filth and disorder.

Gloria ruled the house like the tyrant she was. Some of the rules were completely irrational, but as a child you accept things the way they are. It's only later that you look back and see the gruesome absurdity of it all. We weren't, for instance, allowed to have lights in our bedrooms. Perhaps it was an economy measure, or perhaps they couldn't be bothered to install the bulbs, but looking back now I think it was more likely they wanted to exercise their power over us and let us know they were the masters and we were just mistakes. We may have been great when we were cute little puppies, but as young dogs we needed too much looking after.

The bathroom was on the ground floor with an outside toilet, but we weren't allowed downstairs in the night in case we stole whatever food there might be left in the fridge, so if we needed the toilet we had to use a bucket, which was left out at the top of the stairs. Because it was so dark upstairs we didn't always manage to hit the bucket, and the puddles were allowed to soak into the bare boards, creating a tacky patina of stains. Sometimes the smaller children didn't even make a pretence of using the bucket, they just peed wherever they felt like it. The whole house stank of urine.

There was no paper on any of the walls, or if there was it was hanging off in strips. If anything was broken or stained it stayed that way. The bedrooms were just bare, dingy cells where we tried to hide from Gloria's tempers. The walls were drawn on and sometimes smeared with human excrement, where small children had had accidents and no one had bothered to clear it up. The floors upstairs and downstairs were always sticky with grime and in the few areas where there were remnants of carpet, they were black with filth and ragged with years of wear and neglect. It was like living in a derelict house, one that was just waiting for the demolition crew to arrive or for homeless youths to move in and squat. But it wasn't derelict, it was our family home.

Electricity and gas were always a problem. We had to have meters installed because Gloria and Dennis never paid the bills, and even then they were always robbing the fifty pence pieces, breaking in and then wedging the fronts open. We'd sometimes go for days with no power at all because they'd broken the equipment or had run out of money and we'd have to wait till the following Monday for the same ritual of waiting for the postman to arrive. Since we never had any money, we always owed people. Whenever the gas, electricity or rent people came knocking we were told to hide, diving for cover behind the sofa, or simply pulling a pile of clothes over us, hoping that if they peered through the windows they'd just see a scene of deserted chaos. If that failed, and they managed to get into the house, there would always be a shouting match with accusations flying back and forth and Gloria boiling with righteous indignation at the unfairness of life.

Occasionally my older brother Wayne and I would pluck up the courage to steal from the fridge while our parents were preoccupied somewhere else in the house, driven on by the ache of hunger that constantly gnawed at our insides. We trained ourselves to creep downstairs in the dead of night, knowing what floorboards to avoid treading on in order not to be heard. There was never much to choose from, but anything we found we would cram into our mouths, swallowing it as quickly as possible in case we were caught and forced to spit it out. We'd wolf down raw sausages if that was all there was, or raw potatoes. Dennis had a liking for veal and ham pies and if he left one overnight in the fridge we'd try to get it, willing to brave the consequences in order to lessen the pain of hunger.

Like many small boys I used to wet the bed almost every night and I would call out to my mother, scared of telling her but not knowing what else to do. I soon learned not to tell Gloria because then she would smack me on my wet skin, which made the blows sting even more, and she would push me downstairs and force me to sleep in the bath with just a dirty towel as a blanket to teach me a lesson.

'You dirty, fucking cunt!' she'd scream into my sleep-fuddled ear in the early hours of the morning, furious at being woken up from her own exhausted slumbers, pushing and pinching and slapping at any part of me I didn't manage to get out of her reach.

I'd do as she told me as quickly as possible, lying in the cold, hard bath until she'd gone back upstairs, and then I'd creep out on to the bathroom floor, trying to find another towel to lie on as it was warmer than the cold metal of the bath. Desperate not to fall too deeply asleep, in case I didn't hear her coming back downstairs in the morning, I'd then doze fitfully for the rest of the night. The moment I heard her stirring upstairs I'd climb back into the bathtub and feign deep sleep. I soon learnt not to wake her when I had accidents if I could help it. I discovered that if I lay long enough on the wet patch the heat from my body would dry it. She would never notice the stain because she never changed the beds. The smell of dirt and urine permeated us as well as our surroundings, travelling with us to school the next day in our clothes and hair and on our skins.

My nights were often as frightening as the days, haunted by nightmares. I would sometimes wake up in the dark room and cry out for my mother without thinking, but as soon as I heard her stamping towards the room I would instantly regret it, curling up into a ball, pulling the covers over my head to counteract the inevitable blows that would rain down. I had to learn as early as possible to curb my natural childish instincts to turn to my mother when I was frightened or unhappy. I had to learn to hold the fear and misery inside, to cope with them myself, because if I annoyed her in any way with my problems I would simply make everything worse.

'You make another fucking sound, you fucking cunt,' she would scream at the top of her voice as I tried to hug her and tell her what had frightened me, 'you'll get the shit kicked out of you, and you'll be sleeping in the bath.'

Nightmares were punishable in exactly the same way as bedwetting. She would drag me down the stairs by my hair to the bathroom. I learnt to cling on to her hands when she had hold of my hair, to take off some of the weight and lessen the pain. There are always tricks you can employ, usually instinctively, to increase the chances of survival in any situation. The more I screamed and pleaded for mercy the more furious she would become, so I learnt not to cry, to keep as quiet as possible. I reasoned that if I took the punishment in silence it would all be over quicker, but sometimes my silent acceptance of the punishment simply fuelled her fury. I would stand there flinching, my lip trembling and silent tears running down my face. She would see it as some sort of dumb insolence and keep attacking me until I was unable to stop myself from crying out in pain. I think she needed to hear the screams of pain to prove she was in control.

Her anger always and immediately erupted into violence; sometimes she'd lash out at us with her hands and feet, sometimes she'd grab a stick or a belt or anything else that came to hand in order to make the beatings more effective. If she hit me with her hand, the blow was so hard there would be a raised imprint of the palm and big fingers left on my skin for hours afterwards. In some of the worst furies she would be biting and scratching us in the sort of frenzy you might associate with a wild dog. The best way of defending myself was to curl up into a ball, guarding my face and vital organs. I was too young to defend myself, just pleading for mercy, 'Sorry, Mummy! Sorry, Mummy! Please no, Mum! Please no, Mum!' and on and on.

One night – I must have been no more than six years old – I woke from a deep sleep with an unfamiliar feeling. Someone was holding me, but it wasn't the usual sort of holding. I wasn't being restrained, or pulled painfully in some direction I didn't want to go. There didn't seem to be any anger involved or shouting. I was confused in my half-awake state, knowing that I felt comfortable and protected, but not knowing why. As I came round I realized the house was full of unusual activity. The arms I was cradled in were unfamiliar. They were a man's arms and although he was taking care not to alarm me he was hurrying. There was a sense of urgency and I could hear voices and the noise of running engines outside the house as we made our way downstairs. As we came into the illuminated night I saw that the man who was holding me was wearing a helmet and uniform, and I realized he was a fireman. I didn't feel frightened because he seemed so calm as he took me out into the street. I didn't appear to be in any danger.

There was a smell of smoke and a lot of noise coming from the fire engines that were parked by the curb, putting out the fire that had broken out in the tin house next door. I was sad when he put me down to watch the goings-on with the others. I'll never forget the feeling of being carried for those few moments by that fireman; I'd never experienced anything so gentle or caring before.

My brother, Wayne, was just a year older than me and, below us, were Sharon and Julie. Robert and Brenda came along later. Gloria always preferred Wayne to me, and Sharon and Julie were much quieter and less likely to annoy her. So it was me she hated with the greatest vehemence, until Robert arrived to share my role as her scapegoat. Brenda, the baby of the family, would always be her other favourite, along with Wayne. It was a situation we all understood and accepted. It was just the way things were.

Gloria didn't confine herself to physical bullying. As she punched and kicked, scratched and slapped me, pulling my hair and some-times even biting me, she would also rain down abuse, telling me I was 'pathetic', that I was 'gay'. 'Kevin is a gay little bastard,' she would repeat over and over again. All the time she was telling me how useless I was, her face would be an inch away from mine, her teeth gritted in fury and the four-letter words punching into me. All the frustrations and hardships that were constantly building up inside her own head would spew out over me every time I came near her, every hour of every day. The aggression never relented. Her dislike for me was so intense that even when she was in a good mood she couldn't bring herself to speak kindly to me or to hug me or kiss me. I never heard a single word of praise or kindness pass her lips. Sometimes she'd become so incensed with me her false teeth would jump loose as she shouted. Whenever that happened I could never resist laughing, which would add even more fuel to her rage. To me this was normal life.

The moment Dennis came back into the house from work she would be screaming out lists of my misdemeanours. 'Your fucking son's done this, and that . . .' It was the same every single day. Her endless tirade would drive him straight through to the kitchen as she pelted him with hysterical complaints and abuse until he could get his tape machine going and a bottle open, to drown her voice out with Elvis and beer.

I don't remember what my crimes were in those early days. I was a lively, boisterous boy, so they could have been anything from breaking a cup to slamming a door or eating something that was forbidden, giving her a bad look or being overexcited because I was going outside to play. Sometimes it was nothing at all. It didn't matter what I did or didn't do, the reaction would always be the same.

There were social workers coming to the house now and then, but they never stayed for long, and if any of my marks or bruises were visible they could always be explained away with some invented accident or other. 'He fell over in the garden!' she'd say and they'd look out at the three-foot-high grass with the debris poking out of it and decide they had no reason to doubt her story. The moment they walked through the door she would be pouring out her tales of hardship and streams of bile against anyone who had upset her. You could see the panic in their eyes as they tried to get away from her barrage of complaints and grievances about us, about Dennis, about the neighbours, the council and anyone else who had touched her life in the previous few days or weeks. They couldn't wait to get back out of the house into the fresh air, so they didn't prolong their visits unnecessarily by talking to me or asking me how I was.

They could see she and I hated each other, but they had no proof that she was hitting me. If they did ask me how I'd come by a particular cut or bruise, I'd lie for her, because if I didn't I knew I'd be beaten to even more of a pulp the moment they were out of the door. She would be standing there, towering over me as the social worker knelt down to talk to me. I never knew why they came to us or what they did, but whenever they were there Gloria was on her best behaviour, like a child being good for sweets.

There was no escape for me. I couldn't outrun her. I couldn't hide from her. I had no choice but to continue to live in fear and stay silent about it.

Once Dennis was home and in the kitchen she still wouldn't allow him to listen to his music in peace. She'd be determined to involve him in the disciplining of his children. No one in the family ever spoke quietly. There were never any reasonable conversations. Everyone would be screaming at once and he would inevitably be dragged into the affray, his patience stretched as tightly as hers by the endless noise and foul language. Eventually, particularly once he'd got a few drinks inside him, he'd start hitting out as well. Because she wouldn't let up, going on and on about everything that was wrong in her life, everything that was wrong with him and with me, he would be unable to withstand the pressure any longer. After a long hard day, or night, of physical labour he would snap and they would start to argue. They would hit each other and, if we were within reach, they would both hit out at us as well.

Once tempers were lost we were all in real danger of being seriously hurt by both of them. Both lost all sense of judgement when their anger bubbled over. When Wayne back-chatted him one time, Dennis threw a knife at him. Wayne can't have been more than six or seven. We were all there in the room; Gloria, me and Dennis shouting, the girls watching in nervous silence. He could have thrown anything in his fury; it just happened to be a knife that came into his hand at the moment his temper snapped and he didn't have the control to stop himself. The blade dug into Wayne's leg and the blood immediately started to flow. A loud panic mixed with anger filled the house as they tried to work out what they should be doing and calm themselves enough to act responsibly. When they finally realized they couldn't treat the wound adequately themselves, they were forced to take Wayne down to the hospital to be stitched up. They must have been nervous that they'd be asked awkward questions. When the harassed doctor asked what had happened they told him it had been an accident and he accepted the explanation. It continually amazed me how people in positions to rescue us were always happy to believe whatever they were told by adults. It must have been obvious from the state we were in that things were out of control, but all the people we came into contact with were always willing to take whatever explanation Gloria or Dennis came up with. Maybe it was pressures of time or workload that made them so anxious to move on to the next problem, or maybe they didn't want to interfere, or maybe we were just too scary a prospect for most normal people to be able to face.

Dennis was a very strong man physically. When he was hitting me he would lift me up by my wrist, leaving my other hand free to frantically try to block the blows as I squirmed and wriggled in his grip, but it was impossible and my efforts at self-protection and my refusal to remain a stationary target only made him angrier. Wayne, Julie and Sharon would become afraid when he lost his temper with me, screaming at him to stop hitting me, but their noise would only annoy him more, like a dazed, confused bull being taunted in a bullring. Once he'd smacked me with all his strength he would toss me aside like a piece of dirty laundry. But his eruptions would pass, unlike Gloria's, and he would never scream abuse into my face or tell me what a useless little bastard I was. I got the impression he liked me, that I was his favourite, but he just couldn't handle the strain of the constant noise and the screaming and the anger. He just wanted to be left alone with his beer and his music.

The constant noise must have been like a torture for him, gradually driving him further and further inside himself. He became quieter and more withdrawn with every passing year. There were moments when we got glimpses of the sort of father he might have been if he hadn't been under too much pressure from us all. Once, when Wayne and I were squabbling about something, he gave us both boxing gloves and told us to fight properly if we were going to, believing that the only way to sort anything out was through violence and abuse. Sometimes, if I'd taken a real bashing from Gloria, I'd walk past him and he would put his hand on my shoulder, but he never said anything. When that happened I thought that everything would be all right, but it never was. I thought that he would protect me and look after me, but he never did.

As the years went by his drinking became worse. He moved from beer to gin, coming home every night with half bottles tucked into his pocket and staying in the kitchen until the small hours just drinking and listening to the music. None of us went in there; we knew he wanted to be left alone. The harder he drank the angrier and more depressed he became, withdrawing further into himself.

There was nothing in the house except anger and unhappiness, nightmares and rows, beatings and abuse. There were no saving moments of laughter or forgiveness, no kind words or encouragement for any of us. Life under those circumstances beats down a child's self-esteem and gives them no hope for the future. There is only endurance, never enjoyment. If something or someone else doesn't come along to save them, the children of such families have no hope of escape and merely repeat the pattern set by their parents.

2. The Tramps

If home life was a continuous nightmare, there was no escape for us when we got to school either. The other children called us 'the tramps' and excluded us totally. It was obvious we were different to them, and everyone in the area knew of Gloria so we were branded with her reputation as well. I'm sure the parents of other children were warning them to stay away from us. No one would have wanted their children to become involved with us. If I'd been one of those parents, I suspect I would have been discouraging my children from having anything to do with us.

We were enrolled at Wolsey Junior, the school that lay just behind our house, so the other kids could see the way we lived with their own eyes. Our garden only had chicken wire around it, so we couldn't hide the squalor from anyone passing by. Just the other side of the wire the parents would gather twice a day to drop off and pick up their kids. They would be standing in groups talking, as parents do, and right beside them was the glaring evidence of how far out of control our home life was. I burned with shame when I saw them looking through the wire at the bombsite inside and heard them lowering their voices to exchange anecdotes about us. I became certain that every pair of eyes that ever came to the school was irresistibly drawn to the horrors of our back garden.

The parents might have lowered their voices when they talked about us, but kids don't bother about being polite or sparing people's feelings. They're just looking for reasons to put other people down before someone puts them down, and my parents provided plenty of those, from the way we dressed to the way we smelt, from the squalor of the house to the constant shouting.

Sometimes Gloria would strip wash us in the kitchen sink in front of the window, so anyone going to or from the school could see us, naked and humiliated, being washed down in the kitchen amongst the filthy plates and pans. Sunday night was bath night. If we were out playing on the grass of the Horseshoe when she was ready to start the ritual, we'd hear her bellowing for us to come in, her ugly voice drowning out every other sound. We didn't dare to loiter once she had called, knowing we would receive a beating once she got us if we made her wait.

If I wasn't the first in line for the bath I would have to sit and listen to the inconsolable screams of the others, staring at the television, trying to concentrate on *Playaway*, or some other programme, to dull the noise, completely silent, knowing what was coming as I waited my turn. They were genuine screams of fear and pain.

Once she had hold of us she'd scrub us painfully hard and dig out our ears with a hairpin – you never knew how deep she'd push that pin in and I always feared she would break through my eardrum and make me deaf. If I tried to struggle she'd pin my arms to my sides with a towel and finish the job by force. Once I'd given up the fight and was restrained, I lay still and silent because if I'd moved my head the hairpin would have gone deeper and the damage and pain would have been worse.

The agonizing discipline of those ritual cleansings still clings to me and I find I have to clean my ears out every day, even when I know they don't need it, although I now use cotton buds not pieces of metal. We didn't have any shampoo or decent soap so the baths barely scraped the surface of our dirt, and we then climbed back into stinking clothes and bedding, so our distinctive family smell remained undiminished.

Sometimes the other kids would set up a chant in the playground when we arrived: 'Tramp! Tramp! Tramp!', or any other choice phrase they decided to bellow at us. There was nothing we could do to stop them. We had to brazen it out. There was nowhere to run to and we couldn't fight all of them. There was nothing we could do to improve our appearance; we were who we were and we couldn't do anything to change it. There was nothing we could do about the dirt or the smell because we didn't know how to fumigate the house or launder the sheets and clothes any more than Gloria did. None of us owned a toothbrush or knew what toothpaste was, or even used soap regularly. The stigma of an undignified poverty clung to us as stubbornly as the smells and the other children didn't intend to let us forget our place.

There is no shame in not having money, but even at the poorest levels of society there are still social grades. There are those who work honestly to give their children the best upbringing they can within their limited means, lavishing them with love and keeping them clean, helping them with their schoolwork in the hope they might later be able to escape the poverty trap, even if their parents can't. These people have self-respect and they know there is a better life to be striven for. Then there are the families who just don't care, who seem to wallow in their own squalor, and who've given up all hope of ever improving their lot in life. The children of poor families have no difficulty in distinguishing between the two types. No prizes for guessing where the Lewis family fell in this hierarchy of poverty.

We lived in social isolation. No other children ever invited us back to their homes to play and we were too frightened to invite them back to our house because of what they would have seen. The shame of opening the door to anyone else would have been too much to bear. How can you invite a classmate to your bedroom when you know it stinks of urine because there is an unemptied bucket of the stuff at the top of the stairs, and when there isn't even a light bulb so they could see to play? I suspect their parents wouldn't have let them come anyway.

We never went to anyone's birthday parties. It always puzzled me that I knew these parties went on because I would hear the others talking about them in the playground the day after, but I never actually saw them happening. They were something that existed outside my little world. In my imagination they became something wonderful, like everything else that I felt excluded from. I longed to be someone else, someone who was invited to parties, someone who was popular and had friends and wasn't different. The other parents wouldn't encourage their children to be kind to us. They didn't want to become involved with the aggressive Gloria and her miserable, silent husband. Looking back now, I really don't blame them. They were just protecting their children. But it meant there was nowhere we could turn where we would get any respite from the beating and bullying at home and the taunting of the playground. We were outsiders in every area of our lives.

Not only did we not get invited to other children's birthday parties, we didn't have any of our own either. Gloria would never have been able to organize anything like that. Where would she have got the money? How would she have persuaded anyone else to set foot inside our house? Where would she have put guests amongst the dirty clothes and other detritus of our lives? How would she have known, any more than I did, what a party involved? She didn't know any games. She couldn't cook. Where would she have got a cake from? None of this was part of Gloria's world. Dennis wouldn't have been any better. How could a man too shy to talk to his own family cope with playing games with other people's children? The whole idea would have been impossible.

I have no memory of ever receiving any birthday presents at all.

Wayne and the girls used to get something from Gloria, but whenever it was my turn there was always a problem with the Giro 'not clearing'.

'I'll get you something next week,' she might promise if she felt the slightest twinge of guilt when I came hurrying downstairs on my birthday morning. 'When I get the money.' But she never did.

Despite the evidence which built, year upon year, I always lived in hope that things would change and that my next birthday would become a celebration, a day when I would be special for at least a few hours. Children are optimistic creatures at heart. It takes a lot to convince them that the world is really against them and that things will not improve one day. The day before my seventh birthday I was brimming with ideas of what I was going to receive the next day. As Wayne and I came downstairs to get ready for school I was burbling away to him about everything I was expecting to get.

Gloria must have heard me; I was not a quiet child, used to shouting to make myself heard over everyone else. Perhaps she felt I was criticizing her by listing the things she'd never have thought of getting me and wouldn't have had the money for anyway. Perhaps she felt momentarily guilty, or angry at my presumption. Whatever the reason, she caught me by surprise, stamping across the hall and grabbing me by the back of my jumper before I had time to wriggle past her. She hauled me up off my feet, the neck of the jumper cutting into my throat. I couldn't breathe. As I flailed around in the air, desperately struggling to get some breath into my lungs, she yanked my trousers down with her free hand and started laying into me with my own belt.

I tried to put one hand behind me to intercept the blows, while I struggled to pull my collar away from my windpipe with the other hand. My feeble attempts at defending myself seemed to stoke up her fury. She hurled me to the floor and the moment I was able to

fill my lungs I started to scream with pain and shock. All my determination not to cry in front of her again had deserted me. My
screams seemed to make her even angrier. She came after me again
before I could get away, grabbing my hair and dragging me into
the lounge, my trousers and pants still down round my knees, my
buttocks and back burning from the blows.

As I struggled to get free she picked me up as if I was a pile of
old clothes and chucked me across the width of the room. I remember those few seconds of hanging in the air, like I could fly, before
I crashed down on to the window ledge, hitting my head on the
corner. It was like an explosion going off inside my brain.

I stopped screaming, feeling dazed and disoriented, unsure
exactly what had happened to me. I don't know if I passed out.
There was a splitting pain in my head and I could feel the warm
wetness of blood on my face. I put my hands up to touch it and
they turned red in front of my eyes. Gloria had stopped shouting
too and I could hear her panting in the silence that had fallen over
the house. After a few seconds Wayne recovered from the shock
and started yelling and the girls were crying again. I wasn't making
any sound, just shaking uncontrollably and staring at the blood,
trying to work out what I should do, wanting someone to take me
in their arms and sort me out.

She turned and stamped out of the room, returning a few
moments later with a dirty flannel from the bathroom, which she
threw down to me.

'Clean yourself up and fuck off to school!' she snarled.

I went to the bathroom and tried to mop up the mess. My face
was a shocking sight and the water just seemed to spread the blood
around. It was still coming out and I held the flannel tightly to it
to stop the flow. I was anxious to get out of the house without
making her any angrier. My legs were wobbling as I made my way
to the door. Wayne opened it for me and we stepped out into the

fresh air, both shaking and shocked. We turned left past the next-door house and then turned left into the alleyway that ran between the houses that led to the school entrance. It was about a hundred yards long, with high fences and hedges on either side, so no one could see us. Once we were out of sight of the window I felt Wayne taking hold of my hand as we walked together without saying a word. This tiny gesture of kindness made me want to cry, but I held on. I didn't want anyone to see tears when we reached the playground. As soon as we stumbled out of the dark alley into the school grounds we let go of each other and I took a deep breath, determined to keep going and not faint.

I must have been conspicuous amongst the other children, even by my standards, because one of the teachers came straight over to me. She gently turned my face with her fingers and looked at the side of my head.

'I think we should get that looked at by the nurse,' she said, leading me away from the others. Wayne watched me go, but didn't say anything. I followed her, just wanting someone to take control and make everything better.

As I sat in the nurse's room on my own, waiting for something to happen, I could hear school life going on outside the door. Inside the room it smelled clean and safe, an antiseptic place where people were comforted and made well. In the cruel world outside bells rang in a familiar fashion, but didn't seem to be anything to do with me. For a few moments I had been lifted out of my troubled life and allowed to rest. There were the sounds of running feet and voices shouting and laughing. I'd had trouble sitting down when we first came in because of a pain in my lower back and I saw the teacher looking at me in a curious fashion before she went off to find the nurse. For a short time I'd been absolved of the responsibility of being part of the school day. It was like a respite; time to gather my thoughts and my strength. I must have been in a fair amount of shock, everything had happened so fast. Just a few minutes earlier I'd been coming downstairs, chattering about my approaching birthday, and now I was hurting all over and receiving special attention. I must admit that the attention felt good, even with the attached pain. I wanted to stay in that safe room for as long as possible.

Other grown-ups started coming into the room, looking at me. I can't remember who they were or if I recognized them. Someone asked me to lift up my shirt at the back and pull down the waistband of my trousers. I knew I hadn't said anything to give Gloria away. It wasn't going to be my fault if they'd seen I couldn't move properly. I hadn't betrayed her trust. They were very matter-of-fact about it all, but I could tell they were taking things seriously. I was worried they might be going to say something to Gloria. If they did that I'd be in for an even worse beating when she next got me on my own in the house. The only option I could see was to run away at the end of the school day. I began to lay plans for where I would go to and how I would survive the night. There were some woods a mile or two away, surrounding a golf course. If I could get myself there I could live in the woods like I'd seen children doing in programmes on the telly. I didn't think Gloria or Dennis would bother to come looking for me, and I doubted if they would want to tell the authorities that I'd disappeared. I could stay there until it was time to come back to school.

The nurse carefully patched up my head and cleaned the rest of the caked blood away. She was so kind and gentle and caring, so different to Gloria whose hands never touched me unless it was to slap or pinch or punch. I began to feel better. The shaking had stopped and I thought I could manage to go into school with the others. The nurse said she'd take me to the dining room to get a drink. As I came out of her room I had to walk past the queue of children waiting to go into assembly. Every pair of eyes turned to look at me; not just the children but the teachers as well. No one said anything. They just stared as I walked through the gauntlet of eyes. I stared back, not able to understand what was so fascinating about a bit of sticking plaster on a head wound. It'd been a bad morning, but not particularly out of the ordinary as far as I was concerned. Why were they all so transfixed?

The school day went on as usual, but my fear of going home increased as the time passed and I continued to refine my plans for running away. It was a scary prospect, but not as scary as the thought of Gloria waiting for me behind the front door. At the end of lessons, however, the decision was taken out of my hands. I was told to wait because I wasn't going to be going home. My first reaction was relief at the thought that I wasn't going to have to run away and live in the woods with all their strange noises.

'We're going to take you somewhere safe for a little while,' a teacher told me.

I was now scared again, this time of the unknown. If life was bad at home and at school, and even in my nightmares, it might be even worse in whatever place they were planning to take me. I had no reason to believe that there was anywhere where I would actually be happy.

'Can't I go home?' I wanted to know. It felt like I was being punished, but I didn't understand what I'd done wrong. Despite everything that I went through at Gloria's hands, it was still my home, still the place that was most familiar to me, and the place where Wayne and my sisters would be. I didn't know where they were going to be taking me and the unknown is even more frightening than the known, especially when you're not quite seven and all your experience tells you that the world is an unkind place.

They reassured me and a woman I didn't know led me outside to a waiting car. I'd never been in a car before. It was exciting climbing in through the opened door. The interior smelt clean and different from anything I'd experienced before. When the door slammed shut I was cocooned into a new world, a means of escape from the tiny life I was used to, which consisted of my house and school. They were all I'd experienced until that moment and now I was being taken into the unknown with no preparation. As the car set off I almost immediately felt queasy from the unfamiliar movement.

Despite the excitement of the car journey and the anticipation of an adventure, I still felt a strong urge to run back to my dark, dreary little bedroom and hide my head under the musty, familiar smelling sheets. I missed Wayne, Sharon and Julie. I had no idea what to expect next. It was 1977 when I was first taken into care.

3. The Bear Under the Bed

I was taken to an emergency children's home in Croydon. Because it was going to be my birthday the next day, someone gave me a little koala bear and a Womble. I could hardly believe they were for me. I clung to them as if my life depended on it.

By the time we reached the home, which stood opposite Selsdon Station, it was dark. I was given a bath, some clean clothes, a fresh white bandage for my head and something to eat. There was a nasty looking bruise around the cut, making it look more serious than it probably was. All evening I held on tightly to my new friends, the koala and the Womble, watching wide-eyed as the other children and the staff went about what must have been their normal evening routines.

I was nervous because I was in unfamiliar surroundings, but it was a different nervousness to the one I felt at home. It was more exciting, as if I was on the brink of a great adventure. I was also on my guard, expecting someone to be nasty to me at any moment. Experience had taught me that sooner or later I always got hit or shouted at by someone, no matter how careful I was to stay out of the way. I waited to see what would happen.

The evening passed without anyone doing or saying anything unpleasant and I felt encouraged. When I was taken up to bed I was struck by how different the bedclothes and mattress smelled to the one at home. It was a clean smell that I'd never experienced before, more like the nurse's room at school than any of the bedrooms in our house. There was a bright light, so I was able to see what I was doing as I got into clean pyjamas, brushed my teeth as they showed me and climbed into bed. I lay between the stiff, freshly laundered white sheets and breathed deeply, sucking in the aroma, wanting to remember it for ever. It was a beautiful feeling. I must have fallen asleep very quickly, exhausted by a day that had been so strange and so draining, both physically and emotionally. I hugged the koala and Womble tightly to me, my two new best friends.

The next morning I met more of the staff and other children, all of whom looked older than me, and they all sang 'happy birthday' to me over breakfast. It was a nice feeling to be the centre of such pleasant attention, but disconcerting; I didn't know how I was supposed to react. As soon as the meal was over I made my way back up to my little bedroom to find the koala and Womble. They weren't in the bed where I'd left them, carefully tucked up. I lifted the sheets and rummaged around for them, but the bed was empty. Feeling a twinge of panic, I looked all round the room and knelt down to peer under the bed. My two new friends lay on the floor in the darkest corner, their stuffing hanging out of their slashed stomachs, their severed limbs hanging loose. They'd been ripped beyond hope; there was nothing that could be done to repair them. I think someone on the staff gave me something to replace them, but it didn't feel the same because the first two friends I had ever had had been cruelly murdered. Now I knew that even if someone did give me something, someone else would always take it away or destroy it. I didn't want to get attached to anything else, only to lose it the next day.

When I found them I sat on the floor and cried, unable to stop the tears that I'd been holding back for so many hours. It seemed that there was nowhere I could go that would be safe. I wished I was back home with Wayne and the others, at least then I would know what was going to happen next. Now I was facing an invisible and unknown enemy.

As the days passed my enemies became all too visible. Having waited to see what sort of victim I was likely to be, they pounced mercilessly. Being so young, and so naïve, having had no experience outside my own limited family circle, I was a sitting target for the other, bigger children, many of whom needed no excuse to pick on someone younger and more gullible than themselves. Gloria had taught me that it was futile to stand up to bullies because if I ever stood up to her I'd just be beaten all the harder. The other children soon realized that I was an easy victim, someone who was used to taking whatever punishment they cared to dole out without fighting back. I guess these were children who had suffered at the hands of others themselves and were all too keen to pass their suffering on down the line. I was the one at the end of the line.

Those few memories are fairly sharp, although they may be tinged with inaccuracy due to the fact that I was so young and so many years have passed, but around them has settled a fog of half-remembered scenes and faces that populated the following months. I wasn't taken back home. I remained in a no man's land of different children's homes, schools and short-term foster parents, all with their different smells and sounds; all bringing on different memories of anxiety and unhappiness. Sometimes, even now, a whiff of a particular institutional floor polish or disinfectant will bring back a sharp stab of remembered fear and trepidation. Through the fog I can make out a memory of going to a juvenile court. It must have been something to do with the authorities wanting to gain an emergency custodial ruling. Gloria and Dennis were both there. It seemed strange to see them outside the setting of the home; Gloria dressed to face the outside world instead of in her usual grubby dressing gown. It was puzzling to see her but not frightening. She always behaved well towards me when there were other people around. I was physically safer now, even if I didn't feel emotionally secure.

Each time I went to a new foster family I arrived with the

knowledge that I would soon be moved on, so I held a bit of myself back every time. I didn't want to allow myself to feel too at home if I was going to have to say goodbye a few weeks later. I knew that all these people were being paid to have me, that I wasn't really part of their families, just a boarder. I knew that none of them actually wanted me for myself. None of their faces has remained clear in my memory.

I learnt a lot about how other families worked, and I was an eager pupil, watching everything, always wary in case I did or said the wrong thing and turned them against me. I was desperate to please and sometimes my eagerness irritated people. One set of foster parents had a boy and girl of their own, both older than me, so the parents can't have been that young. What astonished me about this couple was that they kept kissing each other. They didn't seem able to keep their hands off one another. I'd never seen Gloria and Dennis show each other the slightest flicker of affection, either physical or emotional. I couldn't work out what these two were up to. They took me to visit one of their mums and as we went up to her flat in the lift they went into a clinch, with me staring up at them, open-mouthed. That, I decided, must be what love looked like.

I don't suppose I was an easy child for other people to take into their families. Having been a virtual prisoner in a few rooms for so long the scent of freedom was very heady for me. I was a boisterous little boy and I would have considered it normal to behave with my foster families as I did at home. There was never any love or affection shown between any of us, it was all spite and violence, and I dare say some of the families found me too aggressive towards their children as I tried to adjust to the outside world. I tried to behave as I thought they wanted, but sometimes it just didn't come out right. Despite all this, it was still a hundred times better than being at home with Gloria.

My new nomadic life went on for a year, while everyone tried to make up their minds what to do with me. It's my impression that had I been younger someone would have adopted me, but an energetic seven-year-old with a difficult family in the background is a lot for anyone to want to take on permanently. After a year everything changed again. It was now 1978.

4. The Birthday Party

The day before my eighth birthday I was told I was going to be moved again, to another home called Yarborough Children's Home. It was in East Grinstead, a genteel, market town in East Sussex. I was nervous about moving back into an institution from the foster home I was in, remembering how unhappy I'd been at the first place in Croydon. I would rather have stayed in family homes, even if I still had to move around every few months.

'We've had to work hard to get you into Yarborough,' the social worker told me. 'It's a very nice place and they don't often have vacancies. You're a lucky boy.' I decided to reserve my judgement until I'd seen what lay in store.

After we'd driven for a while towards East Grinstead the woman asked if I was hungry. I said I was and she pulled off the road into a car park beside a country bakery and café, which had signs advertising its homemade bread, pies and cakes. We went inside and the warm smell of baking was almost overwhelming. I'd never been inside a place with such delicious smells. There were trays on display filled with cakes, pastries, buns, pies and loaves of bread. The woman asked me which one I'd like and I pointed to one, having no idea what any of them were as I couldn't read the labels. It didn't matter what it was, just the texture of freshly baked pastry was more than enough to excite my taste buds. We returned to the car and I ate my treat greedily as we drove on.

As we drove into East Grinstead I could already see that it was unlike the areas I was used to. Although we were in an area which I guess you would call suburban, the atmosphere was very different.

The houses, many of them substantial Edwardian and Victorian red-brick villas, were set in large gardens and surrounded by mature trees which gave them privacy. The streets were quiet and well maintained. There was a feeling of space, solidity and greenness. I didn't think that anyone like Gloria lived near here.

We eventually drew up outside one of these red-brick buildings, although this one was a little larger than the others. It didn't look like a family home, but it didn't exactly look like an institution either. On one side an unmade road full of potholes disappeared past playing fields and trees, on the other stood the smart gates of a small private school.

The social worker told me we had reached our destination and we climbed out of the car. She led me through the gates and up to the house. My first impression was of big white double doors in a glazed wooden porch, which we stood in while we waited for some-one to answer the bell. When the doors eventually swung open a man who looked, to me, like a giant, towered over us. I stepped back in shock. I stared up at him in awe and he looked me straight in the eye, taking no notice of the grown-up accompanying me. He then crouched down to my level and shook my hand firmly.

'You must be Kevin,' he said. I nodded. 'Will you call me Uncle David?'

I nodded again, dumbstruck. He gave me a wink, pulled himself up once more to his full height, picked my bag up in one hand and held out his other hand for me to take. I gripped it as tightly as I could, terrified at what new experiences I was about to encounter, and he led me into my new home.

The house was fairly quiet, all the children still being at school, and he took me around, introducing me to the staff and showing me the big rooms filled with games and toys. I felt overawed and didn't say much. As the afternoon wore on the children came back from school and I was introduced to them. It wasn't a big home, no more than twenty or so children, but it meant a lot of new faces to take in all at once. I needn't have worried. The others swept me up and took me off. We immediately started running around, laughing and playing while the grown-ups prepared tea. For the first time in my life I felt I'd reached a safe place and the fears I'd come to think of as normal simply drained away. The social worker had been right. This was a very nice place indeed and I was a very lucky boy.

Behind the house was a garden with climbing frames that seemed enormous to me. There was a games room with a billiards table and the whole place felt like one large home rather than an institution. High fences and walls surrounded the premises and we could often hear the happy sounds of the little children laughing and screaming as they ran around the school playground next door.

'How long will I be here?' I asked Uncle David that evening, dreading the answer, never wanting to leave such a wonderful place.

'There are no plans to move you anywhere else, Kevin,' he said. 'We want to keep you here, if you'd like to stay.'

'Yes, please,' I replied, happily.

Although I hadn't told anyone, they obviously knew from my case notes that it was my birthday the next day. I hadn't bothered to mention it to the other children, as I still didn't think it meant anything. My birthdays had never worked out very well in the past, so I thought it best not to get my hopes up. My optimism on that front had finally run out. That night I was sleeping in the same room as two brothers, Mark and Chris Wallace, who had already become my friends. Mark, who was the same age as me, woke me up in the morning.

'Kevin,' he said, shaking me, 'Kevin, it's your birthday. Come on, we've got to go downstairs.' It seemed like a ritual they'd performed many times before.

Immediately awake, I went down with them to find the breakfast table covered in presents and cards. I'd never seen so many, and they were actually properly gift-wrapped, with my name written on them. All the cards and labels had signatures of who had given them, but I couldn't make them out because I still hadn't learnt to read. If anyone in my family had ever received a present the only wrapping was likely to be the carrier bag it had come from the shop in.

I couldn't stop opening the presents, spreading the brightly coloured paper across the table and on to the floor as I discarded it, revealing one toy after another. Nearly every card I opened had a badge attached which I immediately pinned to myself until I clanked when I moved, and everyone kept calling me 'birthday boy'. I was delirious with joy. Uncle David told me I didn't have to go to school that day, that I could stay at home and play with my new toys all day long. From the moment the others left I just sat in the midst of my booty, staring at them, playing with them, pulling them apart and putting them back together. One of them was a little brown bear, which sat beside me all day, sharing the excitement. The staff just left me alone to wallow in my happiness.

When the others came back from school in the afternoon everyone started to prepare for a birthday party, the first I'd ever been to. It felt so strange to be the centre of attention. We played pass-the-parcel and stick-the-tail-on-the-donkey, and everyone became overexcited and loud. This was a party like the ones I used to hear about in the school playground, the ones I never got to see for myself, and it was every bit as exciting as anything I'd ever imagined.

Suddenly all the lights went out and I felt a stab of fear in my stomach. All the bright colours of the decorations and the presents disappeared and everyone fell silent. A wave of panic threatened to overwhelm me. I couldn't work out what was going on. It was like being back in my bedroom with no light, and then I saw the glow coming in through the door. Uncle David was bringing in the cake from the kitchen. It was big enough for everyone in the house to have a piece. It had 'Happy Birthday, Kevin' written across it in icing, with eight candles. They all began to sing 'Happy Birthday' to me as I blew out the candles.

The lights came back on and I started to cry. Eight years of pent-up emotion and bottled unhappiness poured out uncontrollably and all I could think was that I missed the brothers and sisters I hadn't seen for a year. I felt so happy and imagined them still trapped at home with Gloria and Dennis, with all the shouting and hitting, the violence and the unhappiness, the darkness and the hunger, the dirt and the smells. It was all too much for me to cope with and the tears streamed out.

Uncle David scooped me up and carried me upstairs to the bedroom. He gave me a cuddle and assured me everything was all right. When he told me that, I believed it was true.

Life at Yarborough gave me a great sense of freedom. Bit by bit I was becoming a normal, inquisitive child, a happy child, playful and looking for adventure. We often played football in the backyard. If a ball was kicked over the fence into the lane the person who kicked it had to get it. We were playing one day when I gave an almighty kick and the ball flew straight over. I clambered up the fence and when I got to the top I had a good look around. Slowly I stood straight up, suddenly filled with confidence and happiness. I spread my arms out like I was free and standing on top of a mountain. All around was the green of the trees and I felt a breeze on my face. This, I thought to myself, is what freedom feels like. I felt dizzy with excitement, lost my concentration and fell to the ground, breaking my arm. I had to be taken to the local hospital to be plastered up. I didn't care. A broken arm was a small price to pay for finally being free.

5. A Chance

With the move to a new home came an inevitable move to a new school. This one was not far from the home and was called Baldwin's Hill. To get there we just had to walk down the unmade lane beside Yarborough to the next road. It was a very different atmosphere to Wolsey Junior, more like an old-fashioned Victorian village school and I immediately felt safe and comfortable there. I was kitted out with a brand-new uniform and sat next to a boy called Guy Monson who showed me around and we became firm friends. I was so happy I thought I might burst. Here I had everything I'd been missing at home. At Yarborough I was secure and well cared for, never afraid I would be hit or humiliated in any way, and at school I was as clean and smart as every other boy, with a real best friend of my own. Just to have a regular supply of clean underpants was a luxury, let alone clean bedding. I no longer smelled different to everyone else, even though I still had problems with bed-wetting. No one would have dreamt of calling me 'tramp' at Baldwin's Hill. I'd become a part of normal life, no longer odd and different or an easy target for anyone who wanted to give someone a hard time.

My friendship with Guy grew and he started to invite me back to his home to play after school. His house was a cosy little bunga-low down another bumpy lane, buried amongst high hedges and trees, a short walk from the school in another direction. It was difficult to imagine that we were still in the outskirts of a town when we had farmland just across the way and no signs of any traffic. I met his mum, Gini, who was everything a mum should be. She and her husband were divorced. She was bringing Guy up on her own, and she was doing it brilliantly. She couldn't have been more different to Gloria. She worked in the media in some way, I think it was public relations, and the house was full of books and stacks of magazines I'd never heard of before like *Punch, Private Eye* and *New Statesman.*

Our friendship grew and I started to go there for sleepovers. Sometimes when I stayed there for the night Guy and I would creep outside after we were supposed to be in bed, slipping through his bedroom window and down the lane in the eerie darkness, being adventurous as all boys are, only sometimes we only succeeded in frightening ourselves so much we had to scuttle back to the bedroom and spend the rest of the night imagining green monsters knocking on the windows. The only thing that spoiled these nights for me was the fear that I might wet the bed and I would try to make myself sleep lightly in order to be aware of the danger signs like dreaming about a toilet.

The staff at Yarborough gave us a great deal of freedom and we were allowed to go out and about in the surrounding roads and woods as long as we were with older children. *Grease* was a popular film at the time and we all used to imitate their way of dressing, walking about with our collars up, feeling like real little dudes. There was a pond not too far from the house, surrounded by trees and some distance from the nearest houses. It was a cold winter and the pond had frozen over. A group of us, including some girls and my roommates, Chris and Mark, decided to go down there and slide on the ice, even though we'd been told it was out of bounds. I guess all children will be tempted by the forbidden occasionally and the lure of that smooth expanse of slippery ice was too much for us. We were tentative to start with, gingerly putting our feet on to the surface to test its strength. Once we knew it would take our weight our courage grew and we ventured further and further from the edge as we played our games, laughing and falling over, grabbing hold of one another and skating around as best we could in our boots and shoes.

Chris was being particularly daring. He'd spotted a barrel on the other side that must have been floating in the pond when the ice came and was now stuck fast. As he became braver he was sliding closer and closer to the barrel. As more of us poured on to the ice it held fast. The odd cracking noises around the edges didn't seem to develop into anything serious and so we became less and less cautious.

The presence of the barrel must have weakened the ice on that side of the pond. We heard a crack and splash at the same time as Chris's shout. We looked over and saw him disappear from sight. Before we could do anything he'd bobbed back to the surface. Other people were screaming and some had scrambled back to the bank, pursued by the sounds of cracking ice, and were already running back up the hill towards Yarborough to get help. Chris was flailing around, trying to find something to hold on to, but there was nothing, only ice that was too slippery to grip. The weight of the water in his clothes was pulling him down and I could see he wouldn't be able to stay up long enough for Uncle David to be found and to run down from the house. Even when he got there it would take a few minutes before he was able to work out a way to reach Chris. An adult as heavy as him would also be much more likely than one of us to go through the ice somewhere else. I didn't pause to weigh up the odds for long, I just knew we had to hold on to Chris to stop him going under, and then we could try to drag him out.

I walked gingerly towards him and felt the ice cracking beneath my feet. I realized I had to distribute my weight more widely. It was instinctive. I lay down as close as I could get to the hole he'd made, shouting at Mark to grab my legs. The freezing cold water from the surface immediately soaked through my clothes to my skin. I reached out my hands and yelled at Chris to catch hold of them. He lifted his hands from the ice and tried to stretch, but he just floundered more and slipped further away. His face was going under and then coming back. His teeth were chattering and I could feel the same piercing cold that must have been enveloping him.

I wriggled closer, the ice making ominous clicking sounds all around, and Mark edged forward behind me, his fingers digging desperately into my ankles. Everyone else was on the bank screaming advice or just panicking. Chris lunged at me again but missed and disappeared beneath the surface once more. This time I didn't think he would have the strength to come up again. I plunged my arm into the water and grabbed a handful of his clothes. It was hard to get a grip when my fingers were so cold they had gone numb.

'Pull me back!' I shouted at Mark who skidded and slipped as he put all his strength into hauling me away from the edge of the hole, while I clung on to his brother with frozen fingers. Mark somehow managed to get enough strength to pull me back a few feet and Chris began to come up out of the water. Every time he put his elbows on to the ice it would crack beneath the weight and plunge him down into the water again, but at least we were edging towards the shore. Gradually, as we moved away from the barrel the ice became stronger and I was able to haul his top half out, but from the waist down he was still below the surface. He seemed to be almost unconscious, his eyes dazed and every part of him shivering and shaking as he coughed up filthy pond water. He hardly seemed to have any strength at all. It was like trying to lift a dead weight. Mark kept pulling and now the screams of the others were turning to cheers of encouragement.

By the time we were dragging him on to firm ground several members of staff had come running down from the house with blankets and towels. I knew we were going to be in trouble for this, but I was so relieved just to be back on solid land and to have a dry towel wrapped round me that I didn't care about anything else.

When we got back to the house Chris was taken off for a hot bath and the rest of us had to explain what had happened. The others gave a vivid account of the rescue and that evening Mark and I were given extra helpings of pudding, as well as being told off for disobeying orders. Once the excitement was over and I had time to reflect over the adventure, I felt pleased to have accomplished something so good, even if it was in desperation. I felt proud of myself and it was a wonderful feeling. Perhaps I wasn't quite as useless as Gloria had been telling me.

6. A Lesson Learned

Although we were all very happy at Yarborough, we still used to talk about running away. It just seemed like the right thing to do, especially whenever *Huckleberry Finn* or *Stig of the Dump* had been on the television. It wasn't that we wanted to get away from the house; it was just that a life of freedom, sleeping under the stars at night and being free to wander wherever you wanted during the day, seemed so romantic. We wanted to be masters of our own destiny, or at least we thought we did. Whenever a programme like that was on the staff would be extra vigilant, knowing that at least a few of us would try to clamber out through the windows after dark. Once or twice I was one of the escape party and we were actually successful, but we were always back within a few hours, having realized that we weren't going to be finding a paddle ship like Huck's anywhere near East Grinstead, and that life was better when you had access to table tennis and billiard tables, not to mention a warm bed.

New children would come and go from time to time and one girl, Kimberley, who came for a few weeks to give her parents a rest, seemed to be slightly retarded. She couldn't talk very much but she made a big effort to communicate with me, mainly in 'umms' and 'ahhs', but always with a big smile. I rather liked her and we got on well. She was a big girl, probably fifteen or sixteen years old, and looked more like one of the staff than one of the children. For some reason Mark and Chris didn't like her at all. She was too different for them and they really didn't want anything to do with her. They seemed to find her irritating and I noticed they were picking on her sometimes, being spiteful, calling her names and egging her on.

Because she was a bit simple she made an easy target, and they gradually grew more vindictive, like children sometimes do when they find an easy victim. They got into trouble about it more than once but it didn't stop them. They just couldn't resist the temptation to tease her when they got her on her own.

One evening I was walking past the games room when I heard noises coming from inside. I looked in to see what was happening and saw Kimberley cowering in a corner of the room like a frightened animal, with Chris and Mark taunting her. The boys were gleefully sliding knives across the floor at her, making her wide-eyed with terror. I had visions of the knife that was thrown at my brother, but now I knew this shouldn't be part of normal life.

'Leave her alone,' I said.

'Go away,' Mark said. They were having too good a time to stop and they certainly didn't see why they should do what I told them.

'Leave her alone,' I repeated, certain that what they were doing was wrong and that Kimberley needed help.

I guess they didn't like having their authority challenged in front of their victim and they turned their attentions on to me. They both picked up billiard cues and moved towards me threateningly. 'Go away,' Mark said again.

I definitely wasn't going to go anywhere now or I would have marked myself out as a coward for ever. In fact the thought of deserting Kimberley didn't enter my head. As they advanced on me I picked up a billiard ball and hurled it at Chris with all my strength. It was a brilliant shot, hitting him square in the middle of his forehead. There was a loud crack of ivory on bone and he crumpled to the ground. He lay still, with no sign of life. Mark glanced at his brother and then rushed at me, brandishing the cue furiously. I felt a surge of anger and, grabbing another ball, drew back my arm to throw again when I felt a pair of adult arms wrapping round me and I was lifted off the ground. The ball fell from my fingers.

'Calm down, Kevin,' Uncle David instructed me, as someone else ran over to tend to Chris on the floor where he was still out cold.

The room was suddenly full of staff, followed by the other children, all of them sensing some excitement and eager to see what was happening. Kimberley was still whimpering in the corner, frightened now by all the shouting and rushing around. I'd lost all control of my temper by then. I was kicking and screaming, shouting and swearing, memories of a hundred past confrontations with Gloria and Dennis going through my mind. Uncle David carried me to another room, still telling me to calm down and pinning me firmly in the crook of his arm so I couldn't escape.

Eventually I managed to get control of myself and sat, shaking, as Uncle David gave me a glass of milk and asked what had happened. I described the scene I'd witnessed.

'Why didn't you come and get me?' he asked.

I shrugged. It hadn't occurred to me. That would have been like snitching. It seemed like a situation I had to deal with myself.

'You mustn't take the law into your own hands,' he counselled.

I listened and nodded because I respected him, but it didn't sound right to me. I thought that if you wanted to get anything done in life, if you wanted to survive, you did have to take the law into your own hands. If you were hungry and no one would feed you, then you had to steal food from the fridge at night; that was how I believed life worked. If someone fell through the ice you did your best to get them out. If you wanted someone to stop doing something you had to make them. What he was saying didn't make sense to someone who had spent the early years of his life with no one he could turn to for help. I thought it was better that I followed my instincts and used my initiative in a difficult situation. But I didn't say anything.

My punishment for knocking Chris out was to be sent to my bedroom straight after getting back from school the next day. It wasn't too serious, compared to the sort of punishments I had been used to at home, and I suppose it was fair because I could have done Chris a serious injury. But it was also humiliating. My meal was brought up to me. It was a sunny evening and I stood at the window watching the others playing outside in the garden. I could see that Chris had a lump the size of a chicken's egg on his forehead, surrounded by a huge bruise.

Even though I'd been punished I didn't regret what I'd done. It still seemed like the right thing to do under the circumstances. A few days later I came back from school and found Kimberley had moved from the home. I was upset that I hadn't been given a chance to say goodbye.

7. Going Home

A few months after settling into Yarborough I was told that I could start making weekend visits home. I had mixed feelings about this. I still missed my brothers and sisters, but I had no wish to spend any time with Gloria and Dennis, sinking back into the noise, the dirt and the aggression that I was so relieved to have escaped from. Given a choice I would have preferred to stay with Guy or my friends at Yarborough. I wasn't, however, being offered an option and I didn't feel able to say that I didn't want to see my own family. The visits were to become a regular part of my routine every other weekend. Staff from Yarborough would drop me off on a Saturday or Sunday morning and then pick me up in the late afternoon. It was just a question of enduring the hours in between.

Now that I'd been away and experienced another life, I felt a real outsider at home. The house felt small and claustrophobic compared to Yarborough and there was nothing to do, no billiard or table-tennis tables, no toys or games. I had new clothes now and had grown used to living in nice, clean places. I had seen how the rest of the world lived, which made the sights and sounds of my own family all the more oppressive and depressing. Whereas I had once accepted life amongst them as natural, I could see that it was anything but. Now I was seeing them in almost the same light as other visitors to the house, like welfare workers and debt collectors, and the sight did not make me proud to be one of them.

I was doing well at my new school so I could read and write and I was used to being able to talk to people without being shouted at. I was used to groups of people interacting normally, not all yelling at once. It was a culture shock to have to go back to the old way of living, even for a day at a time.

When I arrived back at the tin house I felt completely different to the rest of them. Nothing in the way they behaved to one another had changed from the moment I'd been taken away, over a year before. Everything looked the same, sounded the same and smelt the same, only to me it seemed worse because I was no longer accustomed to it, and there was the same chaos everywhere. Everyone was still screaming and shouting at one another, with Gloria at the centre of the storm all the time. Whereas at Yarborough there were dozens of different things to do, at home there was only the television blaring away. I didn't know what to do with myself from the moment I arrived to the moment I left. It was just a question of waiting for the hours to pass.

Robert and Brenda, who had been little more than babies when I left, were both getting older and so there were two more mouths to feed and two more mouths to shout. The only difference now was that Gloria and Dennis couldn't hit me, because there was always someone coming to pick me up within a few hours. They knew that if they had bruised or cut me it would have been spotted and they would have been in trouble. I was protected from them, but that added to my separateness, as if an invisible glass shield was keeping me from them. I was grateful for that protection, but it made things more uncomfortable. I would play with my brothers and sisters all day, but be hugely relieved when it was time to go back to my friends at Yarborough.

To make matters worse, Dennis had had to give up work. It had been discovered that he was epileptic. He'd suffered a fit while working on the lines, so British Rail had laid him off with a bit of redundancy money, which he was using to buy more and more drink in his attempt to escape from the horrible reality of life at home. The more he drank the sadder he became.

When I was ten years old, two years after arriving at Yarborough, Uncle David gave me the worst piece of news possible. He told me I was going back home on a permanent basis. Gloria and Dennis must somehow have been able to convince the authorities they had mended their ways, that they were now fit parents for me, that they wouldn't be abusing me any more. How anyone looking at the state of the house and them could have believed that I will never know. Even then I didn't for one moment believe that anything would be different once I was back in their power. Although they were being nice to me when I visited, and I liked seeing my brothers and sisters, I didn't want to go back to living in dirt, with no decent regular meals or drinks, no lights in the bedrooms and all the other restrictions. I was sure that once they had me back in the house everything would return to how it had been when I was little and I would lose all the advantages that my stay at Yarborough had given me. I was so happy where I was I would have stayed there for ever if they'd allowed it. I'd grown used to mixing with other children and I wasn't sure that I would be able to cope with the constant screaming and shouting again, let alone the physical and mental torture.

It's hard to imagine how the authorities could have thought that things would be any better. There were now six active children to feed and virtually no income at all. We didn't have any breadwinner in the whole family and it was obvious, even to us children, that Dennis had a drink problem. The pressures were bound to be building up again, so why did they think it was the right place for me to be?

When the time came for me to leave Yarborough, Uncle David gave me a toy car to take with me. He hugged me tightly as we were saying goodbye.

'You're a very special boy, Kevin,' he said, 'with a kind heart. Nobody can take that away from you.'

I hugged him back, said goodbye to all the others, who had been my family for two years, and was taken out to the car by a social worker. I felt like I was being driven to my execution. I was scared, my stomach churning round and round, visions of my earlier life flashing into my mind and taunting me. The journey to New Addington seemed to take for ever. It was teatime when we arrived and as we walked up the path Gloria opened the door to greet us, the other children milling around her legs. She was being as loud and friendly as she knew how. The social worker only stayed a few minutes and I went through to see my father in the kitchen. A terrible air of sadness hung around him. It was as if life had finally defeated him, as if he'd tried everything he could think of to make a success of things and had realized that none of it was going to work, that there was now nothing that could save him from the reality of the life we were all living except the gin bottle.

To begin with things weren't as bad as I'd anticipated. I went back to my old school, although I didn't remember any of the other children very clearly, and my experiences at Yarborough meant I was now able to mix more easily with both boys and girls. When I was tiny I'd looked on all women and girls with fear, now I realized I didn't have to do that, that they could be my friends too.

Within a couple of weeks, however, things had slipped badly downhill. Gloria gave my new clothes and toys away to Wayne. If I protested that anything was mine she'd go mad at me, so I learned to keep quiet and never complain. My father's drinking was a constant strain on everyone. Although he no longer had a job, he couldn't stand to be in the house all day so he used to go up to Battersea in London and just sit in the Mason's Arms, a pub by the bridge over the Thames, where all his old workmates used to meet. He was too shy to make new friends, but he had to escape from Gloria's ranting and raving for at least part of the day. He would always dress up in his suit to go out and at weekends or in school holidays we'd all start screaming and shouting at him as he left the house, begging him to take us with him. If I didn't get picked, after making so much fuss, I'd have to scarper out of the house the moment he did, or Gloria'd beat me half to death for trying to get away from her.

Sometimes I would be picked to go with him, and I loved those days. There would always be an argument before he left, but once we were out of the house a sort of peace settled on us both. The Mason's Arms was a dark, smoky pub and I'd sit in a corner seat with an orange squash, while he sat at the bar with a pint. Occasionally, he'd glance over to check I was all right, or one of his mates would send me on an errand, like buying a newspaper. I knew that on those days I was safe because I was away from Gloria. Dennis and I would go up together on the train, because he still had a concessionary ticket which allowed him to travel for free. We could even sit in the first-class carriages if it was outside rush hour, but I always had to be quiet and on my best behaviour. I had to sit straight and look respectable and he would hiss instructions at me from between gritted teeth. But I didn't mind that, as long as I was out of the house and safe.

On one of the return trips home, after Dennis had been in the pub, drinking from before midday until after six in the evening, we headed for the train to Victoria station as usual. From there we could get a fast train to East Croydon, then a bus on to New Addington. It was the rush hour still and as we made our way across Victoria there were people rushing everywhere. They reminded me of ants hurrying away when water is poured on them. We managed to get two seats in first class, but we weren't supposed to be there at that time of day so Dennis told me to sit up straight and keep quiet. The corridor outside our compartment was packed with people anxious to get home. I felt uncomfortable, sure that they were wondering what we were doing there. I looked over at Dennis and saw he was starting to shake uncontrollably. The other people in the compartment became aware of it too. Soon it was too serious for them to politely ignore and they got up, confused and embarrassed, not knowing what to do. I'd seen it many times before and asked them to give him space. He was throwing his arms about, bumping into the people in the other seats. I tried to loosen his tie for him, but my fingers weren't strong enough to undo the knot. A man offered to help and I told him what needed to be done.

'You need to undo his tie and his top shirt buttons,' I said. 'He needs to lie on the floor, on his side so he doesn't choke.'

The man asked another passenger to help and together they laid my father out on the floor of the compartment as he jerked and frothed. Outside I could hear a voice coming over the loudspeakers: 'If there's a doctor on the station, would you please make yourself known to a member of British Rail staff.'

The train remained stationary and the crowd around us waited with barely concealed annoyance for something to be done so they could get back to their homes. A few minutes later a doctor came into the compartment and checked Dennis over.

'He suffers from epilepsy,' I explained, trying to be helpful.

The doctor nodded his understanding and did his best to make my father comfortable as we waited for the fit to pass. There was nothing else we could do as the minutes ticked past agonizingly slowly. As Dennis came round things started to get back to normal. The doctor helped him back up into his seat and other people sat down cautiously around him, trying not to look nervous. For a man as shy as Dennis it must have been a horrible experience to become such a public spectacle. I sat back on my seat and noticed everyone staring down at me, the same way the children and teachers had done so often at school. I guess they were now wondering what we were doing in a first-class compartment. I felt uneasy and averted my eyes outside the windows to escape their stares, but there were even more people peering up at me from the platform. This time it seemed as though I was looking down at them, but it didn't make me feel any better about it. I glanced at my father, who was still getting his composure back and avoiding my eyes. I turned back to the window and poked my tongue out as far as I could make it go. The faces on the other side of the glass didn't look too pleased, but then the crowd began to break up and the train prepared to start its journey.

I was used to Dennis having fits, but not in public places. Sometimes they gave me a chance to exact a modest revenge on him for all the times he had hurt me or turned a blind eye when Gloria did. I'd learned that if he was having one and I put my hand up to his face, it would completely freak him out. Sometimes, if he'd been giving me a beating and I was feeling spiteful towards him, I used to do that on purpose, just to punish him for what he did to me. Sometimes I suspected he was putting the fits on just to get out of an argument with Gloria – even she found it difficult to continue shouting abuse at a man when he was lying on the floor frothing at the mouth.

On the walk home from the bus stop each day he'd always pick up a half bottle of gin in the off-licence, and spend the evening standing in the kitchen with it, listening to the same Elvis tracks I'd been hearing all my life. As the evenings wore on he would turn up the volume to drown out every other noise in the house. To buy those bottles each day must have cost more than the rest of our household expenses added together; and he was smoking as well. Even at my young age I could see that it would be impossible for us to ever climb out of the pit we'd fallen into as long as Dennis had such a bad habit. The only hope was going to be for me to find ways to earn money myself which I could keep away from him and Gloria and use to buy food for the rest of us. But I couldn't see any way that I could do that with any regularity for at least another couple of years. I was completely trapped and pined terribly for Uncle David, Yarborough and all my friends in East Grinstead. When I had been there I had been able to be a child, if only for two years.

8. Sliding Downhill

When I first arrived back at my old school I must have seemed to the other children more like one of them, but they could soon see that I wasn't, that I was still one of the tramps.

My new teacher, Mrs Larkin, was very kind to me. She was slim and softly spoken. She seemed to me to be everything that a mother should be and I was always desperate to please her and win her approval. I could tell that she liked me; that she could see through the façade I put up to the person underneath. As I started to look and smell like a tramp once more, my clothes obviously out of fashion and down at heel, the other children began to distance themselves and the taunting began again. They would cuss at me whenever I passed, in the playgrounds or the corridors, the classrooms and the changing rooms; there was no escaping their taunts. They would shout insults about my mother; insults that I knew were based in truth. Whatever I might have felt about Gloria in private, however, I still believed I had to defend my family against the outside world and I would attack anyone who bad-mouthed her. I'd inherited a bad temper from her, which often got me in trouble with the teachers, who always felt I was an unruly child. There just didn't seem to be any break from the stresses and strains, from the moment I woke in the morning to the moment I fell back into unconsciousness at night I was fighting or being attacked by someone. Even when I was asleep I wasn't safe because of the nightmares. The stress built up inside me like a tight spring and every so often I would lose control.

As my social acceptability went downhill, so did my schoolwork.

I found it impossible to concentrate in class, which also got me into more trouble with the teachers, and it was impossible to do homework at the house in the evenings since there wasn't a single quiet room and no clear surfaces to work on. With no light in the bedrooms I couldn't even go there. I've heard of children from poor families in the Third World having to sit underneath street lamps in order to work after dark because there is no light strong enough in their homes. I can understand exactly what drives them, but in the suburbs of South London there is no such option. My time was taken up with dealing with my hunger, hiding from Gloria and Dennis, not making a noise so as to avoid a beating. The work just didn't get done and my results slid back down to the bottom of the class.

I was hungry all the time because we always left the house in the morning without breakfast and then had to wait for lunchtime in order to use the council tokens we'd been given. I found it impossible to resist the temptation to steal bits of food from other children's lunch boxes during the morning to try to stave off the pains in my stomach.

Everyone knew it was me who was stealing and so I became branded as a thief as well as a tramp. I regretted having to do it, but I was just so hungry and the boxes of food looked so tempting. I would try to remember Uncle David's words about not taking the law into my own hands, but then the hunger would take over again. I don't think it is possible for a small child to resist taking food if they're that hungry. I don't believe it is a test that they should ever be put to or judged for.

At home the television was always on, competing with the shouting and banging, and the images I saw on the screen provided a desperately needed escape route from reality for me. I'd sit for hours on the grimy floor, amongst the piles of dirty washing and litter, attempting to be as small and quiet as possible in order not to attract Gloria's attention, trying to lose myself in the programmes that showed me a better life. Even basic kids' stuff like *Playaway* on Sunday afternoons provided a simple escape before bath time.

But the best programmes all came from America. They had a sense of fun and drama and simple storylines of good versus evil. My favourites were *Mork and Mindy, Starsky and Hutch, Kojak, Dukes of Hazzard, Chips* and of course *Huckleberry Finn*, where everyone was always happy, doing whatever they wanted to do. Good always triumphed over adversity and everyone had something witty to say in every situation. Everything seemed so much better in America, bigger, freer, more relaxed and more open. But it was always hard to lose yourself in the programmes when there were so many people around making so much noise and trying to pick fights.

Often, when I was down, I'd imagine myself going to America, the land of Huckleberry Finn. I had a fantasy that one day my real parents would turn up at the house, explain there'd been a terrible mix-up at the hospital and take me away. I imagined they came from America and were planning to take me back there for a life like the ones I'd seen on television. One day I knew I would go there and it was that thought that kept me going. When everything around you is against you, you have to have a dream and mine was America. As soon as the credits rolled on one programme I couldn't wait for the next one to start. Well-meaning people sometimes criticize children for watching too much television, accusing them of being 'couch potatoes', but in families like mine the small screen was the only place where I would find any intellectual stimulation at all. The idea of reading a book was laughable and there was nothing else, just the endless repetition of Elvis songs in the kitchen, cigarettes and gin. At least television gave me a glimpse of what was possible in life, gave me some hope that there might, one day, be a light at the end of the tunnel.

What little money we had coming in from the state was getting used up earlier and earlier every week, leaving us having to scrounge whatever we could get from other people. Sometimes there wasn't even enough money in the house to buy Gloria and Dennis their cigarettes and we would be sent out to search for butt ends in the gutters or on the floors of shops. We would bring our booty home to them, like the kids in *Oliver Twist* returning to Fagin's lair, and they would then extract the tiny amounts of unburned tobacco and roll it in Rizla cigarette papers just to feed their habits for another day, until they could afford another packet.

Life at Yarborough soon began to seem like a distant dream; something that had happened to someone else and not to me. With six hungry, unruly children and two unbalanced adults all in one small pre-fabricated house there could never ever be any space or peace for any of us, no time to recover ourselves from the constant fights and arguments. We hardly ever went out, since there was nowhere to go, so we were rubbing up against one another all the time. Weekends, especially Sunday afternoons, were the worst and the school holidays at Christmas, Easter and during the summer, seemed to stretch on for ever. There was no escape for any of us. At least on normal school days we could get out of the house and away from one another for a few hours. However bad things were at school, it was always better than being at home. Wayne and I just tried to stay out of the house for as long as possible each day, desperately trying to think of ways to earn money for food to fill our permanently empty stomachs.

9. Fighting to Survive

Wayne, Sharon and Julie now tended to side with Gloria and Dennis against me if there was a fight. I could understand why they did that; I was bigger now and more able to take care of myself, and if they sided with me they were likely to be beaten for their trouble. But their defection made things harder for me and sometimes I hated them for the small amounts of attention they would get that I was denied, particularly Wayne and Brenda. Sometimes Gloria would let the others go outside to play, but tell me I had to stay in. So I'd have to sit by the window, watching them playing, just like the time at Yarborough, but when Gloria did this there was no justice or reason to it, just spite.

I must have got on Gloria's nerves almost from the moment I walked back through the door from East Grinstead, and she was soon unable to resist beating me whenever I came near her. I was simply too annoying for her to be able to bear. Because I was bigger now I was even more determined not to cry, and that seemed to infuriate her further; she must have seen it as some new kind of defiance of her power over me, because she would keep going, hitting and punching and shouting until eventually I was unable to hold the tears back any longer. My father would also join in the beatings, driven to distraction by her goading over his 'fucking son' and her accusations that he wasn't doing anything about disciplining me. To avoid arguing with her he would just lay into me for whatever imagined crime I'd committed. What I couldn't understand was that the majority of the time I didn't do anything wrong. Why would I, knowing what terrible punishments I would receive if I did?

The bruises rose all over my body, but she wasn't happy just to abuse me physically. As she did it she would constantly be shouting into my ear, her face an inch away from mine, 'Kevin's gay! Kevin's gay! He's gay, he's gay, he's gay!' All the time biting, pinching, kicking and punching me to give force to her words. 'You fucking queer!' Just as she had done a few years earlier.

I had no idea why she thought that. I don't know if I looked a bit feminine or whether she just picked it as a random insult. I had a rough idea what it meant, but I couldn't see why it applied to me. I wondered if there was something wrong with me that she knew about and I didn't. Was I gay? I would ask myself.

Now Dennis was at home all the time, if he wasn't in the pub, the friction between them increased to a permanent boiling point. When we were at school and there was no one else to attack, they would go for each other. One day, when I came home from school I found them fighting each other in the front room. She didn't fight like a woman. It was like watching two men in a pub brawl. They were grabbing hold of one another and punching as hard as they could, just like the staged fighting I saw in the American cop series, except that with Dennis and Gloria I could see the damage that was being done. They were pulling each other's hair, sending chairs and clothes flying as they ricocheted around the room. The other children were all screaming at them to stop, panic-stricken at the sight of their parents ripping each other to pieces.

I joined in the shouting, trying to make them listen to reason and back off one another; sure they were going to keep going until one of them was killed. My voice must have got through to them because they paused for a moment, his eyes dazed with drink and from the blows she'd landed on him, her spitting with anger, and they turned on me. Suddenly united in their anger they grabbed me and pinned me down, punching, kicking and biting me as the others screamed at them to stop. It was as if their hatred of me united and overcame their anger with each other. The screams of the other children grew louder. They must have thought I was now going to be killed, but eventually the pair of them exhausted themselves and I was able to crawl out of the room and up to my bedroom.

Such incidents were becoming more and more frequent and more and more violent with every passing day. Sometimes Gloria would come up with new ways to inflict pain on me. She had an old-fashioned, top-loading washing machine, which had an automated mangle on top. It consisted of two rollers that would squeeze the excess water out of the clothes to make them dry quicker. Wayne and I used to play a game of daring one another to touch the rollers when they were turning. Catching us doing it one day she became so incensed she pushed my fingers into the mangle. The pain was instant as the rollers pulled my fingers relentlessly through, crushing them.

'Mummy, no!' I screamed, over and over, hysterical with fear, believing I was going to lose my fingers. The more I screamed the harder she pushed. My yells must have been louder and more urgent than usual because Dennis appeared beside us, barging her aside and pulling my fingers free before the joints were crushed beyond mending. I learnt not to call her Mummy any more.

As everything in my day-to-day life grew grimmer, I kept one lifeline to the outside world open. I was still in touch with Guy and Gini Monson, the friends I'd made in East Grinstead. We'd exchange letters and every so often Gini would come and fetch me for a day out with them. Gloria would open Gini's letters before she gave them to me and tease me with them; no one else in our family ever received handwritten letters, but she could do nothing to stop these treats without giving away to outsiders how spiteful she was being to me in the privacy of the family. When I was with Gini and Guy I would go along with the pretence that everything was all right at home because I didn't want anyone feeling sorry for me, and because if Gloria knew I'd been saying things about her that would be another excuse to beat me. I suspect Gini guessed from the bruises I often carried, but if she asked about them I'd just say I fell. I'm sure she must have known something terrible was happening to me at home, but she respected my privacy and didn't ask any questions I wouldn't have wanted to answer. She just let me know that she would always be there for me if I needed a friend. That meant an awful lot to me.

I loved my stays with them. The only things that spoiled them for me was that I was still wetting the bed. Although Gini would never be angry with me for something like that and would help me clear it up as discreetly as possible, it was still mortifying. My relationship with Guy was not as strong as it had been when I was at Yarborough and Baldwin's Hill. He was moving ahead at school, like most children of our age, whereas I was now slipping backwards. Each visit showed that we had less and less in common. I was becoming different again and there was no hiding that fact. As the gap widened between us I realized I was actually going to their house more because of my friendship with Gini than my friendship with her son. She was almost like a guardian to me, letting me talk and showing me that there was a world out there in which parents were kind to their children, supported them and did all the right things for them. But even when we were talking I still didn't tell her how badly things were going at home; I wouldn't have dared, in case she said something to Gloria when she dropped me back. But I guess, deep down, she knew.

As well as wetting the bed, I was having nightmares again, just as I had when I was small, waking up in the night sweating and crying, the same images vivid in my mind. There were two in particular. One of them featured hordes of ants. It was like watching a film, but the picture kept changing with a jolt, focusing in closer and closer until it was a tight shot of one horrible ant and I would be jerked awake in a panic. In another there were a king and queen, sitting on tall chairs, having their heads chopped off. The same scenes came to me, over and over again. I could never get used to them. I could never escape.

10. Losing Control

The pressure kept building inside my head. At home there were the constant beatings and the taunting: 'Kevin's gay! Kevin's gay!' And at school more taunting: 'Lewis is a tramp! Tramp! Tramp!' Even when I was asleep I couldn't get away from the nightmares.

It was relentless, hammering away at my brain with no break or respite for weeks on end. Gloria must have been able to exercise some self-control because she hardly ever hit me anywhere where it would show. Although my body was covered in bruises, none of them were visible when I was dressed, so no one at school spotted them except at P.E., when they would be explained away. Most of the time no one took any notice and there was nobody I could turn to for help because I didn't dare to betray Gloria for fear of the repercussions.

Eventually I couldn't take any more and the volcano erupted. We were on our way to assembly and a boy who seemed to me to have everything in the world just wouldn't let up on me. He kept on chanting, 'Tramp, tramp, Lewis is a tramp!'

He pushed it and pushed it until my temper exploded in a vast, boiling eruption and all hope of self-control was gone. I flew at him, just as my mother would fly at me, not holding back any of my strength or anger, blind and deaf to everything except my desire to silence him. Every ounce of the frustration that had been building inside me went into the punches I landed on him. My anger gave me a strength way beyond my puny, malnourished frame's normal abilities. My opponent had not been expecting any sort of response and collapsed to the floor immediately, but I couldn't stop hitting him even though I already had him beaten. That must have been how Gloria felt whenever she started hitting me, just not able to stop, wanting to pour every tiny bit of anger and frustration and unhappiness out. There was screaming and crying all round and a teacher called Mr Robinson appeared behind me. He probably ordered me to stop but I was past responding to orders, just a ball of anger in action. He grabbed me, holding me tightly, like Uncle David had at Yarborough when I was going for Chris and Mark with the billiard balls. He propelled me along to the main hall where people were coming into assembly. Everyone was using the other door to avoid the mayhem I was causing as I fought and kicked all the way. He threw open the doors and we stumbled in, me still struggling with all my strength, him trying to calm me. I kept fighting and he forced me down on the ground to get more control, whispering in my ear for me to calm down. Eventually I realized I was overpowered and I stopped struggling. I lay on the floor suddenly exhausted and burst into tears. Looking up I could see that the assembly room was now full of children and teachers.

Every pair of eyes in the room turned to look down at me. By the time I'd managed to get control of my sobbing the whole room was silent, everyone's attention fixed on the problem child on the floor, everyone excited by the drama of the situation, grateful for the distraction from the tedium of the normal routine. Yet again I'd been singled out from the crowd and shown up to be something different, something bad and wild and uncontrollable. I just wanted to shrink away to nothing. I wanted to change places with anyone else in the room. I didn't want to be Kevin Lewis for a moment longer. I never wanted to be Kevin Lewis, I always wanted to be someone else, someone with hope and a future, not someone for whom there was no escape.

Even after such a dramatic scene and such a public humiliation, I had no choice but to pick myself up and keep going with my life, knowing now it was only a matter of time before the same thing happened again. My teacher, Mrs Larkin, seemed to understand a bit of what I was going through. She always spoke to me in such a kind voice and I used to fantasize that she was my mother, instead of Gloria. One day, after swimming, when we got back to the class, I was so hungry I stole some pieces of food from a lunch box. A little girl saw me and started to call me 'tramp'. She was a red-haired girl who suffered from asthma and I should have been able to control myself, but I panicked. I'd had a bad time with Gloria the night before and so I punched her. I panicked more and was shaking nervously, not knowing what was going to happen next. She started crying and Mrs Larkin came through to see what was happening. She asked me for an explanation and I had none. She got hold of me and I became scared and kneed her in the groin, the one person who'd shown me any kindness and affection. I immediately knew I'd done something terribly wrong.

Mrs Larkin looked at me with sad eyes. 'Is that it, Kevin?' she asked and I burst into tears. 'Come on,' she said. 'Headmaster's office.'

I'd hit a teacher, and a woman as well, and I'd hit a little girl. I knew now I'd gone way beyond the line of acceptable behaviour. They couldn't possibly avoid punishing me for this, and in a way I wanted to be punished, because I'd hurt Mrs Larkin, who'd always been on my side. Maybe I was as bad a person as Gloria said I was.

In the headmaster's office I just kept saying 'sorry' but it was far too late for that. Someone was sent to fetch Gloria and I knew what I would be in for. I begged them not to, but I guess they had no choice.

When Gloria arrived in the headmaster's office she was acting the concerned parent. Even though I'd kicked her, Mrs Larkin gave me such a look of warmth as they all explained to Gloria what had happened and I just wished I could turn the clock back an hour, so I could put everything right. The headmaster said I was suspended. It was the worst possible verdict because it meant I'd be trapped at home with Gloria for days on end. I felt sick with fear. She continued to act like a model parent as we left the headmaster's office.

As we walked across the school playground behind our house Gloria took my hand. To anyone watching it could have looked like a firm maternal gesture, but her fingers just kept squeezing harder and harder and my arm was nearly pulled out of its socket as she dragged me towards home. By the time we were into the alley between the houses, and out of sight of both the road and the school, I was begging her to stop crushing my fingers, but she took no notice. She couldn't hold back her fury a moment longer and my head exploded as her fist crashed into it. The pain was blinding and I would have fallen to the ground if she hadn't been holding me up by the arm. She kept dragging me towards the house, smacking my legs and pinching my arms as I stumbled along, trying to clear my head and keep up. She seemed unable to summon enough violence to make herself feel any better, to relieve whatever pressure was building in her own head. A continuous stream of swear words poured from her mouth and I felt that I was in serious danger. I knew that as soon as I was behind the closed front door she'd lose all self-control, just as I had done with the boy at school and she might just kill me.

As we came out of the alley I managed to break free and ran as fast as I could in the opposite direction along King Henry's Road. I could hear her voice echoing down the road after me in a screech of frustrated fury, unconcerned who else might be able to hear in the surrounding houses.

'You'll be sleeping in the fucking bath tonight, you fucking little cunt, if you don't come back here, now!'

Sleeping in the bath was the least of my fears. I was sure I'd be dead long before it was time to go to sleep. I was filled with fear, from the roots of my hair to the soles of my fleeing feet. The traffic roared past as I ran on, past the anonymous rows of houses and the ugly tower blocks of flats. I glanced over my shoulder. She was still shouting at me to come back, but her voice was growing fainter and she wasn't following me. I got to the end of the road and looked around frantically for somewhere to hide, not just from her, but from anyone else who might feel it their duty to take me back to her. I headed off towards the woods around the golf course that Wayne and I sometimes played in, the ones I'd planned to hide in many years before. Crossing the busy road at the top of the hill I came out on to the open grass that played host to local football matches. There was a sweeping view across the green valley with tiny figures of golfers in the distance. I just wanted to get as far from the streets full of houses and cars as possible. I ran on until I came to the first line of trees and threw myself down beneath the bushes, panting, my chest aching with the effort of running so far and so fast, my heart thumping. My fingers still hurt from where she'd crushed them and my head was spinning from the first punch. I needed to rest for a while. Once I'd recovered I spent the rest of the afternoon mooching about under the cover of the trees. It was pleasant to be alone and not to have to deal with anyone else. I liked the tranquillity of the woods. I imagined I was Huckleberry Finn and that I had no home to go back to, that I could wander in any direction I chose, enjoying whatever adventures turned up. It felt good to rest for a while and just be free, even though I knew it couldn't last.

When the sun went in it started to feel colder and the valley, which had looked so green and inviting a few hours before, was now full of shadows. I wondered if I could make myself a shelter somewhere, like they did in television programmes. I was beginning to feel desperately hungry and tried to think where I might be able to find something to eat. Even the idea of Gloria's fat-soaked chips was starting to seem attractive.

The shapes of the trees began to merge into one another and, as the rest of the world outside the wood grew quieter, I could hear the rustling of leaves and branches all around me. I began to imagine what might be hiding in them, watching me, waiting to pounce. Something screeched in the trees above my head and something else rustled past my feet unseen. My heart pounded in my chest. I knew that if I went home. I'd be beaten, but at least I'd be in the safety of my own home and I'd be able to crawl into my bed once she'd finished with me. There might be something to eat, even if it was only leftovers. God alone knew what would happen to me in the wood if I stayed out all night. Reluctantly, I made my way home, the headlights steadily passing as I dragged my feet back along the pavements I had been running on just a few hours before.

Gloria must have been watching for me from the window because she opened the front door as I came into view. She stood still and threatening in the doorway, leaving just enough room for me to squeeze silently past.

'Your fucking son is here!' she shouted through to Dennis in the kitchen, and shut the front door behind me.

He came out to look at me and I saw his face was covered in scratches. I guessed they'd been fighting again and the thought made me even more frightened. Everyone else had eaten their chips and mine were standing on the table, waiting for me. They were cold, the fat going solid on the edges, but I was so hungry I would have eaten anything. When I'd swallowed the last mouthful Dennis told me to go to bed so I wouldn't irritate Gloria any more. As I went past him on the way to the door he put his hand on my shoulder, as he sometimes did. It was as if he was trying to communicate with me but couldn't find the words. I tried to stop myself crying, but I couldn't. Even a gesture as small as that was more than

I could bear. He lifted me up and put his arms around me, holding me tightly. For a few seconds I felt safe, even though I knew she was waiting in the background and that she'd still be there the next day, once he'd gone out to the pub to see his friends.

She left me alone that night and I slept soundly. Maybe she was tired out from fighting with everyone else. The next day I wasn't able to go to school because of the suspension and I knew she wouldn't be able to stand having me around the house all day. I was right. Every day of the suspension she laid into me with whatever she could find; her hand, her belt or a broken broomstick. Eventually she hurt me so badly that I couldn't crawl out of bed the following morning. I stayed in bed all day and that evening, when Dennis came home from the pub, I heard them talking downstairs. He came up to my room and lifted me gently out of the bed without saying a word, carrying me through into their bedroom where there was a light. He examined the marks on my body while she stood watching in the background with her arms folded. I could see they were both nervous about something.

It was a bad day for her to choose to damage me so noticeably because a social worker was due to call the following day. They only came by every two or three weeks, so usually she left me alone for the few days before a call was due in order to allow the bruises to fade. This time she'd left it too late, although my face was still unmarked. They were obviously worried that this time she'd gone too far. Dennis carried me back to my bed.

The next day she left me in bed, tucking the covers up under my chin, and told me not to pull the covers down, whatever happened.

'If you say anything to the lady you'll get the fucking stick once she's gone,' she warned, and I had no reason to doubt her word.

I heard the social worker arriving downstairs. Apart from Brenda and Robert, who were still too young for school, the other children were out, leaving the house reasonably quiet with just the noise of the television playing in the background. I could hear Gloria's loud voice downstairs pouring out all her complaints and moans. All visitors to the house got out as quickly as they possibly could. I just hoped that this time the woman would pull down my bedcovers before she went. If she did that then it wouldn't be my fault if she saw the marks, and then perhaps they'd send me back to Yarborough. I waited, my heart pounding, as the voices came closer up the stairs. Gloria had left the curtains drawn so it would be difficult for the woman to see anything without a light. She was telling the woman about how I was feeling poorly and the woman was making sympathetic noises.

They arrived in the bedroom and the social worker asked how I was. I said I was fine, far too scared to say anything else for fear of the reprisals that would come after she'd left. She obviously wanted to believe me, because if I was all right then she could get out of the house as fast as possible, I concentrated with all my strength, trying to will her to lift the sheets that hid my broken body, but I could see she was already backing out of the door, probably trying to escape the smell as much as anything else.

'I hope you get better soon, Kevin,' she said, and was gone, taking all my hopes of escape with her.

The following week I was back at school and Mrs Larkin was behaving as if the whole incident had never happened. She was in the middle of organizing a talent contest.

'What would you like to be in the contest, Kevin?' she asked.

'Worzel Gummidge,' I replied, knowing that Gloria would never let me do something like that. Worzel was a scarecrow character who had his own popular television series at the time. All day I felt really sad that I wouldn't be able to join in the fun with everyone else.

When the bell went at the end of school Mrs Larkin asked me to wait behind.

'Would you like me to help you with your costume, Kevin?' she asked.

She must have known that all the other children would be getting help from their parents, and guessed that Gloria and Dennis would not be up to that sort of challenge.

'It's all right, Miss,' I said, my eyes on the floor. 'I'm not allowed to enter the contest.'

'Okay,' she said, putting her hand on my head. 'Would you like me to have a word with your parents for you?'

'No!' I said, more sharply than I wanted to. I could just imagine how Gloria would turn on me if a teacher came to the house, and I didn't want Mrs Larkin to see the way we lived either. I thought that if she saw our house she'd see me as the other children in the school did; she would see that I was just a tramp, and not someone who was worth bothering with.

All the other children kept talking about what they were going to do and be in the contest, but no one asked me, so I didn't have to confess that I wasn't going to enter. It was coming to the end of my time at Wolsey Junior and I comforted myself with the thought that maybe things would be better at the next school.

A few days before the contest there was a knock at the door after school and Mrs Larkin was standing there when Gloria opened it. My heart sank and I slunk out of sight. The two of them stood talking on the doorstep and I stayed right out of the way, straining to hear what was going on. Mrs Larkin's voice was so quiet I couldn't hear what she was saying and Gloria didn't say anything to me after she'd gone. I knew better than to ask any questions. I was just relieved that the visit hadn't resulted in me getting a beating.

The next morning, during our break, Mrs Larkin asked me to stay behind.

'I've got something to show you,' she said, pulling a plastic carrier bag out from under her desk. Inside was a complete scarecrow outfit, with straw up the sleeves and patches all over. 'This is your costume for the contest tomorrow.'

'But –' I protested.

'It's all right.' She cut me short. 'Everything's been sorted out with your mother. But you'd better think up some lines to say if you want to win.'

That afternoon I wrote myself some lines. I spent ages over them, feeling like a real child, just like all the others instead of an outsider.

The next day the assembly hall was packed with parents, staff and visitors. I peeked through the side of the curtains, searching the sea of faces for Gloria and Dennis, but couldn't see either of them. I don't suppose I really expected them to be there and in a way I was relieved that they weren't, but it would have been nice to think they would see me doing something. Perhaps then they would have realized that I wasn't as completely useless as they were always saying I was. There was a real buzz in the air as we waited backstage to perform. I was in costume like everyone else. I was part of the action and everyone seemed to have forgotten that they despised me while I was hiding behind the Worzel Gummidge character. It felt almost unbearably good, like being back at Yarborough and part of a community. The straw itched horribly, but I didn't care.

When it came to my turn to perform I strode out on to the stage and there was a ripple of laughter at my costume before everyone fell silent, waiting to hear what I would say. I froze. I couldn't think of a thing to say, my head was empty, all my carefully prepared lines gone. I looked down at the front row and saw Mrs Larkin and Mr Robinson both looking up at me with encouraging smiles. After what seemed like an age words started to come out of my mouth, and then there was the most wonderful sound I'd ever heard. It was laughter, and it was for me. But it wasn't the cruel laughter I was used to. They weren't mocking me, they were enjoying my act. They were pleased with me. I tried a few more words and added an expression or two and movements I'd seen Worzel do on television and the laughter swelled up, lifting my confidence still further. There were people shouting out. It was uproar, such a happy noise. I was so thrilled they had trouble getting me off the stage. I could have stayed there all night. Eventually I took my bow and left, walking on air.

As soon as the show was over I ran home, so proud of myself and so excited by the experience.

I shouted to Gloria as I barged in through the front door, 'I had such a great time at the contest. You should have come!'

'Should?' she sneered, and I immediately knew I'd said the wrong thing. 'Should?'

I wiped the smile off my face and averted my eyes quickly. I ran straight upstairs to my bedroom to keep out of the way. Sitting on the edge of the bed, replaying everything that had happened in my head, I was unable to keep the smile from creeping back.

My time at Wolsey Junior was due to finish a few weeks later. Before I left Mrs Larkin gave us all a card with a twenty pence piece inside. My card simply said, 'Don't forget to count to ten before you react. Love, Mrs Larkin.'

11. Out to Work

School holidays were always difficult because it meant we were all imprisoned together in the house twenty-four hours a day. At least school gave us a breathing space of a few hours, even if it brought its own form of hell with it. When the holidays did come round I was always looking for excuses to go out and I was always hungry; so from the age of ten or eleven I started searching for ways to make some money to buy food for myself and for my brothers and sisters. This was around 1980.

It's hard to make money when you're that young, not only because there aren't that many jobs you are allowed to do, but because there are always people looking for ways to cheat children, trying to get something for nothing. I used to go to the local golf courses and offer my services as a caddy. Although golf courses are very pleasant places to be, particularly on fine days, caddying is hard work, particularly when you're still small and not as strong as you should be because of your appalling diet. I would spend all day lugging bags of clubs around for players and quite often they would realize they were out of cash at the end of the game. They would always have some excuse and would tell me where to find them later to collect my money. On several occasions I went search- ing for the addresses these men had given me, spending hours walking around the streets trying to remember exactly what the name was that they'd given me. Sometimes I'd have to take a guess and ring a doorbell, only to find it was the wrong place. It would have been so easy for these people just to give me the few pounds they owed me. It would have meant nothing to them; no more than the price of a small round of drinks, but it would have meant I could have bought some food. Every time someone pulled a stunt like that we just had to go another day without.

Even when I did manage to get my hands on some cash, there was never any point bringing it back into the house because Gloria or Dennis would take it off me to buy drink or cigarettes. They would always promise breezily to pay it back, but it never happened. So the moment any of us earned anything we'd buy sweets, or fish and chips, or whatever we could afford to stave off the pangs for a few hours. The people at the chippie up in the shopping precinct used to store their spare chippings of batter and sell it to us by the bag, which was cheap and filling.

If I did manage to get some money and didn't want to take it into the house, I would go home and wait outside in the phone booth opposite the house, trying to attract Wayne's or Sharon's attention, so we could all go down to the chippie together. It involved a lot of walking for a small boy; all the way back from the town or the golf courses with the money, and then all the way back up again with my brother and sisters. But the thought of food can drive a hungry child a long way.

Our diet was always terrible. Gloria didn't have any idea how to feed children. We lived pretty much totally on chips; we certainly didn't have any fresh fruit or vegetables. The chip pan was never washed; it just sat on the side in the kitchen, waiting for the next batch to be thrown in. The stale smell of frying clung to everything in the house and everyone who came there.

In the first summer holidays after I went back home from East Grinstead I also wanted to make enough money to buy myself a birthday present. Being at Yarborough had taught me how good it felt to be given something and I knew my parents wouldn't do it. So I decided to buy myself something, wrap it up in its plastic bag and then open it on the day as if it was a surprise, pretending to myself that I couldn't remember what it was. It was a ritual I would be repeating a great many times in the coming years. It's a habit I still haven't broken, even after all this time. It drives my wife mad when I buy myself something I want just a few days before my birthday, not thinking that she might have had the same idea.

Another of the early jobs I did was being a milk boy. I would wake myself up at four or five in the morning, while the rest of the family was still asleep, and I'd quietly get dressed, creep downstairs and let myself out of the house. Even though I never had a watch I always knew roughly what the time was and waking up has never been a problem for me. I liked the quiet of the early mornings and the freshness of the air. I would then run around the streets looking for milk floats, listening out for the distinctive hum of their electric engines and the rattle of the bottles in their crates, so that I could offer to help the milkmen with their deliveries. If I managed to find one they nearly always agreed, and paid me for my trouble, but it wasn't always possible to hunt them down in time. Some mornings I'd spend an hour or two searching the streets, until it was too late, and then I'd have to return home empty-handed and already hungry in order not to be late for school. The milkman I liked best sometimes used to pay me with food he carried on the float, rather than money, which I was always happy about because it gave us something for breakfast, which would mean we could get through the morning until lunchtime with full stomachs.

There was an open-air market every Friday in New Addington, filling the car park between the main road and the shops with stalls and vans selling everything you can imagine from wonderful fruit and vegetables to cheap clothes and electronic gadgets. There was a meat auctioneer who would turn up in a huge lorry, let down the side and set up shop right there. I would sit and watch in awe as the men up in the lorry, behind the counter, worked the crowd, shouting out their wares, taking bids, exchanging jokes. Everyone who worked the market seemed to have ready money and to be enjoying what they were doing. I loved the buzz of a world where you lived by the deals you made that day, and the crush of shoppers and browsers as they meandered their way through the tightly packed stalls.

I used to get up early and walk the mile or two up to the precinct to get there as they were arriving in their vans, to offer my services. There was a guy with a toy stall who would give me a couple of pounds to help him set up and lay everything out, which I loved doing. The market would be there in all weathers and I can remember doing it in the snow one year. I only had plimsolls and my feet were so cold I thought they were going to drop off. The full-time workers in the market all had padded moon boots, which were the fashion in the early eighties, and I really wanted a pair of those, but there was no way I could afford them, not even the pairs they sold cheaply in the market. All the money I made had to go on food before it went on keeping my feet warm, so I just had to keep quiet, stamp my feet to keep the blood circulating and get on with it.

In the summer holidays the funfair would come to town and Wayne and I would both go up to help them set up. We would go from stall to stall asking if anyone had any jobs they wanted doing. It was hard physical work. Earning the money was great, but being out of the house and amongst friendly, happy people was the real treat. A few years later my little brother, Robert, ran off with the funfair, just to get away from the torments of home. I think he suffered pretty much the same treatment as I did and the world of the fairground offered him a way to disappear.

When I was eleven I moved to another school. I'd been looking forward to moving from Wolsey Junior, thinking it would give me a fresh start and that I'd be able to make friends at last and be like everyone else. I forgot that all the same children would be moving with me, so nothing would actually change. Even though we were not right behind our house any more, people still knew about my mother and about my nicknames and the stealing and the tempers. It wasn't a nice school. I always found that when other children were on their own they'd talk to me and be quite friendly and normal. As soon as they were in a group, however, they'd ignore me, or hurl insults. It was as if they believed they'd be tainted if they were seen associating with me, as if they might catch my unpopularity and be forced to be outcasts along with me. I could understand why they felt that but it still hurt, and I couldn't see how I could break the cycle of exclusion and unpopularity.

There was one particular girl who'd been quite nice to me on a number of occasions. One morning, as I was coming in late in a bit of a hurry, I passed her as she was waving through a window to her friends inside the classroom. At just the same moment two boys came out of the building, called me a name and pushed me. I fell against the girl, knocking her into the window and banging her head. I was horrified because I could see she'd hurt herself quite badly and the other two boys had disappeared, leaving me looking like the guilty party. The girl was crying so hard no one asked her for her opinion of what had happened. Because of my history it was immediately assumed I had attacked her and I was dragged in front of the headmaster, who had a reputation for being a cruel man. I tried to explain what had happened but he wouldn't listen. Nobody believed I'd been pushed; they were all convinced I'd just shoved her into the glass for no reason. Why would I do that? I thought to myself as they went on and on at me. She was always nice to me. Why would I attack one of the few people who showed me friendship? Any protests I made were brushed aside, so I fell silent, horribly aware that there was nothing I could do to change their perception of me.

The two guys who had pushed me were also friends with all the other kids who'd witnessed the scene through the window, so no one from in there was going to speak up on my behalf against them, even though they'd seen exactly what had happened.

The headmaster liked to give the impression he was a stern disciplinarian and made it clear that he intended to cane me for this offence.

'But I'm not going to do it immediately because I need to get permission from your parents,' he said. 'I want you to spend a little time thinking about what you've done and about what's going to happen to you.'

'Please don't phone my mother,' I pleaded, knowing that this would give her one more excuse to lay into me herself once I got home, but he was adamant. I guess it was a legal requirement.

And so I had to wait outside the headmaster's office until he was ready to cane me. Getting permission from Gloria, of course, was no more than a formality. Beating me was an activity she thoroughly approved of, whether she did it herself or delegated it to Dennis or anyone else, so I knew there wouldn't be any salvation coming from that quarter. Waiting for pain, when you know it's coming, makes it a hundred times more frightening.

When it was finally time for me to go back in and hold my hand out he didn't spare me at all. It was not enough for him simply to bring the cane down on my outstretched palm. In order to exert maximum force he pulled up a chair and climbed on to it, jumping off each time he brought the cane down on my hand. The pain was incredible and I wasn't able to hide it. I yelled fit to burst as each of the four strokes descended and he climbed back on to the chair again for the next. By that time I was quite seriously malnourished from the appalling diet I was living on, and I was developing anaemia, although I didn't know it, which meant that my resistance to pain was lower than it should have been. My screams could be heard in all the classrooms that lined the corridor up to the headmaster's office.

I was completely unable to hide the tears, even after the caning had finished, because the pain continued to pulse through my hand, making me feel faint and sick as I slowly made my way back to the classroom. Every pair of eyes turned to stare at me as I opened the door and walked in. They all knew what had happened with the girl because they'd witnessed it through the window, and they'd all heard my screams. For the first time ever I thought I saw guilt in some of their faces. It was as if they were beginning to grow up and realize that the way they were treating me was wrong. All of them knew that it had been within their power to speak up and save me from the beating, but none of them had had the courage to do it. I guess that didn't make them feel proud of themselves.

I didn't say anything, just sat down and tried to catch up with whatever was happening in the class. They were all writing something so I picked up my pen, but I wasn't able to hold it because my hand was burning so fiercely and I couldn't think straight because my mind was in such turmoil.

Soon after that incident we were moved to another council house a few miles away in Norbury. I think our neighbours in the Horseshoe had been complaining about the trouble Gloria was always causing and so the council decided to give us a fresh start. Our standard of living didn't improve as a result, and the house, although it was built of bricks rather than tin, was no nicer than the wreck we had left behind us. I did now have a room of my own, but it was the smallest room in the house, designed to be a box room, I would imagine, rather than a bedroom. As far as I was concerned it was just another undecorated and unlit cell. There was one small square window, which allowed the moon to shine through and give me some light to find my way around at night.

Wayne and I were moved to a new school in Mitcham, which I felt hopeful about, seeing it as a chance to make a new start amongst people who knew nothing of our history. But it wasn't long before our new classmates realized the sort of family we came from and we were excluded socially once more. Wayne went to the new school first and had already started to play truant each day by the time I arrived. I could see the attraction of staying away; at least it freed us from the taunts and the disdainful looks, so we would go off together. Gloria always claimed it was my bad influence that led Wayne astray, which gave her another reason to lay into me at home. But she knew he'd been doing it before, and he carried on after I'd been moved to another school.

Sometimes Wayne and I got on really well and sometimes we loathed each other, like most brothers, I guess. Because he got more new clothes from council clothing grants than I did, being the older one, he tended to be less conspicuous at school. So he hated it when I was around because he got stuck with the same 'tramp' label as me. When he was on his own he could sometimes win people over.

To separate us off I was moved a few months later to Ingram High School for Boys in Norbury, in the hope that I would do better away from Wayne's influence. This was a much nicer school and it was there that I met a teacher called Colin Smith. He seemed to look at me differently to other teachers. He was a tough disciplinarian, a teacher of the old school. He was an immaculate man in everything he did; very firm and no one ever mucked about in his classes, but he was also very fair, and he seemed to think there was something worthwhile about me.

The beatings and jibes were still going on at home and no one at school took any interest in the bruises I was always covered in. Now I was getting older perhaps they assumed they were just the result of normal boyish rough and tumble, but I noticed Colin Smith looking at them when I was in my P.E. kit one day. He asked me about them and I made the usual excuses about falling over and bumping into things. He didn't say anything, just nodded thoughtfully, and I could tell he didn't believe me. I hoped he wouldn't follow it up. I dreaded anyone going round to the house and saying anything, because I knew it would lead to me getting a worse beating once they'd gone. I was also keen that no one at the school got to see how we lived.

Because of the start I'd got at Baldwin's Hill in East Grinstead, I'd managed to stay in the third highest class when I went to secondary school even with my gradually slipping standards. But now, as the pressure was being put on academically, I was finding it hard to keep up, because I still couldn't do homework in the same way as the other children and there was more and more emphasis being put on the work done at home. When there is nowhere to sit, and there is constant shouting and fighting going on all around, it's impossible to concentrate on anything. I couldn't even retreat into my bedroom to work because there was no light once the sun had gone down. Before long I had slipped all the way down to the bottom class.

I was receiving a council token each day to pay for lunch at school, while other children had packed lunches. Although it marked me out as different, I was still very grateful for it. Had it not been for that free meal my health would have deteriorated even more quickly than it did. We still rarely had any breakfast at home and there were chips for supper every single night.

Colin Smith asked me to stay behind after lessons one day. I went to his office, wondering what I might be in trouble for now.

'How's life at home, Kevin?' he asked, as blunt and to the point as always.

'Fine,' I lied, not able to look him in the eye.

'If there are any problems you can always come and talk to me, you know,' he said.

'Yes, sir,' I said, and beat a hasty retreat.

It was a kind thing for him to say, but I didn't think I would ever have the nerve to actually tell anyone outside the family what went on at home. In fact, things had been getting worse, although at least now I was able to get out of the house for several hours at weekends in order to work.

In my early morning searches I'd met a milkman called John. He was a young guy and I thought he was great. He told me he was a jazz funker and that when he was off work he would wear the hat and the Farrers that were all the rage at the time; driving a squared off Cortina when he wasn't on the milk float. He was exactly the sort of man I wanted to be. He told me his full name was 'A Hundred Per Cent John, because there are so many Johns working in this area'. I worked with him on Friday and Saturday mornings because they were his busiest days, when he had to collect the money from his customers as well as make deliveries.

I enjoyed the work, even though it was hard in the winter because the cold glass of the bottles would stick to your hands and you couldn't wear gloves or the bottles would slip out. I was always trying to find those fingerless gloves that old people wear. I liked the feeling of being useful and of being rewarded fairly for my labours.

John noticed the bruises on me from time to time, just as Colin Smith had, and would sometimes ask me about them. I always had an excuse ready, but I could see he didn't believe me any more than the teacher did. At the end of the round he'd always take me for breakfast at a café opposite the police station and I would have a giant fry up, or even a spaghetti Bolognese if it was nearer lunch-time. The people working in there got to know me and would always give me a bowl so huge even I couldn't finish it. I guess they could see I needed feeding up. By the time they'd finished with me I could hardly move. It was great.

One day during the summer holidays I turned up at John's milk float with a huge bruise around my eye. John didn't say anything;

he just looked at it and stayed silent when I offered my usual unconvincing explanation. When we'd finished the round and had had something to eat he told me to hop into his car.

'I'll take you home,' he said. 'I want to have a word with your dad.'

I sat in terrified silence as we made our way back to the house. John was a strong lad and I could see he was spoiling for a fight. I dreaded to think what would happen once he'd gone and I was left to their mercy. He didn't say anything either. He seemed to be seething with anger.

'Please,' I said eventually, as he turned into our road, 'just leave it.' But he still didn't reply.

There was a concrete path from the pavement through the open, debris-strewn front garden. Sometimes that path felt like the longest walk in the world. I could see John glancing at the chaos all around and averting his eyes so as not to embarrass me. He knocked loudly on the door as I stood beside him on the step, trembling. We could hear raised voices inside.

Eventually Dennis opened the door and I breathed a sigh of relief that it wasn't Gloria. The two of them stood looking at one another. Neither of them said anything. I guess John thought he'd made his point just by being there for me. Without so much as a nod or a smile he turned and walked back to his car. I went into the house. Dennis closed the door behind me and said I wasn't to work for John any more. He must have known exactly what message John was conveying with that meaningful silence. I never saw A Hundred Per Cent John again.

As well as working as a milk boy in the early mornings, I would team up with Wayne and try anything to make extra money in the evenings, weekends and holidays. We didn't mind how many hours we put in because it always meant we were out of the house and earning money for food. We'd do 'penny for the guy' in October and in December we'd go carol singing. We were terrible singers. On Christmas Eve one year we were doing our rounds and were working some houses on a busy roundabout. I doubt if anyone inside the houses could hear us over the traffic noise, but we were giving it our best shot. In a moment of high spirits I put my foot on a wall outside one of the houses we were singing at. The wall collapsed beneath me and we ran for our lives.

We were still laughing about it a few minutes later as we walked past a church. From inside we could hear people singing carols. They were doing it properly, not like us, and it was a very attractive sound. Neither of us had ever been inside a church before and our curiosity got the better of us. We crept up to the door, summoning up all our courage. It had a huge iron handle, which I turned cautiously. I pushed open the door and peered through at the dimly lit interior. We stared up in amazement at the tall ceilings, which stretched above the small congregation. Flickering candles lit the scene and a rich musty scent of age and polish filled my nostrils. The singing came to an end just as we looked in and I dropped the door handle, sending a mighty clang echoing round the quiet building.

The vicar looked up and saw us, frozen in embarrassment on the threshold, and smiled welcomingly, gesturing for us to come in. We obeyed, curious to see what was going on and comforted by the atmosphere of the place, and sat down in an empty pew at the back, listening attentively as they went back to their singing. As we sat there, in that beautiful place, Wayne and I exchanged looks and we both knew at the same moment that we loved each other. No matter what we'd been through in our short lives, or how much we resented one another from time to time, we knew that much. We didn't stay long, the moment was never repeated and neither of us ever mentioned it, but I've never forgotten it.

Christmas came and went as usual. While other children wanted it to last as long as possible so they could be with their friends and families, giving and receiving presents and enjoying big meals, Wayne and I just wanted it to be over so we could go back out looking for new work. It was beyond any of our capabilities to generate a festive spirit in a house so steeped in hatred and misery.

A local newsagent in Thornton Heath high street said we could do a newspaper round for him if we wanted, but said we'd have to be at the shop by five in the morning. The next morning we were there, dead on five, having walked all the way from the house, but he didn't turn up till after seven. He didn't offer any explanation or apology. It seemed an unnecessarily cruel and inconsiderate gesture, but we weren't in a position to complain because we wanted the work and knew that if we didn't do as he said he'd have no trouble finding other kids who would. He must have been able to tell how desperate we were for money and he offered us other jobs around his house, cleaning up leaves, walking his Dobermann (or should I say allowing the Dobermann to take us for walks), or whatever needed doing. Even though we didn't like the man we were grateful for any chances to earn.

Wayne had managed to get a couple of second-hand fishing rods and, because it was him, Gloria hadn't made a fuss about bringing them into the house. If they'd been mine she would have beaten me with them until they snapped. Sometimes the newsagent would pay us with drink and crisps instead of cash, which we'd take with us and go fishing in a nearby pond. Occasionally we'd use the free train passes we got because of Dennis having worked for British Rail and travel down to Brighton to fish in the sea. They were always great days out. We never caught anything and we wouldn't have had a clue what to do if we had, but it made me feel, at least for a few hours, like we were Tom Sawyer and Huck Finn on an adventure. I loved the feeling of freedom when we came out of Brighton station and I could smell the sea air and knew that we could please ourselves for the whole day. Even though we didn't have any money to do anything on the pier or in any of the amusement arcades or snack bars, we could still use the beach and watch the waves and the other holidaymakers. It gave us a chance to empty our minds and dream a little of what life could be like once we were finally free of our parents. It felt a long walk back up the hill to the station when we knew we were on our way home again.

I was also cleaning cars on Sundays on my own. From nine o'clock in the morning I would walk to a nearby street and be knocking on doors with my bucket, sponge and Fairy Liquid, offering my services around the neighbourhood. I'd work right through the day, ignoring the traffic that passed a few inches from my back as I lathered and rinsed and rubbed the parked cars with every ounce of energy I could muster. I built up a number of regular customers who I would do first, before going in search of new business. Although I didn't realize it, my health was beginning to seriously deteriorate due to the way we lived, which meant that by the end of the day I was completely shattered. But I enjoyed the work and the freedom that the money was starting to give me.

One of the houses I knocked at was occupied by two men. It was a Victorian semi in a row of identical houses. I cleaned their car every week and they were always very pleasant, giving me a biscuit and a glass of milk while I worked. The house had a black door, which I would come to early on in my round. One Sunday morning I was chatting to one of the men while I was collecting my money, having finished their car, and he asked if I did any other work.

'I might do,' I shrugged, quite willing to try anything that would earn money, even though I was still only twelve years old.

It was summer time and I noticed he was wearing shorts as he led me down the side of the house and through the back garden to a shed. I wondered if he wanted me to do some gardening, or clear out the shed. I didn't mind what it was as long as he paid me.

'Do you like young men?' he asked once we were inside the shed and he had carefully closed the door behind us.

He might as well have asked me if I liked green Martians. I didn't have a clue what he was on about, but a feeling of disquiet was stirring in my stomach. Something about this scene didn't seem quite right. It didn't seem to be the sort of question he should be asking. I don't think I said anything, although I may have made some sort of non-committal noise out of politeness. Whatever my response was, he obviously took it as encouragement. He rummaged around in a drawer and pulled out a magazine, indicating that I should have a look at it. I did as I was told and the stirrings of disquiet in my stomach tightened into pangs of panic. The pages were covered in glossy pictures of naked men in sexually provocative poses. I didn't know where to look. I felt scared and sick and wanted to run away, but I had to stay because he hadn't paid me my money.

'Do you like that?' he asked, pointing to one of the pictures and my stomach did a somersault.

I said nothing, my throat having closed down and my brain gone numb. I realized he was holding my hand and I froze, not knowing what to do or say, trying to think how to snatch it away from him without offending him and losing my car-washing money. I felt him guiding my hand towards his shorts and realized they were undone and he was wearing nothing underneath. I was suddenly galvanized into action, pulling my hand out of his grip. Now that I'd finally reacted he must have realized he'd made a mistake because he stepped back and apologized. I left as fast as I could, grabbing the money that he held out to me and running back down the garden and out past the house into the safety of the busy road outside.

There was a park across the road, which I ran over to and sat down on a bench, trying to compose my thoughts and calm my thumping heart. I felt furious because now I was frightened to continue with the cleaning round, and it had been the first thing I'd ever done that made me feel totally free and independent of anyone else. It seemed there wasn't anything I could do, or anywhere I could go where other people wouldn't interfere with me in some way. At home I had the beatings and the taunting, at school there were the jibes and now someone else had tainted my work. Even though I was out of the house and out of the school and earning money, I still wasn't free.

As I sat there, gathering my thoughts, I grew determined not to let one man mess up the best day of my week and so, once I'd recovered from the shock, I continued working, attacking the cars with twice the usual vigour, my strength fuelled by my anger. I ended up earning £13 that day, more than I ever had before. I continued building the round in the coming weeks, but from then on I went past the black front door at the speed of light, and I never told a single soul about what had happened in that shed. When I got home Gloria took the money off me, promising to pay me back when the Giro came through, but I never saw it again.

12. It Has to Get Worse Before It Can Get Better

I knew Colin Smith, my teacher, had worked out what was happening to me at home. I could feel his eyes resting on whatever new bruise or mark I was unable to hide whenever I went into school. He would occasionally ask me about them, but he was always willing to drop the subject when I made it obvious I didn't want to talk about it. I could tell he didn't believe my stories, but I couldn't find a way to tell him the truth.

The social services were still visiting us, but their calls were becoming less and less regular and Gloria was always able to cover up whatever was wrong with me on the day they showed up. By this time I wasn't just taking whatever beatings were doled out to me. I was defending myself; kicking and punching back with all my strength. It made things worse because it fuelled her temper, but I had to do something, I couldn't just lie there and accept whatever she wanted to do to me. It seems incredible now to think that I had to physically fight my own mother in order to defend myself, but at the time it just seemed like part of my normal life.

One morning, when I arrived at school late, I was particularly badly shaken by whatever had happened at home before I came out and it must have been obvious to anyone who looked at me that something was wrong. Colin called me into his office.

'Are you being hit at home?' he asked, bluntly.

'Yes,' I replied, no longer feeling able to lie to him. I was reaching the end of my tether. I was almost ready to stand up to my tormentors once and for all.

He must have passed the information on to social services but, as usual, they didn't get to the house for a few days, by which time my bruises had faded again.

They must have been suspicious and wanted to talk to me away from the noise and interference of the rest of the family because eventually a male social worker arrived at the school and questioned me there. I thought that maybe this time they would realize their mistake in returning me home and I would be able to get back to Yarborough, but at the same time I was wary. I didn't want to say too much about what Gloria did, in case they didn't take me away immediately and I had to face her on my own with her knowing that I'd betrayed her.

At the end of the school day the man came home with me to talk to Gloria and Dennis. I was absolutely terrified; imagining how mad Gloria was going to go the moment the social worker had gone. Dennis was there, as silent and sheepish as always, and the man faced both of them, telling them that the social services were thinking of taking me into emergency care. To my horror I could see Dennis was near to tears and Gloria started pleading with me not to go, promising that things would get better. I just wanted to turn round and walk out of the house with the social worker, but I could see that he was wavering, unsure what to do in the face of such emotion.

'All right, Kevin,' he said eventually. 'Tell us what you would like to do. Do you want to stay here with your family, or would you like us to take you into care?'

My heart sank. How could I say, in front of my weeping father and pleading mother, that I wanted to be taken into care? What if the social worker didn't take me immediately, what sort of revenge would Gloria wreak on me the moment the door closed behind our visitor? And in the back of my mind a nagging voice was saying perhaps things would get better now that there had been a warning, maybe she really would make an effort.

Unable to say what I really felt and betray my parents so totally, I mumbled that I wanted to stay at home. The trap had sprung shut on me. The social worker had put me into a position where I had no choice but to seal my own fate. Not only did my parents now think I was shopping them to the authorities; the authorities thought I was messing them about and didn't want to be helped. I felt completely desolate.

Colin Smith wasn't fooled when I told him what had happened the next day. He could see the man had put me in an impossible position. Although I didn't know anything about it at the time, I think I must have been put on a list somewhere as a potentially endangered child, and he was watching my every move at school, ready to report anything suspicious.

The warning had had no effect on Gloria or Dennis and they forgot their emotional appeal almost immediately the man walked out the door. The fighting was getting worse and worse as they got increasingly on each other's nerves. One day they were coming to blows upstairs in the girls' bedroom. As with other fights that I'd witnessed between them they weren't holding anything back, both of them punching and kicking as they screamed foul-mouthed abuse at one another. We were all shouting at them from outside the room to stop and the girls were in tears. It looked as if someone was going to end up being killed.

At that moment something inside my head snapped. I started to scream, so loudly that I was no longer able to hear myself. It was as if I'd gone beyond hearing anything that was happening either around me or inside my own head. It felt as if I'd stepped out of my body. I'd had enough of this life. I just wanted it to stop. Despite all the noise the others were making, this terrible wail silenced them. Both the grown-ups stopped, mid-punch, and stared in amazement at me as I stood there with my mouth wide open and this fearful sound howling out, as if I'd just had thousands of volts shot through me. People must have been able to hear me from several streets away.

The next thing I knew I'd been knocked to the floor and Gloria was dragging me into the room with them. Both of them left the other one alone, all the grievances that had caused the fight in the first place apparently forgotten, and they started laying into me with more force than they ever had before. It was the worst beating I'd ever had and it kept on going. Their anger seemed to give them superhuman powers and they kept punching and kicking and slapping me. The other children were going wild with panic, thinking their brother was going to be killed in front of their eyes.

'Leave him alone!' I heard them shriek. 'Leave him alone!' Some of them received passing smacks for their interference if they tried to venture into the room to rescue me. Both the grown-ups were lost in a frenzy of violence.

Eventually, after what seemed like an eternity, they seemed to wear themselves out and I felt the strength ebbing from their blows. Dennis gave up first, going off downstairs, puffing, physically unable to do any more, while Gloria continued biting me with whatever strength she had left. Finally she too ground to a halt, panting and exhausted. In the stillness that followed the storm she must have realized she'd gone too far, that this time she just might be unable to hide the damage she'd done to me. She left the room while I was curled up on the bed, unable to move.

Some moments later she came back in. With an awkward shift in mood she put her arm round me. It was the first time I'd ever known her to show me any affection at all, either physical or emotional, and it felt very strange. Perhaps she hoped she could cajole me into staying silent for a little longer, knowing she'd gone too far and might this time be found out. Strains of Elvis came up from the kitchen. I left my arms at my side, not wanting to touch her. The next day I heard her boasting to the whole neighbourhood how Kevin had gone up to her and cuddled her. She never held me again, and I certainly never held her.

The next morning I was still in terrible pain but dragged myself out of bed, not wanting to be trapped in the house with her any longer. It was hard to stand up. I was covered in marks and bruises. I had over twenty bite marks on my neck, shoulders and arms where Gloria had bitten down with her gums, using all her strength. If she'd had her teeth in she would have ripped my throat out with the power of those bites. There was no way I could cover all these up. They looked like love bites, which meant the other boys at school noticed them immediately.

'Lewis's been kissed by Dracula,' one shouted and the others caught on, repeating the mantra and repeating it, over and over again. This was an all-boys school; a boy covered in hickeys wasn't going to be shown any mercy.

Getting myself from the house to the playground had taken all my energy and once I was there my legs gave out underneath me. I collapsed on to the tarmac and dissolved into tears. I didn't feel I could go on any longer. One of the teachers came over and picked me up, seeing that I winced in pain as she touched me. I was taken into the nurse's room and Colin Smith came in to take a look at me. I could see he was shocked by what he saw and he went away to call social services. But when he spoke to them they told him I'd expressed a wish to stay in the family home and they were reluctant to interfere with my decision. I knew I wanted to go, but only if they would take me away immediately. I didn't want Gloria to know I was going but still have access to me, even if it was only for a few days.

Colin must have protested and insisted that the social worker came to look at me again. But he didn't come round to the house again for a couple of weeks, by which time the marks had faded once more. The social services must then have reported this back to Colin because he took me into his office again the following day.

'I'm sorry, Kevin,' he said, and I could see from his face that he meant it. 'I'm afraid it has to get worse before it gets better.'

I could tell he was choked up at having to give me the news. I don't think he could quite believe they were going to allow me to go back home for more of the same, but he'd obviously discovered he couldn't do anything about it. He'd done everything he could and nothing was going to change. The news didn't shock me as much as it did him. I'd come to expect nothing from social services, because it was them that had delivered me back to Gloria from Yarborough and they didn't seem to have done anything to help me since then.

Even though I was still weak for my age, I was now getting bigger. I was starting to learn how to defend myself better from the blows, trying to kick her away. Sometimes I'd be in my bedroom on my own and I'd hear her thumping up the stairs, swearing and screaming abuse back down at Dennis, and I'd know she was heading for me. I would prepare myself to fight back as hard as I could, hunching myself into a ball to protect myself. But by doing that I was increasing her anger and she was still much stronger and much more vicious than me, so the punishment I received was far worse than it had been when I had put up no struggle. I was also trying harder and harder not to cry now that I was growing up, and that seemed to make her all the more determined to keep going until she'd managed to draw tears from me.

I felt totally alone. I was still excluded by the other kids at school and even my brothers and sisters tended to avoid me in case they got a smack from Gloria for associating with me.

My smallest brother, Robert, was now six or seven years old, and she seemed to have taken as great a dislike to him as she had to me. She'd pick on him in just the same way, hitting him and taunting him. In an attempt to escape from the house Robert had befriended an old man who lived nearby and worked for the council. The man used to take Robert to the swings a lot, giving him a break from the house and from Gloria's bullying. Sometimes Robert would even stay over for the night at this man's house. On one occasion I was invited to go round with him. It was a much more comfortable house than ours and there were enough bedrooms for us to have one each so I was perfectly happy with the arrangement. It was like a little holiday.

I'd gone to bed already, enjoying the smell and feel of the clean bedclothes, when I heard noises coming from Robert's room next door. I thought I should check he was all right and went in without announcing myself. The two of them were sitting side by side on the bed and Robert had his pyjama trousers down around his knees. I felt a chill of fear run through me, as I had with the man in the shed on the car-washing round.

'Leave him alone,' I said, feeling deeply protective of my little brother, in a way that no one in the family had ever felt about me.

The man jumped up and I could see he was worried. At the time I didn't have any idea just how much trouble he would be in if I told on him, but he must have known. Once I was sure Robert was safely tucked up in bed I went back to my own room, but I didn't sleep well that night, half listening for any suspicious movements on the landing outside. The next morning the man took us both out to the shops and gave us every treat imaginable before taking us home.

I thought about the scene I'd witnessed a great deal and decided I had to do something, if only to protect other children who might be lured into his house. I couldn't trust Gloria or Dennis to protect Robert from this man, so I would have to do it myself. When we next got a visit from a social worker there was the usual uproar of everyone trying to have their say at once, but I eventually managed to catch his attention and told him what I'd seen. He seemed to be listening, but nothing ever happened. I don't think he believed me, or if he did they must have thought my evidence would never stand up in court. A few years later Robert's friend was arrested for an offence against some other child. If they'd only believed me they could have spared that child, and maybe others in between, from all that trauma. But I suppose there was just too much going on in our house for them to be able to act on everything. It must have been like walking over the threshold into hell for them every time they passed our front door. They certainly acted as if we were some alien and slightly frightening species and, I guess, from their point of view, we were. It never felt as if they believed anything we told them, and they gave off an air of arrogance, as if they always knew better than us. I suppose they did know better about most things, but I never felt confident they would help me, even if I asked them directly.

From time to time I'd play with other children in the street. There was one boy, Errol, who I befriended for a while and we used to play together on a local cricket field just across the road. One evening, after school, we went up there with his younger sister. We were playing around the pavilion when we saw two dogs mating. Errol and I were probably sniggering, like small boys do at such things, but his sister went over to pet the dogs. Obviously they didn't want to be disturbed and one of them went for her. She turned and ran, her face contorted with fear, as the dog snapped and snarled at her heels. It managed to get her dress in its teeth and ripped the material. I grabbed a stick and a stone and chased the animal without a second thought. I felt no fear whatsoever. I went after the dog to protect the small child. I threw the stone first, missing the dog but giving it enough of a fright to make it run off in the opposite direction.

It didn't seem like anything special at the time, just a natural reaction. I felt proud of myself for that. One day I knew I was going to be brave enough to stand up to Gloria once and for all.

13. New Horizons

Colin Smith must have been more worried about me during that time than he let on; perhaps he was afraid he'd made things worse by interfering, that he shouldn't have stirred up trouble that would rebound on me. Although he was so kind to me personally, he never showed me any favouritism inside the school. Quite rightly, I had to behave just like everyone else. He was always totally fair like that, but outside the classroom he did the most amazing thing, something completely unexpected that opened up a whole new world for me. I guess that's the definition of what a good teacher should be able to do for his pupils.

He called me into his office at the end of a school day and said he had something that he thought I would like. He then gave me a Walkman personal stereo and a tape of popular classical songs that he'd made for me in his own time. At first I was simply touched to receive any sort of present at all. If nobody ever gives you anything it really is the 'thought that counts' when they do. I was puzzled as to why he'd think to give me a Walkman, but was intrigued by the idea of trying out something new. Although it was a second-hand machine it was probably the most generous gift anyone had ever given me, and the fact that he'd gone to the trouble to make a recording just for me of something he thought I would like made it priceless.

My immediate problem, as with anything I managed to acquire, was how to get it into the house without Gloria spotting it and taking it away or smashing it out of sheer spite. I hatched a plan to smuggle it past her in my pants, the bulge carefully concealed by my blazer until I got upstairs to my poky little bedroom. My heart was pounding as I came into the door, trying to look natural as I picked my way through the debris that always greeted anyone who stepped through the door. I didn't say a word, or even look in her direction. The worst thing that could happen would be for me to draw attention to myself and annoy her, because if she started hitting me she would either discover the stereo, or smash it with one of her blows. Out of the corner of my eye I could see her giving me a look, like a vicious old guard dog too lazy to raise its head when someone passes by, and I kept walking. I reached the stairs, which were just as covered in junk as the hallway, and made my way up, forcing myself not to go too fast, not to look suspicious, not to attract her attention in any way. Once I was safely in the bedroom I could breathe again, and remove my prize from its sweaty hiding place.

Since virtually every possession I'd ever had had either been taken from me or destroyed, I was always meticulous in my security precautions with anything I did smuggle into the house. I'd developed a habit of hiding the few possessions I'd managed to acquire inside the mattress of my bed. I knew they were safe there because Gloria never changed the sheets, so I'd made a slit in the mattress and I now pushed my worldly possessions, including the Walkman, inside. The stained, worn mattress became its home. I would even leave it in there while it was playing, so that only the headphones would have to be hidden if someone came in unexpectedly. From then on a large percentage of my earnings had to be set aside each week to buy batteries, so that I never ran out.

I'd never stopped to really listen to music before and Colin Smith's tape was a revelation. I would lie in bed at night with the headphones on, lost in the classical music, letting my mind wander as far as possible from the reality of my surroundings. It was so peaceful, as if the orchestra was serenading me on my way to Amer-

ica. The first time I listened a song came up called 'Ebben? Ne
andrò lontana'. To begin with it scared me but as I played it more
and more it grew on me. It soon became my favourite; so tranquil
and eloquent, as if the mummer was singing just to me, sending
me to sleep each night.

I could never tell anyone else about my growing passion for
classical music because they'd think I was weird to be listening to
it at my age. I had enough of a reputation for being different without letting people know I had 'nerdy' tastes in music as well. So for
a long time I would only use it to go to sleep at night, my head full
of images of escaping to America as I let it roll over me. Even in
those limited doses, the music was changing my life. It felt as if
until that moment I'd been trapped in a cupboard with no doors,
and suddenly a door had opened. At the same time it was frustrating because although the door was open, showing me a view of
another world, I was still sitting inside the cupboard and unable
to step outside. My love for music increased with every waking
moment. As I became braver, I would smuggle the Walkman out
of the house and sit in the park to listen to the music in the fresh
air, surrounded by greenery. I was able to get into a new world that
was mine and mine alone. For the first time I'd discovered something that allowed my mind to rest. I could finally understand why
my father had wanted to spend all those hours in the kitchen listening to Elvis, how it would have soothed his soul after all the
shouting and ugliness and given his exhausted mind a chance to
escape from the ugliness into something else.

The best thing was when I went to visit Gini and Guy, because
I could smuggle the stereo out in my pants when Gini came to
collect me: Gloria would never hit me or question me in front of
her. Guy would then lend me his tapes, which I would play all day
long until it was time to go back into the house, when the Walkman had to go back into its hiding place. I never took my own tape

with me in case Guy took the mickey out of me for liking something so strange. I was just as happy listening to the sort of pop music most people our age were into. On Sunday evenings Gini wouldn't take me home until Guy and I finished listening to the top forty charts on Radio 1, taping the whole chart so that we could listen to it again next time I came. I used to get a sinking feeling in my stomach as the programme moved further and further up the charts because I knew the moment of my return home was getting closer. The number-one record, which should have been the high point of the programme, was actually the moment when I knew my day out was over and it was time to get into the car and start the sad journey home to Norbury.

I had managed to acquire one or two other possessions, with extreme stealth. Something I'd always wanted, but knew I'd never get, was a train set. One evening I was passing a parish hall after doing some job or other and had a little money in my pocket. I saw a sign advertising a jumble sale and popped inside. The hall was full of trestle tables, all covered in old clothes and bits and bobs, and surrounded by larger items such as worn-out ironing boards and old-fashioned electric fires. As I joined the crowds, rummaging through the piles of junk in the hope of finding something I could afford with the pennies left over from my earnings, I came across a few pieces of an old train set, all bound together with an elastic band. I think it was priced at something like a pound, which I could just afford. I bought it, almost beside myself with excitement at finally owning my own train set. Once again the problem then was getting it into the house without being spotted, since it was too big to fit into my underpants without doing me a serious injury.

So I decided not to take a big risk and to wait for my opportunity. If I was caught with it I'd not only lose the train, I would also be beaten for my temerity in thinking I could own something the others didn't have. As I walked back from the hall my mind was racing as I clutched my booty under my jumper. When I got to the house I crept round the side into the garden, careful to make sure no one saw me through the windows. I found something sharp enough to dig a hole and buried my treasure. I then waited until a few days later, when Gloria went out to cash her Giro and I knew she would be out of the house for at least an hour, before digging it up. I dusted the earth off and hurried up to my bedroom with it, sliding it into the mattress, padding it carefully with the stuffing to make sure it wouldn't make a noise and give me away if, by some remote chance, Gloria decided to do something with the beds. Then I loosely stitched up the hole.

I had a needle and a length of cotton, which I used to hold together the rip in the mattress cover each time I put something away. Then, once I was sure Gloria was safely in bed or engrossed in doing something else, I'd open up the stitching, get out the train and set up the few pieces of track for it to run back and forth on, lost in my own imaginary world for a few minutes before I had to pack it all away again. I lived in fear of her finding the needle while I was out at school and working out what it was for. I knew if that happened she wouldn't hesitate to stick it into me in order to make the punishment fit the crime.

One night I'd been playing with my train while listening to my music and I was so tired I didn't bother to sew them back into the mattress. It had been so long since Gloria had been near my room I'd been lulled into a false sense of security. So I just pushed everything out of sight under the bed, meaning to secrete it away the next day. Unfortunately she chose that day to go into my cell while I was at school and she found everything. Perhaps she was suspicious of the amount of time I spent in there on my own, or perhaps she was looking for money and thought I might be hiding some of my earnings from her. When I got home and discovered what had happened I was terrified, certain I would be in for a terrible beating. But she didn't explode immediately, as I thought she would, she just gave all my prized possessions to Wayne, except the tape, which she threw away. She wanted to know where the music had come from and I told her that Colin Smith had given it to me.

She must have been brooding on the situation because that evening she decided I did deserve a beating after all, if only for receiving favouritism from a teacher. She wound herself up into a furious temper, convincing herself I needed to be taught a lesson I wouldn't forget, and came after me late that night, when I was already in my grubby pyjamas, lying on my bed and missing my music. She didn't come up alone. Dennis was dragged out of the kitchen and into the row and he started laying into me in a drunken rage that she kept on stoking up. Perhaps he too was jealous that another adult had shown me some kindness, when no one ever did the same for him. Or perhaps he felt guilty that he wasn't able to give me anything I needed or wanted. Or perhaps he felt nothing at all except anger at being disturbed from his drinking. Whatever was driving him, he just kept on hitting me. I was frightened that things were going to get out of control again so I managed to wriggle free of them both and clattered downstairs. There was confusion at the top of the stairs behind me as they both tried to get after me at once, and in those few seconds I managed to throw open the front door and run out into the street, still in my pyjamas. Once there I couldn't think where to go. I didn't want to loiter in the park opposite the house in the dark, and I didn't have any friends whose houses I could go to. The school was closed and I had no idea where Colin Smith or any of the teachers lived. The only place I could think of going to for help was the local police station on the other side of the park.

I must have cut a sorry little figure as I walked into the police station, barefooted and out of breath, and told them what was happening to me. There were three officers on duty, one woman and two men, and they all seemed to be towering over me, looking down their noses as they told me there was nothing they could do to help because it was all happening in the privacy of my own home.

Exhausted, cold and rejected, I walked back out of the station into the night, padding down the road and into the house again on my own. There was nowhere else for me to go. They wouldn't even escort me home across the dark park. Luckily, by the time I got in, Gloria and Dennis's anger had burned itself out in my absence and I was able to crawl back into bed without catching their attention or rekindling the fight.

Next time I went to visit Gini she wanted to know what had happened to the Walkman, because she knew how much it had meant to me and didn't believe I would just have forgotten it. I told her Gloria had taken it away and that afternoon she took me out into East Grinstead and bought me a new one. I no longer had the tape that Colin Smith had made for me, but at least I had the ones Guy and I had made of the pop charts. I was very touched that Gini would do such a thing for me, and nervous that Gloria would take this one away from me as well. When Gini dropped me off that evening she made a point of telling Gloria she'd bought it for me. Gloria was always trying to be friends with Gini and I knew she wouldn't take this machine if she thought Gini had bought it.

Gloria was always looking for friends she could pour her heart out to, and the more she tried to be friendly the more people recoiled from the force and volume of her bitterness. Whether it was social workers or people like Gini who wanted to help me, she was just too much for them to take. Occasionally, she would tease me by putting the new Walkman up out of my reach, provoking an argument for the sake of it, but she didn't dare take it away from me for good, because then she would have had to explain to Gini why she'd done it.

The beatings were still becoming worse and the screaming in my ear was constant, partly because I was getting bigger and trying to defend myself, driving Gloria to ever greater frenzies of violence, partly because the pressures of life were becoming worse for her as we all grew bigger and Dennis slipped further under the influence of drink. She was like a ferocious animal caged in a zoo that couldn't be trusted to co-habit with any others for fear she'd turn on them. She also became careless about where she marked me, not able to control her blows as carefully when I was ducking and diving and fighting back. The bruises and marks on my face and body became impossible to ignore at school and the social services, again at Colin Smith's instigation, couldn't put off taking me away any longer. This time when they came to see me at school and asked if I wanted to leave the family, I said I did. A social worker came home with me to collect my few possessions and to inform Gloria and Dennis what was happening.

My mother only had one question to ask as I was being led down the path to the car. 'Does this mean they'll be stopping his child benefit?'

That summed it all up for me. I guess that was the only reason they'd asked to have me back in the first place.

14. Margaret and Alan

I just couldn't stop saying 'sorry'. It was the word that sprang to my lips at the start of virtually every sentence. I was so used to being wrong, so used to being punished. Apologizing never stopped the punishment, but it had become like a nervous tic. I couldn't stop myself, even when I hadn't done anything wrong. It was an attempt at self-defence, admitting I was wrong from the start so no one would have to beat it out of me.

When they took me away again I'd hoped that social services would return me to Yarborough so that I could take up my life where I'd left off. But no one suggested that and I would never have been presumptuous enough to bring up the subject myself. I didn't feel that I had any power over my own destiny; I just had to do what they told me, go where they put me, and hope for the best. They immediately started talking about fostering me with other families. I was disappointed. I hadn't particularly enjoyed the fostering experience before, always feeling like an outsider in the families I was placed with, knowing I was only there because they were being paid to look after me. But I didn't argue, anything would be better than being at home. I now knew for sure that my parents had only wanted to have me in the house because it brought in more money, so where was the difference?

When the authorities had time to look into my health, once they'd got me out of the house and didn't have to fend off my mother and other members of the family, they diagnosed me as anaemic. It was assumed that it was because of the appalling diet I'd been having for the previous four years, and they were probably right. If you feed people really badly for long enough eventually they will become weak and sick. Everyone agreed that I needed building up, both physically and psychologically. It was now 1984 and I was thirteen years old. I probably wasn't the easiest of children to place. It would take some very special people to be able to handle a teenager who had been damaged as badly as I had by then.

I was told that a temporary family had been found for me in Coulsdon, a few miles away. It looked as if I was going to be shifted around from pillar to post all over again. The couple, they said, were called Margaret and Alan and I was going to be taken round to meet them that evening. The house I was driven to was a nicely kept suburban semi, with bay windows and red tiles on the walls. The road was pleasant and lined with trees, a little like the ones I'd known around Yarborough. It was obviously a good neighbourhood. The moment they opened the door to the social worker's knock I could see Margaret and Alan were the exact opposite of Gloria and Dennis. At the most superficial level they were opposite sizes. Where Gloria had towered over Dennis physically, Alan was a tall, lean man. Where Gloria had been hard and aggressive looking, Margaret was soft, round and maternal. Margaret looked a bit younger than her husband, but I still didn't reckon she was going to be able to hit me as hard as I was used to. I was introduced to them as 'Uncle Alan and Auntie Margaret'.

The house was as well kept inside as out. It smelled clean and everything seemed to be polished and in its proper place. It was a real family home, well used down the years but cherished and cared for. On that first visit, as the social worker chatted to them, Margaret made me a baked potato with baked beans and cheese on top. It was such a simple, basic meal to them, but it was a combination of textures and tastes I'd never experienced before and to me it was the most delicious thing I'd ever had. If you've lived on a diet of chips for four years even a baked potato seems like a feast. I was so hungry and it smelled so good as Margaret served it up, that I stuffed it into my mouth too fast and blistered the roof of my mouth. I quickly swallowed some cold water, anxious not to show myself up.

Alan, I was soon to discover, was a tremendously wise man. He had run his own local business, and was so successful that by the time he retired and sold up, he owned five shops and a distribution business. He was still active in the business world, doing the book-keeping for some of his friends in the trade. Margaret ran the home beautifully, cooked all the meals and helped her husband with the business. They'd worked hard all their lives and they loved children. When their own grew up, they felt there was a gap in their lives, so they decided to take up emergency fostering. It was agreed that I should move in with them for a few months, while the social services worked out what to do with me.

I was very nervous about moving into such a nice house. I was still wetting the bed at that stage, even though I was fourteen years old, and I was still haunted by the nightmares that would make me wake up screaming when everyone else in the house was asleep. I thought it would be embarrassing to show myself up in front of such nice, calm, self-controlled people. But I was so glad to be away from Gloria and Dennis that these seemed like minor worries and I began to believe that maybe I could make a new start. If I was living in a normal home with normal people I would be able to dress like everyone else, and wash like everyone else, and I would be eating the same food and building up my strength. I wouldn't have to look and smell different any more. The change to a proper diet was such a shock to my system that I developed terrible mouth ulcers as a reaction, but they soon faded. I thought I would finally be able to put my 'tramp' image behind me.

I was desperately eager to please them, and Alan and Margaret worked hard to persuade me that I didn't have to say 'sorry' all the

time. I kept asking permission for everything, wanting to know
what I should be doing, terrified of doing the wrong thing and
incurring their displeasure and being sent back home. I had lost
all self-confidence. I thought I must be as useless as my mother was
always telling me I was.

I was continuing at the same school and Margaret suggested we
go out and get me some new bits of uniform to smarten up my
appearance. Because they were an older couple, with grown-up
children, they were slightly out of touch with the way young people
thought and behaved. That would have been all right, I just needed
kindness, nurturing and guidance, which they were both more than
qualified to help with, but I also needed help in not looking different from everyone else. While we were out Margaret spotted a pair
of trousers in a second-hand shop that were ten pence and were
the right colour for school. The only problem was they were bell-
bottoms, and this was at a time when every other boy was wearing
narrow trousers. It sounds like a trivial point, but anyone who can
remember being a school child will also remember how perilously
a child's reputation can hang on these small points. As long as I
was wearing these conspicuously unfashionable trousers, I was still
going to be different; and as long as I was different I would continue
to be an outsider. These trousers were enormous, but I was far too
shy to say anything to Margaret, who was being so kind about
buying me new clothes in the first place, and I was terrified of doing
anything wrong that might lead to me being sent away from their
house. I accepted the hideous trousers without a murmur, but inside
I just wanted to shrivel up and die.

Now that I had less to worry about at home, these flares started
to occupy an inordinate amount of my thoughts. I had to travel a
long way to school on the bus from Coulsdon to Norbury and I
would hunch myself into a corner in the hope that no one would
be able to see my legs, encased as they were in the huge folds of

flapping material. I would try to hide them in class and everywhere around the school, but I was kidding myself – everyone knew I was wearing them.

The other children at school had heard that I'd been taken into care and my nickname changed from 'Tramp' to 'Fosters' or 'Fosters Lager', or sometimes they would call me 'Flares'. So I might have been freed from the violence and the bruises, but I still wasn't free from being different and excluded. People still didn't want to be associated with me, for fear that they would be tarred with the same brush.

At the end of the next term Margaret arranged for me to move to Purley High School for Boys, a more local school in Coulsdon. It was a good school and, more importantly, it was my big chance to shake off my past and start again with a clean slate. All through the summer holidays I had knots in my stomach when I thought about having to meet a whole new set of children, wearing those horrible trousers. A new school seemed like a real chance for me to escape my past, but I knew those flares would ruin my chances of being accepted. The moment I walked through the door in them I would be branded as an outsider.

Just before I went back for the start of term, Margaret and I went out to get me a blazer, and she bought a new pair of trousers as well, normal ones. It was like a giant weight being lifted off my chest. I was suddenly completely normal, from top to bottom. I started the school like any other new boy and was instantly accepted. But Margaret still wanted me to rotate the new trousers with the flares, to get the wear from them. I started secretly making holes in the flares in the hope she'd throw them out, but she was a good housekeeper and sewed the holes up as fast as I could make them. Every weekend I was terrified I'd have to wear the bell-bottoms and when she got my uniform out I would swap them over in secret. I was determined to be a normal child from now on. I treated the new pair as if they were the most precious things in the world. If they got the slightest mark or crease I would take them off and clean them up. I wouldn't run in them or bend my knees if I could help it. I had to be sure that nothing happened to them. On one occasion, when Margaret insisted on me wearing the flares to leave the house, I smuggled the other pair out in a bag. As soon as I was out of sight of the house I dived into the bushes on the golf course and changed them.

There was another family living next door to Alan and Margaret with a daughter called Charlene, who I got on with very well. She went to a girls' school. Her parents, Gary and Diane, had the same respect for Alan that I did and I used to get on with them really well. I wasn't allowed to go out to work any more, but both Margaret and Diane found me jobs to do around their houses and gardens so that I could earn myself some money. I was saving up in the hope that, eventually, I would have enough to buy myself another pair of spare trousers. Money had taken on a new meaning for me. I no longer needed it to get food, because there were always good meals on the table, and I was starting to be given toys so I was like other boys my age there. But I still wanted to earn money for clothes and other things that teenage boys need.

'What are you going to do with all this money you're earning?' Margaret asked me one day.

'I'm going to buy a pair of school trousers,' I said.

She was obviously shocked. 'Why?' she asked.

I took the plunge and told her the truth about the flares. I could see she was puzzled, because Alan wore trousers like that and never had any problems. As I told her how I'd felt in the trousers all through the summer there were tears coming into my eyes and she listened in horrified silence. That weekend we went out together and we bought a twenty-pound pair of trousers, paying half each. She threw away the bell-bottoms for me and suddenly I was free to wear my trousers just like anyone else, no longer living in fear of damaging them because now there was a spare pair I could use until they were cleaned or mended. I felt I was a proper boy at last.

Because I'd put so much effort into my anti-flares campaign, I'd never once had to wear them to the new school and, as a result, I never had any trouble at all. It was like a miracle and once I'd relaxed I started to play sports like water polo, hockey and rugby and made friends, just like everyone else. There were always incidents when someone might try to pick on me or tease me, just as there are in any school. I made sure I never rose to any bait, never responded to any taunts. I remembered to 'count to ten', just as I had been advised all those years before. The last thing I wanted was to be blamed for any sort of trouble, in case I was removed from the school and sent back to my old life. I wasn't one of the really popular guys around the school, but I wasn't one of the nerds either, I was just comfortably in the middle somewhere.

I was now able to relax and settle into my new life. I still loved TV and my favourite time was early Saturday morning before everyone got up when I would go downstairs and sit in front of the TV watching *Raiders of the Lost Ark*. I would sit there completely mesmerized by Indiana Jones in his crusade to save the Ark of the Covenant. To me it was pure adventure, an adventure that completely transported me – my mind was free from everything, just Indiana and I saving the world. I must have seen it over a hundred times at my home.

Margaret and Alan were what is known as an 'emergency' foster family; somewhere where children went until a fulltime place could be found for them somewhere else. Their youngest daughter still lived with them. She must have been about twenty, and there were two disabled children who seemed to be there permanently. So it was a full and busy house. Their two eldest children had married and moved to Australia and they'd had one other daughter.

Their son was a bit of a mystery to Alan. Alan Junior wanted to be an actor and had appeared occasionally in small parts in some of the Australian soap operas. Although he was very proud of him, Alan would rather his boy had followed him into business. When I was with him I felt that we had a real father-and-son relationship, talking about subjects that interested both of us. I got a suspicion that he would have liked to be able to do the same with Alan Junior.

There was a big apple tree in the garden and in the autumn we picked the fruit together, me climbing up amongst the branches and passing the apples back down to him. He taught me never to bang the fruit together otherwise it bruises and rots, so we had to pass it gently from hand to hand. I think it was that motion of me passing him the apples, quite soon after I'd arrived in the house, which formed the bond between us. It made us a team.

I had my own bedroom and although I was much happier during the day, the nightmares still rose up from my subconscious to haunt me once I fell asleep. Margaret would come in response to my screams and would find me curled in a ball, protecting myself against the blows that I expected her to rain down on me, and she would sit on the edge of the bed to calm me. The first time I heard the two of them argue with each other I became frightened and scurried up to my room to hide, but then I realized this was a different sort of arguing to anything I had experienced; that they were never going to hit each other, that they would simply exchange words. Later they would make up with a kiss and cuddle and then life would continue as before. I began to lose some of my fear of confrontation.

I grew to admire Alan more and more as the months went past. He was such a wise man. He seemed so safe because of his height and his grey hair. He'd had a couple of heart attacks before I arrived and so had to take life at a sedate pace. During his working years he'd been up at four every morning, working all hours to build a secure life for his family. Now he kept more leisurely hours, even though he hadn't completely retired.

The garden was T-shaped, and round the corner from the house he had a wooden shed that he sat in, doing the book-keeping for his friends with the help of an old-fashioned adding machine. Sometimes I would just sit in the corner of the office and watch him for hours on end. Whatever question I asked he would always have an answer and it always made sense. I was still apologizing all the time, but I was gradually feeling easier about myself. The concept of business fascinated me. Because I'd worked I understood how hard it was to make money and I wanted to find out how you did it and how you built a business that was good enough to support a family and live a solid life like Alan's. I was brimming with curiosity about everything he did. He taught me new ways to add up and explained how money worked. He was also a keen bridge and poker player and ran a bridge club. During the school holidays I helped set things up for the players and prepare and serve the refreshments through the day. I would always be paid for my efforts, but I would gladly have done it anyway, just to be near him and to be part of the family.

I divided my time between their house and next door. Both Margaret and Diane were wonderful cooks. Margaret actually cooked for the local Women's Institute, and there was always enough to eat at every mealtime. Diane made the best profiteroles I'd ever tasted and once she'd discovered I liked them she made them for me all the time, drenching them in chocolate sauce. So many people were being so kind to me it was hard to believe I'd had to wait so long to find such a normal life. One evening we invited Colin Smith round to supper to thank him for all he'd done. To me it was the icing on the cake.

I was so happy in the house and I dreaded being told it was time to move on to somewhere else and having to start all over again. When they asked if I'd like to stay with them until I finished school I jumped at the chance. I couldn't imagine there could be anywhere better for me to go.

Now and again I would go back to my natural family for visits, just as I had from Yarborough, but I no longer felt I was part of it. I felt like a stranger looking in, and Robert and Julie were no longer there. Then I was told that Gloria and Dennis had split up. I think the violence must have got too much for them both and he just walked out. He was given a housing association flat somewhere and lived alone. Knowing how shy he was I could imagine just how lonely he must be, but I guessed even that was better than being in the house with Gloria all the time. At least he'd be able to drink and listen to Elvis in peace now. I had no sympathy for either of them. As far as I was concerned they deserved whatever misery came their way.

One summer the school arranged a trip for us to the Norfolk Broads for a sailing holiday in small wooden boats. Each boat had four to five boys onboard; one would be a prefect and one would be an experienced sailor. There'd been a list of things we needed for the trip so I even had some new possessions to take with me. I was beside myself with excitement. We set off across the peaceful Broads in a dozen or more little boats, drinking in the fresh air, watching the birds rising up out of the reeds around us and feeling very grown up. It was the most wonderful, liberating experience as we all tried to pretend we were adults now.

While we were out on the water one of the other guys fell overboard fully clothed and disappeared under the boat. There was a moment of horror as we all scanned the water to see where he was and he didn't reappear. Then, after what seemed like an age, he bobbed to the surface at the back of the boat. I knew he wasn't a good swimmer and I'd been doing a lot of swimming by then at school. I didn't even stop to think; I just jumped in and got hold of him, swimming back with him in my arms and pushing him up into the boat. He was bigger than me and heavy with the water in his clothes, as Chris had been when he fell through the ice all those years before, and the others had to help me lift him over the side. No one made a big deal of the affair, but I felt chuffed with myself. I was beginning to feel that I handled myself well when it was necessary, and I thought I'd gained some respect amongst the others, increasing the feeling of camaraderie in the boat. The boy I'd helped had some sweets, which he shared with me. We felt good together, although none of us said anything. It was the trip of a lifetime.

I was still in touch with Gini and Guy and one weekend I went with Guy to his dad's house, which was a beautiful old farmhouse near East Grinstead. It smelled of wood and was full of oak beams and nooks and crannies. His new wife was a great cook and there was tons of food for everyone. It was the sort of house and the sort of lifestyle I'd never experienced before and it took my ambitions forward another gigantic leap as I wandered around, drinking in every detail. I felt that I was entering an adult world. Guy's father was a reporter for the BBC and there was a bunch of journalists at the house for some sort of party that evening: they were all discussing the Falklands War and current affairs in general. As they talked about ships and helicopters and fighting they conjured up a world that was big and exciting, and so far from anything I'd experienced. They were the people who created the world that I'd been watching on the TV screen for so long. They seemed supremely confident and at ease with themselves and the world. Guy's father and his wife had two small children, so there was also a family atmosphere in the house. Outside there were haystacks to play in and a ride-on lawnmower that I was allowed to drive around the croquet lawn. This was the sort of place I would want to bring up any children I might have, somewhere with space and quiet and comfort. Somewhere that feels free and peaceful and smells sweet.

The tiny seeds of ambition inside me, which Alan had been gently nurturing into life, started to blossom that weekend. This was the type of life I wanted to have and I could see now that it was possible, that normal people like Guy and me actually could end up living like this. I just had to work out how to get there from where I was.

15. Going into Business

Throughout my childhood my most pressing problems were how to get through the day without being beaten and how to get enough to eat. Now that I'd finally escaped from Gloria and had grown used to regular square meals, I was keen to get on with my life, to start working towards attaining my dreams, which were coming more into focus as I found out a bit more about how the world worked.

Inspired by Alan's sage advice and by everything I watched or heard about the business world, I decided to go into business for myself at the first opportunity. I was sure it couldn't be that difficult, I just needed a good idea to start me off. At fifteen I set up my own advertising magazine and called it *Eye Catchers*. The idea was to charge local businesses a pound to advertise and I would then print up the ads and deliver them to local houses. A friend called Chey helped me with the deliveries and Alan let us print the magazine up in the back of his office. It felt wonderful to be creating something of my own, something that I believed I could develop into a real business. I had so many plans buzzing around in my head.

We produced three editions before economic realities and a shortage of time got the better of us. We were about twenty quid down on the venture and the pressures of schoolwork during the exam season made it impossible to continue. I was horribly disappointed after the high of seeing the simple little magazine come into existence. But even though it hadn't taken off quite as I'd hoped, it had still whetted my appetite for business. It proved to me that it was possible to start something up from scratch. I could see why it hadn't worked and I was confident I could avoid making the same mistakes next time. I was convinced that if I just worked hard enough I'd be able to succeed in life once I worked out what to do and set my mind to it.

Becoming an entrepreneur wasn't my one and only ambition of course. There were other plans and schemes along the way, sometimes inspired by no more than seeing a good movie. For a short while I flirted with the idea of becoming a pilot, after watching Tom Cruise in *Top Gun*. It looked like the most brilliant way to spend your days and I was sure I would be an ace in no time if I were just given a bit of training. I went to the RAF for an interview but they told me I would have to stay on at school to take O levels and then A levels, and Margaret and Alan weren't prepared to look after me for that long, so I gave that one up.

It was now the middle of the eighties and people kept talking about the fortunes being made in the financial markets in London. The film *Wall Street* was showing in the cinemas and I watched documentaries and news items about the trading pits where everyone was screaming at one another, buying and selling stock. The chaos looked fabulous to me. It looked normal, just like home but without the beatings. It excited me and I knew I could do it well if I was given a chance. If there was one gift Gloria had endowed me with it was a big mouth. I could shout with the best of them. I wanted to become a pit trader. No one needed to have an education to make a fortune here, in fact the papers were always saying it was a profession for 'barrow boys'. There were headlines appearing every day talking about million-pound bonuses and champagne lifestyles for people in their early twenties. I could see no reason why I couldn't become one of them.

Things at school got better and better, feeding my self-confidence about my prospects. When I started there I was in the lower band, with kids who weren't very bright and would take CSEs instead of O levels. Each term I went up a class, having started in the lowest one because of my performance over the previous few years, until just before the examinations when I was only one class below the one taking O levels. I knew that if I'd stayed at Baldwin's Hill and Yarborough I would have been far enough advanced to be doing those exams myself, but I'd lost too much ground in the interim and I didn't have time to catch up. I would be taking CSEs instead.

Despite my improved performance at school, the damage had been done and I still only managed to get CSE grade twos. My teachers, and Margaret and Alan, all wanted me to stay on to try to get grade ones, because they would count the same as O levels and would allow me to get a normal job in a company. But I didn't want a normal job. I didn't want to become a lowly cog in some company, heading off to work on the train each morning, sitting in an office, and coming home exhausted at night, just for a paltry weekly wage. I tried to think what I would be able to do that would make the drudgery worthwhile, and I couldn't think of anything. I wanted to be in control of my own destiny, like Alan had been. I wanted to be a pit trader or an entrepreneur. I thought it would be better to just get out into the world and start working to achieve my dreams rather than worrying about getting some rather average exam results.

I decided to ignore all the good, sensible advice I was being given, and take my chances in the outside world. I'd tasted freedom with the *Eye Catchers* venture. I'd felt the excitement of creating something from nothing, of persuading people to buy advertising space and of actually having control of the product. The experience had lit an entrepreneurial flame inside me, even though it hadn't ended up being successful, and I wanted to try again. I didn't know how or where, but I knew I wanted to get out into the big world that I'd been watching for so many years on television. I was sure that once I was spending all my time looking for opportunities and thinking of ways to make money, I would find them.

We all discussed my plans and it was made clear that if I did leave school I would also have to leave Margaret and Alan's, because they were in the business of fostering children, not adults. In fact as I'd grown older I'd found I'd got closer to Alan but drifted further away from Margaret. I think she preferred dealing with small children and wasn't sure what to do with a teenager who was almost a man. If I did something she disapproved of she used a phrase, 'CHM', which meant 'Council House Mentality'. I heard her use it first when I'd been shouting a bit too loudly in the garden and it stung because there were other people listening, and it reminded me, in a gentler way, of some of the jibes my mother used to throw at me. It made me feel like an outsider again, someone who didn't fit in. As I got older I felt this sort of disapproval from her more often, but I didn't think I deserved it.

She and Alan went on a trip to Australia at one stage to visit their children, staying away for a couple of months, and during that time I was sent to stay with a friend of Margaret's called Shona. When they got back I noticed a marked change in Margaret's attitude towards me. I think that getting away from it all, and cruising on the *Canberra*, had made her re-evaluate what she wanted to do with the rest of her life and she'd decided that she'd done enough fostering. I felt that she was anxious to get me out of the house and have some quiet time with Alan, who was obviously growing frailer with each year.

I was also told, however, that if I decided to leave school it didn't mean I was going to be put straight out on to the street and expected to fend for myself. I would be helped to get my own place to live. The social services would pay a deposit and two months' rent to get me started, and after that I would support myself. In my naivety, that sounded fine. I imagined I'd be up and working in no time and would be able to pay my rent and support myself easily after two months. I liked the idea of being completely free of everyone and able to live exactly as I wanted. I was so keen to get started I didn't take the time to really think the situation through and ask myself how I was going to get the first job to start me off on my road to riches.

I plunged ahead at full steam. At seventeen I left school and set out to stake my claim in the world, full of high hopes and boundless ambition, confident I would have the whole thing cracked within a few months. From the small ads in the local paper I found a house to share with three other people. It wasn't as nice as Alan and Margaret's, but it wasn't as bad as the two family homes I'd been brought up in. It backed on to the main London to Gatwick rail lines, which made it a bit noisy since trains rattled past pretty much constantly, but I didn't care, I was an early riser anyway. I was given the deposit, the first two months' rent and £200 spending money to support me until I was earning. I was sure I was on my way.

I didn't see that much of the other people in the house. They came and went from whatever jobs they had and we would pass occasionally in the communal rooms, but mostly I kept to my bedroom with the door closed. They were all much older than me and I was putting all my energy into finding a way to make a living. I didn't have time to start a social life.

I was beginning to realize that getting started wasn't going to be quite as easy as I'd first anticipated. I was searching for every vacancy I could find advertised, and ringing or writing to every employer who I thought might be able to use me. But if you have almost no qualifications there aren't that many options on offer; most of the jobs that made the best promises seemed to involve selling things that not many people wanted to buy. I was happy to take anything anyone was willing to offer, but the first job to come my way involved knocking on doors and attempting to sell carpet-cleaning services to housewives who hadn't realized they needed such a service. I didn't intend to do it for long, but I thought it would give me some useful experience and the money would help me to stay afloat until something better came along. It was a harder struggle than I had anticipated, taxing even my gift for the gab.

The salesmen I'd learnt from had worked in the market, where customers had come to them looking for goods to buy, had actually wanted and needed the products they were selling. They had arrived in crowds, with money in their pockets and a willingness to purchase. I was confronting one reluctant customer at a time and having a lot of doors slammed in my face. I'd have to tell the customers it was my birthday and all sorts of rubbish just to get my foot in the door, but still they didn't want to buy the stuff. Who wants to let some smart-talking teenager into their house to sell them something if they can avoid it? No one. Since I was on commission the job wasn't earning me a bean, but it was costing me valuable time and energy and sapping my confidence as I trudged the streets getting rejection after rejection.

I also had a Saturday job at the Homebase DIY Centre in Croydon, which did at least give me a few pounds each week. I'd started there before I left school, having been given a bike on which I cycled down to the Purley Way early every Saturday morning. It was wonderful to have cash that I could spend just as I chose and, as long as I'd been living with Alan and Margaret, it had seemed like a lot of money. Now that it was my only source of income it didn't seem so much.

Still at the back of my mind I had an idealized picture of where I wanted to go with my life. I still envisaged myself escaping to America, where I knew everyone had big dreams, and I still dreamed of finding my fortune in the financial markets, but I could see I had to find a practical way of supporting myself while I pursued these dreams. I was beginning to feel despondent about the amount of time it was taking me to get things moving.

Before I'd left Margaret and Alan's, I'd put some of my earnings towards taking driving lessons, and Margaret had kindly agreed to help me with the rest of the money. I passed my test quite quickly, so that was one skill I did have under my belt. But not many firms want to trust a seventeen-year-old behind the wheel of a company vehicle.

In the first few weeks of being on my own I found the freedom intoxicating. Having money in my pocket and no one to tell me what I should do or where I should go went to my head. The two months that the social services were willing to fund me for seemed like for ever when I first arrived in the house. I couldn't imagine them ever ending. I decided I wanted to try every sort of food I could find: I tested Indian, Chinese, Italian and every other variation – never stopping to work out how much it was costing each week compared to the amount I was earning. If I'd still been in Alan's house he would have pointed out the error of my ways very quickly. But I wasn't, I was on my own, making my own judgements.

Within a few weeks the money was running out and the landlord was mentioning that the rent would soon be due. The two months were nearly up and the pictures in my head of where I wanted to be were beginning to seem a long way from the reality. I'd been working as hard as I knew how, but I seemed to be sliding down a slippery slope towards poverty rather than climbing up towards the wealth and happiness I'd been anticipating.

The two months passed and the rent became due. My pockets were empty and I was suddenly scared. It felt like I had no one to turn to for help. I had to find the money or I'd be homeless, and then I'd never be able to land a job. As long as I had an address I had my foot on the first rung of the ladder. If I slipped off that there would be no safety net to catch me, I would be homeless and unemployable. There was only one option. I went to see Alan to explain what I'd done. I felt so stupid, coming back after only two months with my cap in my hand. He listened to what I had to say, and pointed out the mistakes I'd made, which I already knew. He said he'd lend me a month's rent, but I would have to pay it back. I would have insisted on doing so anyway. I respected him too much to be able to just scrounge from him, and I desperately wanted to win his admiration by succeeding in life. He knew I had to be taught to take responsibility for myself from now on. I was going to have to give up on the carpet-cleaning job because that was obviously not going to work out. I needed to find something sensible to do, so that I had a firm base from which to pursue my ambitions. It was a relief to have been handed another month in which to get started, but the pressure was still on. I now knew how quickly a month could pass.

My only definite income came from the humble Saturday job at Homebase, wandering around the shelves in green dungarees doing whatever I was told and trying to help customers. I decided to increase my hours with them, so that at least I'd have enough to live on. I could have made it a full-time career, but I knew if I wanted to make it to management I was going to have to stay for years, and that still wasn't how I planned to spend my life. However badly things were going, I wasn't ready to give up on my dreams by a long way.

The world was proving to be a bigger, colder and more frightening place than I'd imagined. As my first Christmas on my own approached, I didn't feel I could go back to Alan and Margaret's for the holiday, because I felt they'd done their job with me and it was time to move on, but I didn't have anywhere to move on to. One or two friends invited me to come over on Christmas Day, but I lied and told them I was busy. I didn't want anyone feeling sorry for me. It was the same with birthdays. I'd been used to dealing with all those things on my own as a child, and so I was able to deal with the loneliness now, but it was still hard. Christmas Day is impossible to ignore. It comes at you from every angle with images of families being together round big meals and decorated trees, giving each other presents and enjoying traditions together. If you are sitting alone with a television in a bedsit beside some railway lines, with no money to buy yourself a decent meal, it's impossible not to feel bad.

I'd found I was losing touch with my old school friends anyway because at the times when they were meeting up I had to work. I had to save my money for the rent so I couldn't afford to go to football matches or to the pub whenever they asked, or indulge in any of the other normal social activities that boys of that age go in for. When I got home in the evenings I was usually on my own, just watching the television, eating take-away food and trying to plan a way forward.

When I got to my eighteenth birthday, which I understood was an age when employers would start to consider my applications more seriously, I launched my assault on the money markets. Being a trader was still my dream and I now knew that no one was going to offer me a job unless I made the first approach. I spent hours planning the letter I would write asking for jobs. I did draft after draft, explaining how it was my dream and why I thought I would be good at it and asking for an interview. I hand-wrote over fifty copies of the letter once I was happy with the wording, and sent it to every company in the City that I could find the address of at the library. I made phone calls to get the right names of the people I needed to contact in alien-sounding places like 'personnel departments'.

From the day I sent the letters off I waited in for the postman each morning, hardly able to contain my excitement and anticipation, certain I'd be flooded with offers of interviews. Each day I made new excuses to myself as to why there was nothing, and became optimistic about the next day. In the end, two companies wrote back to say 'no' and the rest ignored me completely. It seemed that in the world I wanted to join, I was virtually invisible.

It was a couple of months before I gave up hoping and accepted
that I wasn't going to hear from any more of them, by which time
I'd started to formulate a new plan. I was reading everything I could
find about the subject, learning about futures trading and options
and all the stock exchange terminology, and it was dawning on me
that to really make money in the markets you had to use your own
capital. That must be the way forward. If I could just find a way of
accruing some capital, I could launch myself into the career that I
was most interested in without having to rely on anyone else giving
me a job. But how to make that seed money, that was the question
that seemed to elude me. It was taking every bit of energy I could
muster to earn enough to live in one room of a shared house with
virtually no outside life at all. Accruing capital seemed like a very
distant dream.

It wasn't just that I lacked the necessary education for most
careers; I also lacked the aura that confident people have when they
go to interviews. I'd learned a lot by watching Alan, but not enough
to undo the damage that had been done to my self-esteem in the
first fourteen years of my life. The quality that Margaret referred
to as my 'council house mentality' must still have been written
plainly all over me whenever I wrote letters, made phone calls or
turned up for interviews. I had no track record, either educationally
or workwise, that I could point to in order to dispel people's first
impressions of me. The only jobs that seemed to be open to someone in my position were selling on commission, living by my results.

I started buying the London *Evening Standard* and looking for
work in the centre of London. I'd got myself a suit, which must
have looked every bit as cheap as it was, and I started going for
account management jobs and anything else I could persuade
people to interview me for. I was too young for all of them, which
gave everyone the perfect excuse for saying no.

'I'll give you this,' one interviewer said as he was turning me down, 'you've got balls.' I took that as a compliment, but it didn't help me move forward.

It wasn't hard to find a certain sort of selling job, but they were soul-crushingly tedious and usually they were only offering payment on results, which seemed unobtainable. I spent some time selling advertising space over the phone for a magazine I'd never heard of, just working from a script and trying to get in as many calls as possible in the hope that a percentage of them were bound to bear fruit. They didn't and it was costing me money just to get to their office. I tried market research, standing in the street asking people questions – more commission that I didn't earn.

My spirits were sinking fast. If this was the only sort of white-collar work I could get, and I couldn't even make a living at that, what on earth was I going to do?

One of the jobs I went for was as a 'sales merchandizer' for Servis. I think they were offering an £8,000 basic salary and a van, with interviews being held in Birmingham. I sent them a cv in my best writing and rang up to sell myself over the phone. I explained I couldn't afford the ticket up to Birmingham and they agreed to pay my fare. The job involved going round retail outlets checking that all the Servis point-of-sale material was displayed correctly around their washing machines. The interview went like a dream. They invited me back a couple of weeks later and I was offered the job. It was a long way from my dream career, but it was a foot on the next rung of the ladder.

There was a week's training course, where I got to stay in a hotel, which was great because it meant I got proper meals again. I'd been having to cut back a bit in that department in order to pay Alan back his money. One of the things I missed most about moving out of their house was Margaret's cooking. So, every other Friday I went to the Women's Institute market that she used to cook for and bought homemade steak and kidney pies and biscuits. Even though Margaret had stopped cooking for them herself, I still knew many of the other old ladies down there and they'd always look after me.

That hotel room in Birmingham seemed like the height of luxury to me. Although I'd been on holiday a couple of times with Margaret and some other kids, I'd never stayed in a hotel on my own or had a room like this to myself. At the end of the course I got to drive my Servis van back home so that I'd have it there to do my rounds to the retailers. It was the first time I'd driven since passing my test about a year before and I was having terrible trouble remembering all the stuff I'd been taught. I could see the fleet manager watching me with a worried expression as the van crawled out of the service area. I'd forgotten to change the mirrors and couldn't see anything except sky in any direction, but I wasn't going to stop and readjust them in front of everyone.

I drove out in search of the motorway with my suit on and my briefcase and equipment in the back and I felt like I'd finally arrived. When I eventually found the motorway I thought I'd take it easy in the slow lane, but that only lasted about five minutes before I was into the fast lane with my foot on the floor. I had a job and a vehicle and I was ready to go places now.

I stayed with Servis for about six months and I learnt a lot. The most important lesson, however, was that if I wanted to make anything of myself in life it was going to have to be through selling. That was going to be the way in which I'd get together the capital I needed to pursue my real dreams. I realized that everyone had to sell something in order to survive, and that I just had to learn to do it better than anyone else.

When I was passed over by Servis for a promotion to selling that I thought I deserved, I decided it was time to move on and I went to Konica, to train for selling photocopiers. I soon realized I wasn't going to make enough money there and moved on again to another company that people in the business were all talking about. I didn't enjoy the job as much as the Servis job, but it did teach me that in order to make decent money you have to sell direct to companies and not be a 'rep'. There were senior salesmen working at this place who earned over £100,000 a year. There were even some ex-money markets people there, earning more than they had from their trading. It seemed I had finally got myself to the right place at the right time.

When I started there I worked unbelievably hard, trudging the streets looking for business. My efforts paid off because I made £5,000 in my first month, which I then spent in clubs and pubs. I felt certain I was on a roll now. If I could make that much in just a month, I would have no trouble doing it again. I'd broken through the barriers that had been holding me back and nothing would stop me now. My bank obviously agreed and immediately granted me an overdraft facility and I was offered credit everywhere I turned. Before long I was driving a three-litre Supra car and living like a king, all on credit. It was 1989 and boom time in the UK.

The results of the first month, however, proved to be something of a freak. I was still doing better than I'd ever done in my life, but I was not earning as fast as I was spending and the debts were mounting up. All the good advice I'd taken from Alan over the years was forgotten in a surge of overconfidence and relief at finally having broken out of the cycle of poor education and bad beginnings. I'd lost focus on my dreams.

A year later the photocopying industry crashed. There was a problem with the paying of commission within the company. I lost my job, but the debts were still there. I tumbled off the ladder again, back to where I'd started, but with even fewer illusions.

16. Slipping Beyond the Law

My life by that time had changed a great deal, but it was all built on sand. By the time my job in the photocopying business had vanished I'd moved house and was sharing with a guy I'd met at the company. I was also spending time at another friend's house in Horley, a town near Gatwick, and there I'd met up with a man called Paul, who worked for one of the big car rental companies and lived on the same estate.

One day Paul came round to the house driving a brand-new Mercedes S-Class; a seriously luxurious car. It belonged to the rental company he worked for but he'd found a way of getting it for his own personal use without anyone knowing. The way the scam worked was that the car had been booked into the repair shop, although there was nothing wrong with it. Because no one had checked up on it after that, Paul had then been able to drive it away from the repair shop without anyone in the company noticing it had gone. I was deeply impressed by this sleight of hand and by how easy it appeared to have been.

'I've got another car at home,' Paul said. 'Do you want this one to use?'

He explained it was better for him to have the Mercedes driven around than for it to be parked all the time near his house. He didn't want to be driving around in such a luxurious car in case he was spotted by someone from his work. The other car was much less conspicuous.

Since I was by then without any sort of vehicle I accepted the offer gratefully. The car was a revelation, a hundred times better than anything I'd ever driven before. Gliding around the area in such luxury lifted my dampened spirits and reminded me just how much I wanted to be successful, so that I could own these sorts of nice things for myself. Being inside a powerful, solidly built car makes you feel invulnerable and capable of anything. I liked that feeling and wanted more of it.

Since working in London I'd started doing some sparring at a boxing club in the area to keep myself fit and to let out some of the anger that was still trapped inside me. Letting off steam with the punch bag always made me feel a lot better and now took my mind off the fact that I had large debts, no money or income with which to deal with them in the foreseeable future and couldn't find a job. It was almost like being back where I had been at the beginning, since working as a salesman for a photocopying company didn't qualify me for any other sort of job apart from the commission-only selling jobs I'd tried in the past and found to be useless.

I was meeting a lot of different people around the club and one of them spotted the car as I was climbing into it to go home. We started talking and the conversation quickly got on to the Merc. I explained it wasn't mine, that I was just using it from the rental company before it went in for repair.

'I know someone who would take a car like that off your hands,' he said. 'If you ever needed some quick money.'

'Yeah?' I replied casually. 'How much do you think he'd be willing to pay?'

'Couple of grand, I should think.'

By that time I was desperately in need of money to pay off the debts that I'd stupidly allowed to build up, so I promised to give the suggestion some thought. I went back to Paul in Horley and told him what this guy had said.

'They say we can get a couple of grand for this car,' I said.

'Well, no one at the company knows it's gone,' Paul said. 'So we might as well.'

The decision was taken and arrangements were made by telephone. We were told to take the car a few days later and park near a round-about in Chertsey. The man we were dealing with was coming down from South London and would meet us there. We drove to the designated place in both cars. I took mine to the location they'd described to us and Paul parked his round the corner and came to sit with me. Both of us were quiet and jumpy as we looked around, trying to predict what was likely to happen next. Not only were we scared of getting caught by the police, we were also nervous about who we were due to be meeting. We knew they were not going to be people who you messed with. What if they just took the car and didn't give us our money? What if they didn't turn up? What if the police turned up and wanted to know what we were up to? I was very tempted to forget the whole thing and just drive away, but then I remembered how much I needed the money. And anyway, I'd given these people my word I would be there.

There were dozens of unanswerable questions going round and round in my head as I watched the roads outside and I wished I had never got involved. But it was too late to back out now. We were committed to going through with it, and the money was going to solve a lot of immediate problems.

We sat for a while in this state of tension, watching the traffic going by, trying to work out which car would be the one coming to see us. An anonymous looking saloon containing four men went past.

'That looked like them,' I said.

'Nah,' Paul shook his head. 'They've driven on.'

'They're back,' I said as the car reappeared on the roundabout and cruised past once more, the men inside not giving us a second look.

'What are they playing at?' Paul wondered.

'Just checking us out, I guess. Making sure no one else is watching.'

The car circled the roundabout slowly a few more times and we could see that now they were looking at us. We still had no way of knowing what was going to happen next. The game went on for about ten minutes as they checked the coast was clear and no one else was lying in wait. Then the car pulled up a few yards away from us. Two of the men got out and walked briskly over. The remaining men drove away immediately.

We climbed out of the car to meet them. A white envelope was pushed into my hand and the keys were taken away. No eye contact was made. The Mercedes had gone within seconds and we were left standing on our own, wondering what had happened. We made our way quickly to where we'd left Paul's car and drove home. I opened the envelope as we drove and checked the money was there. It was. I felt a mixture of relief that it was over and that we had the money, and disquiet that I'd slipped over the law in order to make a living. I told Paul I was nervous the car was going to be traced back to us.

'How can they?' he wanted to know. 'No one even knows it's gone from the company. When they do find out, how would they trace it to us?'

'The problem is, I haven't got anything to drive around in now,' I pointed out.

'I'll sort you out something,' he promised.

True to his word, he got me another car, a more modest Ford this time, for my own use, and a few days later I lost the key, which also had the car's alarm on it. I rang Paul up and told him my problem.

'Well, I can't get a new key cut at work,' he said, 'or they'll notice the car's out and start asking questions. I'll get you the key number and you can get it cut somewhere else.'

An hour later he rang back with the key number. I went down to a local key-cutting service, gave them the number Paul had dictated to me and told them it was for a Ford. They didn't ask any more questions, they just did as I asked and gave me the key. I couldn't believe it was that simple, although the full implications of it didn't strike me immediately.

A few weeks after we'd disposed of the Mercedes the garage owner who'd taken it phoned up out of the blue. I was a little unnerved to hear from him at first, wondering if there was a problem, not really comfortable with the idea that someone like him knew how to find me so easily. But his tone was friendly and he didn't seem worried about anything. We chatted about nothing much for a few minutes and then he got to the point.

'If you can get hold of a car like that one,' he said, very reasonably, 'you should be able to get hold of others to order.' We decided to meet a few days later in a pub. He had given me a great deal of food for thought. By then the thousand pounds I had got from the Mercedes had gone but none of my debt problems had. I still hadn't been able to find any other way to earn a living. At the same time I was uncomfortable about being involved with people who obviously operated a long way outside the law.

'I can't steal cars,' I told him when we met. 'I just wouldn't be able to do it.'

In my mind there was all the difference in the world between selling something that had come into my possession by dubious means and actually going out stealing things that belonged to other people. The fact that no one at the company had even missed the Mercedes made me feel better about profiting from its disappearance. The act seemed to be one step removed from actually stealing from another person.

'You don't have to go round breaking into them in the street,' he laughed, cajoling me along, making me feel foolish for holding such scruples. 'You could work with your friend, getting them out of his company.'

As he was talking an idea was going through my head. If Paul could get me the key numbers to other cars, and he could also book them in for repairs, I could just walk in and get them from wherever he had them parked up. I told my contact I'd think about it and get back to him.

That evening Paul and I went out for a drink and I told him about the call and about my idea. He thought about it for a few minutes and agreed he could see that the system might work. The garage owner in South London needed to order cars of certain makes and colours to fit the profiles of wrecks that had been brought in and registration papers that he had in his possession. If we could find cars to match his specifications we could supply him.

'Let's try it,' Paul said when we'd talked round every angle of the idea and not found any snags.

'Okay, I'll ring him back,' I agreed, 'and tell him we'll give it a go. I won't make any promises, just say we'll try it out.'

A few days later the garage owner rang with a make and colour he needed. I rang Paul and passed the information on. He then rang back with a key number of a vehicle that fitted the description and a location where I would be able to find it. I got the key cut and went to collect the car, delivering it to a street close to the garage, leaving the key underneath for them to pick up once they'd received a call. The system worked like a charm. They paid us on time and ordered another car a couple of weeks later. We'd created a business for ourselves, supplying cars to order.

Word spreads about this sort of thing in certain circles and I began to get a reputation as someone who could get things that people wanted. I didn't disillusion anyone, just allowed the rumours to persist. The car deals were putting enough money in my pocket to live on, but not much more. I should have been more worried about them than I was, but I rationalized it away as the only person getting hurt was an anonymous car rental company, who would be claiming off insurance anyway. It seemed like a relatively harmless crime, at least that was how I justified it to myself.

Having discovered I had a skill and a growing reputation I began to think of ways of expanding it into other areas that might pay. I was spending a fair bit of time in pubs and clubs, where you can't help but meet a variety of different people. Anyone I met who was involved in the management side, I tried to find out what they wanted, to see if there were other things I might be able to supply in exchange for cash. Acquiring the cars was taking almost no time at all and I was keen to work hard if anyone wanted to use my services.

One thing led to another and I found there was an endless appetite in the club trade for cheap alcohol and cigarettes. I got to know the most influential local club and bar owners and found out what they needed. On the whole they seemed to be willing to take anything as long as it was the right price. I'd then go out and source the products from other contacts who were bringing them in from different places and needed to get rid of them quickly. I'd become a middle-man, doing the deals that the people running the clubs didn't have time to do for themselves and didn't want to get involved with. I would take a cut on each deal.

A lot of my business transactions took place in the car parks of those anonymous service stations dotted along the motorways, where lorries, vans and cars intermingle and no one knows anyone else. In these transient places it was easy to exchange vehicles or move a few crates around without attracting any attention, especially after dark. I'd stumbled into a parallel business world; living alongside the legitimate business travellers, but invisible to anyone who isn't part of it, moving goods between those who have them and those who want them with no paperwork, being paid in nothing but cash.

My operations didn't always go smoothly. There was one incident where I somehow ended up with the wrong van and had a load of seafood to dispose of instead of drink. The neighbours all dined on lobster for several weeks.

It doesn't take long before you get a reputation in this line of work. The criminal world is small and word travels through it quickly. If you're known to have money to spend and contacts to sell to, people will get in touch, offering to supply things. I was aware that the club owners were people you couldn't mess around with, hard businessmen who did whatever was necessary to stay in business and turn a profit. I made sure I never made promises I couldn't fulfil and I always owned up quickly if I wasn't able to get something they wanted. It was business to me, plain and simple, getting cash to live on and to help pay off my debts. I behaved as professionally as if I was in a legitimate business and people respected me for it. I became known as 'The Kid'. I would turn up at a club and calls would be put through to the owners from the doors: 'The Kid's here'. I'd be ushered quickly through. I was useful to them and I didn't mess them about and they responded to that.

Because I provided the club owners with a good service I found that I'd become 'connected'. Word got about and it was generally known that 'The Kid' was protected by powerful people, and so my reputation grew. Very few people interfered with me because they knew who my contacts were. I got into a couple of fights in bars and I won very quickly, partly because I'd been training at the boxing club and was very fit, but also because I'd learnt from my parents to hit hard and fast. As a result I also gained a reputation for being hard myself, which was only partly deserved.

I would never have had the temperament to be a professional boxer because as soon as someone hit me or upset me I'd immediately hit back with no forethought or subtlety, using every ounce of strength I could muster. The anger that had built up in the first twenty years of my life was just sitting there waiting for someone to disturb it. I didn't play any games or exercise any strategic thinking when I fought, which meant any drunk picking a fight with me in a bar because they thought I was a bit young and flash got hit much quicker and harder than they'd expected. But these were isolated incidents. You only have to knock someone out once or twice for word to get around and people to steer clear. Almost nobody gave me any trouble at all. Because I'd been so damaged as a child, and knew I could survive, I wasn't frightened of anything. I wasn't even frightened of dying. When you've got nothing to lose you're in a pretty strong position in many ways. Perhaps other people could sense that about me, perhaps that was why they showed me the respect they did.

More people came to me asking for things as the months went by, and the more deals I was able to put together, all of them putting cash in my pocket. I was staying afloat, I was living the good life, out every night and driving a flash motor, but it was still a business built on sand. I still had no capital or substance behind me. It was all wads of cash passing from hand to hand, creating an illusion of big money and affluence, when in fact it was just quick turnover, small profits and a lot of flash spending. I wasn't building up the money that I needed for all the dreams that now seemed to be on hold.

Despite the lack of solid money, I felt much more secure and protected than I ever had in the legitimate business world I'd tried to make a living in first. Now there were powerful people who had a vested interest in looking after me; that made me feel confident and comfortable. As long as I could get them what they wanted they didn't want any harm to befall me. I loved the feeling of being able to walk past queues waiting to get into clubs and being let straight in. I imagined that everyone left outside was wondering who I was. After a lifetime of being the boy on the outside watching everyone else having a life, I was finally accepted and on the inside. That was a good feeling. I belonged somewhere at last, even if I was only just keeping myself above water financially.

I still kept myself to myself, even when I was socializing. I never told anyone exactly what I was up to, because I reckoned if no one knew then no one could blab on me. I didn't expect to stay in this world for ever, I would be wanting to go back to the straight world as soon as I could get something legitimate together, and so I didn't want to be saddled with any sort of criminal record. I knew that the criminal life wasn't for me, because it was only a matter of time before I would be caught doing something, but I couldn't yet see a way out into the legitimate world.

The car business stopped when Paul left the rental company, and I concentrated on supplying drink to club owners. Although I enjoyed the feeling of being able to strut around the clubs, protected and respected, I was desperate to find a way into a proper business, but I knew it was still a matter of raising a lump of capital with which to back myself. I was only twenty-one by then, but I felt like I'd been fighting to get a foothold in the business world for ever.

17. Bereavement and Disappointment

While I was working as a deal turner I got back in contact with Margaret and Alan. I'd matured a lot since leaving them, having learned to stand on my own two feet, even if it wasn't yet in the way I'd hoped. It put our relationship on a different footing, strengthened it even. Despite my rocky start I'd managed to survive in the outside world and that made me feel like I'd achieved something and could go back with my head held high. They didn't have to know what I was doing; they just saw the surface, the young man who seemed to be looking after himself in the world. They didn't ask me any questions about my work; maybe Alan could guess the sort of things I did.

He'd suffered another heart attack, which upset me badly, and it was beginning to look as if he wasn't going to survive much longer. He wasn't getting out much and it was obvious that he was tired most of the time. There were plans being laid for him and Margaret to spend more time in Australia with the children and grandchildren who lived out there. They'd been trying to sell their house, but without much luck since the property market was depressed. I made sure I spent as much time as possible with Alan because I was afraid I wouldn't have him around for much longer. I went round to the house at every opportunity. Sometimes we'd just sit together in the garden without saying much, comfortable in the knowledge that the other one was there. I went back to staying with them some nights and going off to work from there. One morning, as I left the house, I glanced up and saw him watching me from his bedroom window.

'You take care of yourself,' he called down, as if he knew something was going to happen. I waved back and went to work with a strange feeling of disquiet in the pit of my stomach, unsure why I felt so bad.

When I got home that afternoon I could tell there was a sombre mood in the house the moment I came in through the front door. I could hear people talking in subdued voices. Margaret was in the kitchen with Gary from next door and her youngest daughter, Donna. The disquiet I'd been feeling all day stirred into a painful foreboding. I knew I was about to find out something that would hurt a lot. I pushed open the door and they turned to look at me with faces that explained everything. As I listened in stunned silence they told me that Alan had died playing bridge, the thing he enjoyed more than anything else. Even though I'd been expecting it, the news hit me like a punch in the face. I couldn't think of anything to say, just turned on my heel and walked out of the room, wanting to get away from everyone else so that I could let my feelings out without inhibition. I walked through to the lounge and sat in his favourite chair, put a cushion to my face and wept uncontrollably. Gary came through a little later and patted me on the shoulder, trying to console me, but I was inconsolable. I had no idea how I was going to cope with the grief that was churning around inside me. More than anyone else, Alan had given me the time and support and love that had been missing from my life for so long. I'd wanted so much to have him around to watch as I moved up in the world and achieved all the things I wanted to achieve, but now he'd gone and there would be no more chats in his workroom or bridge parties or quiet afternoons in the garden. He would never see me amount to anything at all, never know how big a part he had played in my life. There were so many things I wished I had said to him, and now it was too late.

I found the funeral particularly difficult because, whereas I'd felt like we had a father-and-son relationship when we were together, I was now relegated to being a friend of the family, no longer part of the immediate family. I did understand this from their point of view. But although I wasn't Alan's real son he'd been more of a real father to me than Dennis. I wouldn't have expected anything else, but being pushed to the sidelines left me with an empty feeling in my stomach, reminded me that I didn't really belong anywhere.

All through the service I couldn't stop crying. It was as if the floodgates had finally been lifted after all the years of holding back the tears and there was no way of closing them again. I found the idea of his body being burnt unbearable. When the coffin rolled away through the doors to the furnace I was completely unable to control myself. I couldn't understand how anyone could be burning the body of someone they loved. I remembered the feeling of being safe in the arms of the fireman as a tiny child and this seemed to go against all that I'd felt that night. Gary tried to comfort me again outside the crematorium but there was little he could do. I covered my eyes with sunglasses and stayed silent.

When we got back to the house again I went upstairs and lay on my bed. I couldn't face mixing with the others downstairs, making polite conversation and handing round sandwiches. I didn't want people to see how much I'd been crying.

Margaret was very businesslike about everything. I think they must both have known it was coming because they'd already transferred all their joint assets over to her. Once the funeral was over she just wanted to pack up and move down to Australia to be where most of her family was, and to put her past behind her. I suggested that if she wanted to get rid of the house quickly, I'd buy it from her to take it off her hands. I don't know how I thought I was going to do it. I guess it was just one of those things you say without expecting anything to come of it. I certainly didn't have the money to run it, let alone buy it, but perhaps I thought I'd work that one out when the time came. Margaret knew enough about my situation to be aware I didn't have the sort of money for buying houses, and she suggested that if I did buy the house from her, she'd loan me £30,000 to start a business.

'It's what Alan would have wanted,' she told me, and I felt choked with emotion.

The moment she suggested it I could see this was my way forward, and that it would have been what Alan would have wanted, with Margaret and I both helping each other to put our lives in order. The £30,000 was exactly the sort of capital I felt I needed to get myself launched into a legitimate business. I could imagine Alan would have approved, given his grasp of business and of the need to have money behind you. If I had that sort of capital to work with I could stop dashing around making a few quid here and a few quid there, and concentrate on making the money work for me, and I'd have something to make the mortgage repayments on the house while I got established. I could give up living on the edge of the law, and really start to build something. It would be the stepping-stone I needed to get to the next stage of my life and I accepted the offer gratefully. I knew that I could work hard and that with the money I would be able to create something that I could grow and build. I was so looking forward to the chance to prove what I was capable of. I already had my eyes on a business. A friend of mine had introduced me to a gentleman who wanted to sell his bar. It was the kind of business that I felt would put me on the road to the success that I wanted in a legitimate line of work. I also liked the sort of life which owning a bar would provide. It would give me a fixed place in the world.

It was not going to be a straightforward deal between Margaret and me by any means. The house was on the market at £125,000 and until Margaret was in a position to give me the loan, I didn't even have the money to pay for stamp duty. But she wouldn't have any money to give me until I'd managed to get a mortgage in order to pay her for the house. With no money for a deposit and no steady income, getting a mortgage was going to be difficult. It was a chicken and egg situation. A friend of mine knew about mortgages and said I could get a 90 per cent one if I could just prove my income, and if Margaret told them the house was actually going for £145,000 and that I had already paid her a £20,000 deposit. I don't know how I proved I had an income, but I did. It was a fraud. But I had no choice if I wanted to lift myself back to the legitimate side of life.

All through the negotiations I kept checking with Margaret that the loan was still on, to the point where I think I was starting to annoy her.

Interest rates were high and the mortgage was going to be costing me over £1,000 a month, but I was convinced I could make the £30,000 work for me and earn me enough to cover it. Margaret went off to Australia just before we completed the deal. The day before we exchanged contracts I spoke to her on the phone in Sydney and I asked again, 'Am I still all right for this £30,000? I can't afford this house without it.'

She assured me it would all be sorted out.

Two days later, with the deal on the house completed, I rang her again to ask about the loan. She told me she'd spoken to her lawyer and been advised against giving me the money. I felt the world caving in around my head as her words sank in. Not only could I see my dreams of starting the business and being truly independent disappearing in smoke, I could also see that I now had outgoings of over £1,000 a month and not enough income to cover them.

I phoned back again a bit later to plead with her and to try to find out why she was doing such a cruel thing.

'I haven't even got the money for the stamp duty or the first mortgage payment,' I said.

She put the phone down on the side, without hanging up, and walked away. I was stuck with an open line to Australia and no one to speak to.

I moved into the house, because at least then I wasn't paying out any rent, but it was a sad experience. All the furniture had gone, missing pictures leaving bare patches on the walls, naked light bulbs hanging from the ceilings and a few old curtains and carpets, now robbed of their previously homely feel, just looking tired and shabby. The only pieces of furniture left were my bed and a chair.

It was coming up to Christmas and I had to spend the festive season alone in the empty house with no money and my dreams a distant glimmer. I had never felt so lonely in my life. My deal for the bar was put on hold and I couldn't see how I could get it up and going again. My disappointment was overwhelming.

18. Down to Bare Knuckles

I was still boxing to keep fit and took out my frustrations on the punch bag. I would never have been able to become a professional because of my temperament, but I was still able to handle myself. I needed a way to vent my frustrations since everything else in my life was going from bad to worse. There were some problems with the law in the area where I lived and worked and the club owners I'd been supplying all went to ground, causing my drinks business to dry up overnight. There were no hard feelings; they just didn't want to buy anything that might be remotely dodgy. I suddenly had no income at all, not even cash in my pocket to buy food, and the debts were building up every day at the house.

Some people knew that I was desperate to earn some money and I had been approached a few weeks before by a guy called Johnny. I'd seen him around a few times but didn't know much about him.

'You're a good fighter,' he said matter-of-factly. 'If you ever need money, I might be able to offer you some work.'

He gave me his number and I put it into my pocket without ever thinking I'd do anything about it. I knew what he was talking about; illegal fights, or 'bare-knuckle' as they're known, where there were no rules except destroying your opponent as quickly and brutally as possible. At that stage I was still concentrating on trying to keep the drinks business going. Now, however, a few weeks later, with mortgage payments and household bills piling up around me, I needed to scrape together money in any way I could if I didn't want to lose everything and be in debt for years to come. I called the number he'd given me, reminded him who I was and told him I needed money.

'Well,' he said, 'if you can handle yourself, maybe you could have a fight or something.'

I didn't think that much of it. I felt I'd tried everything else, why not try this?

'Okay,' I said. 'How much do I get paid?'

'A hundred and fifty if you win, nothing if you lose.'

'Okay. What do I wear?' Looking back, it was a strange thing to ask, but it was the only thing that came into my head.

'Just tracksuit bottoms and T-shirt,' he said.

Once he'd hung up I began to imagine what it might be like. It might be fun to fight; to be up in a ring in some crowded, smoky, illegal den with onlookers screaming and shouting, urging me on, people laying bets and laughing and having a good time. The idea began to grow on me, taking on a sort of seedy romanticism and glamour.

It was arranged that I'd be picked up a few evenings later around King's Cross somewhere. It was getting dark as I waited on a street corner until the car pulled up and I got in. I was already feeling apprehensive; not knowing where I was going or what was going to happen. There were several men in the car and we drove out of London on one of the main routes for about an hour. No one spoke much. The last of the daylight faded and we reached the end of the streetlights. The night was getting very black indeed. We turned off the main roads and drove through a built-up area on to a narrow, unmade track. We went over a hill and started to descend to an area that wasn't overlooked by any houses. I now had no idea where I was. I began to feel nervous, the butterflies churning in my stomach. Eventually we came out on to a field. This was beginning to look very different to the scene I'd been imagining.

There were eight cars pulled up facing into a circle as we bumped across the grass to join them. The men who'd come in the cars were standing around, smoking and talking in quiet voices. I guess they were making bets, but I was more interested in trying to work out what was going to happen to me. The cars' headlights illuminated the 'ring' in which the fight would take place. My opponent was already stripped down to the waist and waiting. He was a bit taller and older than me and didn't seem to have that much muscle on him, but he was covered in tattoos. I knew he'd be happy to hurt me in any way he could and I just had to make sure I got him first.

'What happens?' I asked Johnny, my contact.

'Just get on with it,' he grunted.

There was no whistle or bell or anything to signify the fight had started. I pulled off my jacket and walked towards my opponent. As I got close I noticed he smelt. It was as if he'd been working with horseshit all day and had come straight from there without washing. We grabbed each other, landing punches and kicks wherever we could. I was immediately angry and unable to hold back any of my punches. I just wanted to hurt him badly. I managed to get a grip on his legs and jerk them out from under him. The moment he was down on the floor I stamped on his head. I kept kicking and punching as fast and as hard as I could, determined not to let him get up again. If he couldn't get up I'd won. The audience made no sound as they watched. They didn't cheer or boo or shout anything at all; or, if they did, I didn't hear them. They just watched us getting on with the job.

It was all over in a couple of minutes. My T-shirt was ripped and my tracksuit bottoms were covered in mud. I felt shattered. The men got back into their cars and drove away. Johnny gave me my money and I sank silently into the car they'd brought me in. The ride back was as quiet as the ride down had been. They dropped me back at King's Cross and I made my way wearily home. I had a few cuts on my face but nothing to alarm anyone who might see me. It had been nothing like I'd imagined and I felt bad about what I'd done to the other guy, but I knew he'd have done the same to me if he'd been able to. It had been a reasonably easy night's work.

Johnny rang again a couple of weeks later to see if I wanted another fight. I still needed the money and the memory of the first one was already fading, so I said yes. The pick-up routine was the same and once we were at the location we waited in the car for a few minutes, surveying the scene. My opponent was sitting in another car a little way away. We stared at each other through the car windows, trying to weigh one another up. This time there were more cars forming the ring, and there were some women amongst the onlookers. They seemed like gypsies to me, but I didn't take much notice of them, concentrating on what I was going to be doing. It was as if the first fight had just been a trial and now I was being given a bigger audience. Everyone seemed to be waiting for someone else to make the first move. I wanted to get it over with so I opened the car door and got out. It was as if I'd given a signal and all the other car doors opened as people got out to watch.

I knew what to do this time. I walked straight over to my opponent. He was quite good looking, with dark hair and a toned body. Unlike the first guy, this one looked fit. I smacked him in the face with all my strength. I would guess he was in his late twenties, a little bit taller than me again. I was pretty fit myself from my training and he went down from the first punch. I think I may have broken his nose. There was certainly a lot of blood coming out of it. His tooth had split my knuckle right through to the bone; I heard the skin ripping open as I punched but I didn't feel a thing. I kept hitting him and every time I made contact a spurt of blood came out of my knuckle. He never recovered from the first blow and within what seemed like no time I'd taken him out and he was lying motionless on the ground. When I was sure he wasn't getting up again I looked at my hand and saw the white of the knucklebone poking through the flesh. The pain began to get through to me.

I'd won my money again and this time they gave me a lift back to Coulsdon, dropping me on the A23, just off the motorway, and leaving me to walk back to the house. Once I was inside I sat down and cried at the way my life was going. All the emotions I'd been holding in came flooding out. I'd had so many dreams and tried everything I could think of to make a success of my life, but now I was living in a deserted house, deep in debt and having to fight for pocket money. The thought occurred to me that I just might not be able to do anything better, that I'd been kidding myself all along to think I could ever amount to anything. There was no one I could turn to for help or advice because Alan was dead and I certainly couldn't go back to my parents. I was no longer close to any of my school friends, and the business people who were my new acquaintances were not the sort of people to go pleading to. I felt completely alone. By the time I got to bed the pain from my hand was excruciating and there was no chance I'd be able to sleep.

In the morning I took myself down to the local hospital and they stitched the wound up for me. They didn't ask any awkward questions.

19. From Bad to Worse

One of my favourite haunts for food when I was living back at Alan's old house was the local fish and chip shop. I'd noticed there were three guys who always seemed to be standing outside the shop. I could tell they were as thick as porridge but I had no reason to speak to them about anything so I didn't give them a second thought. There was also a black guy living locally, who was slightly disabled. I didn't know him either, had never spoken to him, but I noticed the three idiots messing around behind him one time, taking the mickey out of the way he walked. None of it was any of my business, since I didn't know any of them, but the sight of it grated somewhere deep inside my head. Maybe it reminded me of when I was a child being taunted by the other children, or of seeing Kimberley trapped in the corner of the room by the boys at Yarborough. I didn't do anything about it, but the incident played on my mind, making me feel slightly sickened when I thought about it. Another time I was driving past at the same time of day and I saw exactly the same thing happening. They were taking the mickey out of him behind his back, which seemed well out of order. I parked the car and went into the shop.

'Give me a bag of chips, will you?' I said to the boy behind the counter. 'And make them hot ones.'

'These are hot,' he said.

'No,' I said, 'I want them still with boiling oil on them. I'll pay you extra.'

He didn't ask any more questions, just did what I asked. I covered the boiling hot chips in salt and vinegar, walked outside and smashed them straight into the face of the biggest of the three, who seemed to be the leader, and then I went after the other two.

'You ever pick on him again,' I warned, 'and I'll fucking kill you.'

I knew I shouldn't be getting involved, but I also knew no one else would if I didn't, and the disabled guy deserved to be able to walk home each day without having to put up with abuse from a bunch of clowns. I sometimes saw them round the area after that, but I never saw them outside the chip shop again.

About a month after my second bare-knuckle fight, when my hand was beginning to heal, Johnny was on the phone again. This time he had a better offer for me. In this fight I'd get a hundred and fifty pounds if I lost and a thousand if I won. I presumed this meant there was something even dodgier than usual about the deal. If they were willing to pay me even if I lost, this fight was probably going to go to a level of viciousness I hadn't had to deal with before. But if I won a grand, that would help me with the mortgage payment that month and buy me some more time in the house to think of some way to get myself out of trouble. By this time the mortgage company was becoming suspicious of why I hadn't paid anything, not even the first instalment, and lawyers were demanding payment for the stamp duty on the house. I agreed to take on the fight.

I was picked up in King's Cross again and driven out to the same place. This time there must have been thirty cars in the circle. Something much bigger was going on and I felt uneasy. I'd strapped my knuckle together with some sticky tape. I knew it was bound to hurt, so I'd swallowed several painkillers in the car in preparation. The moment I saw my opponent I knew I'd been set up. He was completely different to the first two. The others must have been used to build my confidence and make me feel I could win against anyone they found for me. No one who'd seen this guy in advance would have volunteered to fight him. He looked more like an animal than a man. He had no neck and hardly any teeth. His skin was as thick and hard as cheap leather work boots. He was shorter than me but built like a bear.

I glanced around at the onlookers. There were a lot of serious faces. There must have been real money being betted on this one. It was obvious this guy was a professional. I knew they wouldn't let me back out now. If I tried to call off the fight the crowd would beat me up as well as my opponent. There was no option but to try to bring him down quickly or prepare myself for a beating.

I went in as hard and fast as I had the time before, smacking him with all my strength, but it made no impact whatsoever; I might as well have punched a brick wall. I could tell there was nothing I could do to hurt this man. He grabbed me like I was a child and punched me so hard my head seemed to explode. Before the explosion had even finished he headbutted me and a giant silver flash went off in my face. I went down like a sack of rags and he didn't let up for a second, punching, kicking, dragging me around in the dirt. He was enjoying himself. Everywhere I turned he was there, with the glare of car headlights behind him, blinding me as I reeled about in search of an escape route.

At one stage I managed to pull myself to my feet, thinking I might be able to make a run for it, but my legs wouldn't work. He came at me again and I felt myself being lifted off the ground and bent backwards over the bonnet of one of the cars. A metal emblem jabbed into the base of my spine like a blunt knife. I'd thought Gloria was bad, but this beating was beyond anything I'd ever experienced. As I slid to the ground again I responded just as I had as a child, curling myself into a ball to protect my vital organs and waiting for it all to be over. After a while the blows didn't actually create pain as they fell, it was more like the distant thuds of bombs dropping. I could feel their impact on me, breaking my skin and

my bones, but I was spared the pain. That would come later, when
the numbness had worn off.

Then I must have passed out because I don't remember anything
until I came round to find every inch of my head and body throb-
bing. I was desperately thirsty but when I tried to speak my lips
were too swollen to move. My eyes were virtually closed up as I
tried to peer around and see what was happening and where I might
be able to find comfort. Some of the cars were already leaving with
roars of exhaust fumes and sprays of dirt. There was no sign of
Johnny. I later discovered he'd betted on me on the first two fights,
deliberately building my reputation by putting me against people
I could easily beat, and then he'd betted against me on the third
fight, knowing that I hadn't a hope. He must also have known there
was no chance I would ever want to fight again, and so there was
no reason to help me get home. Someone I'd never seen before gave
me my £150 loser's fee.

My opponent was still there and now he'd won his money and
spent his aggression he was as nice as pie to me. He tried to make
conversation but I was in so much pain I could hardly move. My
ribs were screaming with agony and I knew some of them must be
broken. My legs kept buckling underneath me when I tried to walk.
Presumably they didn't want to leave me in the field for any passers-
by to find, so someone loaded me into the back of a filthy white
van. The windows were all boarded up so no one would be able to
see me from the outside. Several of them climbed into the front
and chatted to one another as if I wasn't there as I rolled around in
the dirt of the floor. Every bump the van went over sent spasms of
pain shooting through me.

They stopped at the top of the M23 motorway to drop me off.
I couldn't see how I could look after myself in the state I was in. I
asked them to take me home, but they wouldn't do that, not wanting to get involved any more than they already were. They

compromised and offered to drop me off in Coulsdon high street. By then it was late and the streets were more or less empty. As they drove away I half walked and half crawled into a mini-cab office. Everyone stared at me.

'You all right, son?' someone asked.

'Yeah,' I mumbled through broken lips, 'just get me a cab to take me home.'

A car came round immediately and the driver helped me get in. When he dropped me off I paid him out of what I'd earned. I hauled myself upstairs to the bedroom and collapsed on the bed. I just wanted to end it all. I felt I'd tried my best to get started in life, and I just wasn't succeeding. There didn't seem to be any point in going on. But, unless you're going to kill yourself, you can't give up. You have to keep trying. A few days later, once I'd started to mend, I began to rack my brains for other ways to break out of the destructive cycle of debt and poverty that I'd got myself into.

20. In Pursuit of Quick Cash

Because of the house, my creditors were becoming more and more impatient. I seemed to be receiving summonses almost every day for one unpaid bill or another. Having reached the bottom of the barrel with the bare-knuckle fighting I had two choices as to where I could go next; I could either give up the house and just walk away from the whole mess, or I could keep struggling to achieve my childhood dreams of freedom and prosperity. I decided, once my body had mended enough to support me, to keep trying.

I still wanted to buy the bar and, when I made enquiries, I discovered that it was still for sale. Had I been a more experienced businessman that might have raised some queries in my mind, but I was so desperate to get my hands on it I didn't think too deeply about why no one else had snapped it up after I dropped out. Originally the plan had been for me to pay a £20,000 deposit, and the rest out of the profits the bar produced. The business had done really well in the past but had lost some of its excitement, mainly because the owner had lost interest in it. It's the sort of business where you need to be very hands-on and enthusiastic if you're going to get the right buzz going, otherwise the customers just drift off to the competition. I thought I could revive its reputation quite easily because I was willing to put a great deal of time and effort into it, and I was bubbling with ideas. I had no experience in the industry to base this on, I'd never even worked behind a bar pulling pints. I had no idea how the business worked, apart from supplying dodgy drinks, but I was brimming with confidence that I could pull it off. I'd been planning to use the remaining £10,000 of Margaret's loan to get the stock levels up and do the place up a bit.

I'd been so looking forward to getting started on the venture and had been telling the owner that the money was on its way for a few weeks. Then, when Margaret changed her mind, I'd had to confess to him that I hadn't got the money. It made me sound like an idiot, like some kid who was living in a fantasy world. But I had to keep trying to find another way round, because I really wanted to get into this business, certain that it would give me the foothold I needed to move up in the world and make some solid money. Having pulled myself together, I called him up and we arranged to meet.

'How much can you get?' he wanted to know when I told him I still wanted to make the deal happen if it was at all possible.

'I don't know,' I replied, racking my brain for anyone that I might be able to borrow a bit of money from. 'Give me a few days.'

A few days later I came back, having been to see everyone I knew who might be able to help out. I'd also sold everything I could lay my hands on, even taking the old fridge and washing machine that Margaret had left in the kitchen and selling them to the scrap heap for a few pounds. I went back and told him I could come up with £7,000 if he could give me a couple of weeks. He obviously hadn't had any better offers from anywhere else and he accepted. I would have to make up the difference in payments from the cash flow each week.

I'd managed to raise some of the money by selling things, but I was still five thousand short of the figure I'd promised him, and now I only had two weeks in which to get it. I was going to have to find a quick deal that would earn me a few thousand. It required drastic action. I contacted the South London garage owner who'd been buying the rental cars off Paul and me. It wasn't a contact I wanted to make but I couldn't think of anything else. We arranged to meet.

'I need five grand,' I told him. 'What do you need?'

He pulled out a list of cars that he needed. There were ten on the list. 'If you can get me those in the next two weeks,' he said, 'I'll give you five grand, but they've all got to have keys and be ready to go.'

Since I had no contact in a rental company any more, I was going to have to find the cars on the streets, which was a much more frightening prospect than simply dealing with Paul. I didn't like the idea of resorting to crime in order to raise the money, but I could see no other way. It seemed to me that if I didn't raise enough money to get into a legitimate business I was going to go under anyway. I justified it to myself with the belief that once I'd got myself into the bar business I would be able to stay within the law for the rest of my life. There just didn't seem to be any honest way that I could raise the sort of money I needed in order to lead a good, straight life. I was going to have to do this one last illegal thing to give myself a chance to succeed, not go bankrupt and to earn myself some self-respect. My mind was made up, so now I just had to develop an efficient method of working that would minimize the risks of getting caught while I collected the cars I required.

The first thing I needed was a car of my own to cruise around the streets in, and that car had to be totally legal so I wouldn't get pulled over or attract any attention to myself as I moved around. I did still have an old car of my own, so I made sure everything about it was legal and then set out on the search. I was determined that I wasn't going to stop working until I'd completed the list. It was a bit like an illegal treasure hunt. I drove around for hour after hour, my eyes constantly scanning the sides of the roads. When I got too tired I'd park up in a side street and doze in the car, setting off again on the search as soon as I felt refreshed. I ate all my meals at the wheel as I scoured the streets for the exact models and colours my contact had asked for. The cars were mainly Fords and Vaux-halls; anonymous makes that could be sold easily at auctions without attracting undue attention.

Whenever I spotted a car that was on the list I'd make a note of where it was, and of the garage that had supplied it, the name usually being written under the registration number or on a sticker somewhere on the back window. I would then ring the garage, tell them I'd lost my keys, give them the registration number and make of the car and ask them to give me the key number. I'd make my voice sound as desperate as possible: 'Could you please help me? I'm late for the airport and I've dropped my keys down the drain. Please help. I've been told all I need is the key number.'

I didn't want to make the call memorable for them should the police ever come round asking questions about that particular car. It was like acting and I found I was rather good at it. The garages never questioned it, and it's unlikely the police ever thought to contact any of them when the cars were reported stolen anyway. The people who answered my calls never asked for any proof that I was the owner of the car in question, they just gave me the numbers over the phone. Easy as pie. I could never have stolen a car any other way. I had no idea how to put wires together under a bonnet or break a lock. I couldn't have smashed my way through a window or any of the other methods which street crooks use. It wouldn't have been any good if I had, my contact didn't want to buy damaged goods; he wanted pristine cars with keys.

Once I had the numbers I needed I took them to a key-cutting service and they, having no reason to be suspicious, did the job. Once I had the key I would go back to pick the car up. I'd have a pushbike in the back of my car, which I would transfer to the stolen car, so I could get back to my car once I'd delivered the stolen one to a street near to my contact.

When I took the cars I always wore a suit and looked like the sort of person who would be driving whatever car it was. Some of them I found parked around airports, so I even carried a briefcase, which I'd pop into the boot as I picked it up, to make it look more natural and to attract less attention. Who was ever likely to remember seeing a man in a suit putting his briefcase into the back of a car at an airport and then just driving away in it? I must admit I did look a bit silly cycling back to my car in a suit, a rucksack on my back with the briefcase inside. Sometimes the car was too far away to cycle, so I'd take the train or taxi back.

One of the cars I took was a 24-valve Granada. It was a powerful motor and I was driving it a little too fast as I took it away from the scene of the crime, just as someone who owned such a car probably would have done. As I shot through a side street I came head to head with a police car coming in the opposite direction, narrowly missing a collision. I slowed down and watched in my rear-view mirror. To my horror I saw the police car stopping and turning round. It was possible they would just give me a talking to and send me on my way, but it wasn't a chance I was willing to take. I put my foot to the floor and shot away down the back roads, my eyes constantly flicking to the mirror to see if they were in sight, my heart thumping. When I was a few streets from home and hadn't seen them for a while, I parked up, got out and ran back to the house. I slammed and locked the door behind me. Once safely inside I stayed in for the rest of the night, dreading the sound of a knock on the door. In the morning I sauntered back to the car and it was still there. No one seemed to be paying it any undue attention. I must have lost them almost immediately in the back streets of Coulsdon. I climbed back in and finished the delivery.

Often I couldn't deliver the stolen cars to my contact immediately and had to park them up overnight somewhere. If that happened I needed to change the number plates in case someone spotted them. I'd go through a copy of *Exchange and Mart* until I found a similar model of the same age and colour and I'd ring up and ask for the registration number, giving some story about how I needed to check it out before I came to look at it. I'd then get false number plates made up with the number they gave me. I would take the tax disc off so that there was no way a pair of prying eyes could see there wasn't a match. That way I knew the car would be safe until it was collected. I was becoming a real professional.

By working night and day I managed to deliver all ten cars the day before my two-week deadline was up. I'd made it; I had enough money to do the deal. All my plans were now in place: I would buy the bar, get it going and that would give me enough money to cover the mortgage payments and get my life on the right tracks. I phoned my contact in the garage to ask for the money he now owed me.

'I won't be able to get it till next week,' he said.

I felt disappointed. I was eager to get my life moving, but I could understand that he needed to get paid for some of the cars himself, and I thought I could hold the bar deal off for one more week now that I knew the money was coming. I was terrified of losing the deal, but if the garage guy hadn't got the money to give to me I had no choice but to be patient for a little longer. Why did things never go like I hoped? I rang again the following week. I couldn't get hold of him. I kept trying but I was starting to feel uneasy.

'Where's my money?' I asked whenever I got hold of him and he kept putting me off with different excuses.

Eventually he told me he hadn't got it. 'You've got to wait for the cars to be sold,' he said.

'That wasn't the deal,' I insisted. I was beginning to feel like he was making a fool of me. I didn't like having to ring up and plead for money that was rightfully mine. 'The deal was you paid when I got the cars. You always have money. Just pay me what I'm owed.'

I knew this guy always carried around a wad of notes and had more in the safe. There was no way he was completely cleaned out.

I could see my only chance to succeed in a real business going down the tubes if I let this man mess me about. I was feeling desperate. Every day I had to wait seemed like an eternity. I knew too many older guys who'd left it too long to get going in a legitimate business, who were always dreaming of what they were going to do and never actually getting it together. I dreaded becoming one of them. I'd been struggling for long enough; I now had to get the ball rolling. I'd worked so hard during that fortnight to get the cars; I'd succeeded and now I was being messed about.

Although everyone thought I was connected to the dangerous guys who ran some of the dodgier clubs and businesses, I'd never actually gone to them and asked for any favours. I'd never needed to, just having my name linked to them was usually enough to make people wary of messing me around. I knew they liked me and would probably oblige, but I'd never wanted to put myself in their debt. I liked the relationship just as it was. These were evil sons-of-bitches but I trusted them and they could trust me; that's how we bonded. I kept my mouth shut and they did whatever they had to do. But now I was desperate and I had to do something significant if I didn't want to end up bankrupt and on the street. I had no choice. I went to see them and told them I needed a gun.

21. Guns and Lay-Bys

Guns and drugs were two things I'd never got involved with. I always believed that cars and alcohol were fairly frivolous crimes compared to these. But if I didn't take significant action now I was going to lose what felt like my last chance.

My contacts didn't ask any questions. They simply agreed to help and I was told the gun would cost £200. I said that would be okay and a meeting was set up in a lay-by at the side of a dual carriageway. I was told the type of car I should look out for. The meeting was scheduled for the next evening and everything happened so quickly and efficiently I barely had time to take it in. My nerves were tight. If I was caught in possession of a gun it would ruin any chances I would ever have of leading a straight life, but I could still see no alternative. The guy was never going to give me my money just because I was asking for it. He had to be shown that I meant business.

It was around nine at night as I drove through the dark towards the spot that had been described to me. I saw the car already there and pulled up in front of it, watching my contact in the rear-view mirror for a few seconds before getting out. He was a tall, stocky man in his late forties, dressed in dark, nondescript clothes. He had his bonnet up and was fiddling around in the engine, pretending something was wrong. I went up to him and said nothing.

'It's by the next lamp-post,' he said, without looking up. 'The poppers are at the one after that.'

With that he pulled down the bonnet support and snapped the lid shut, climbed back into the driving seat and started the engine.

He drove off without giving me a second look. I got back into my car and drove on. The road was quiet, just the occasional headlights passing by. My heart was pounding as I tried to see the lamp-post he meant, but there didn't seem to be another one. My stomach was cramping up and the palms of my hands were sweating on the wheel. Then I realized I'd passed it. I had to go back. Every nerve in my body was tight with fear. This was like nothing I'd ever done before. This seemed like serious danger. When I finally got to the place there was a folded black plastic sack lying in the dark at the base of the post. I didn't stop to look inside. It could have contained a dead cat for all I knew, I just wanted to get out of there. I chucked it on to the floor in the back of the car and drove off. I didn't bother to stop for the bullets. I had no intention of killing anyone, or of getting killed myself. As long as I didn't have any ammunition that was less likely to happen. I didn't even need to know if the gun worked, as long as it looked as if it did. This was going to be a game of bluff.

I felt more scared than I had since I was a child as I drove with the bag on the floor behind me. Everything that had happened to me in the previous months had been piling more and more stress on to me, and now I'd reached a point where I was driving about in the middle of the night with a gun in the car. I felt physically sick, but determined to go through with it. I couldn't afford to show weakness now or I'd be finished; I'd never get my money and without the money I wouldn't get the bar and I'd lose the house and end up on the streets. I had to keep going. My first thought was that if I got caught and sent to prison, at least I'd have a room of my own to sleep in, which I soon wouldn't have on the outside if I didn't raise the money. It was all driving me to madness.

When I got back home I went out into the garden, right to the far end, carrying the unopened bag. Everything was silent and black as I scrambled under the fence to one of the neighbours' houses, burrowing beneath their compost heap and pushing the bag deep inside the hole. The rich smell of the steaming, rotted compost filled the night air. I knew they didn't have a dog, so nothing would disturb my hiding place. I straightened up the fence again. At least now the weapon wasn't on my premises and I had time to breathe and think what to do next.

When I got back into the house, all my muscles still shaking with fear, I realized I hadn't eaten all day, my stomach had been feeling too tight with nerves to be able to handle food. I left the silent, empty house and went down to the fish and chip shop, ordering double portions of everything, bringing it back to the house and scoffing it all down as fast as I could get it into my mouth, desperate to fill my stomach and deaden the hunger pains. As I pushed the last mouthful in I sank down into the chair, my stomach now uncomfortably distended, although my hunger had been sated. Every inch of me felt full. An hour later I was kneeling in the bathroom with my fingers down my throat, bringing back every last morsel of the meal, trying to lose the uncomfortable, unhealthy feeling of being stuffed. It was the first time I'd ever done such a thing, but it wouldn't be the last.

I knew I had to act fast. Firstly I didn't want the gun around for a moment longer than necessary and secondly I needed the money to do the deal. Once I'd calmed down, and dozed a little, I went outside to bring the gun back in before dawn broke. I didn't want to be seen rummaging around in someone else's compost heap in the daylight. I brought the bag back into the house and opened it. This was the first time I'd studied the weapon. It was heavy and cumbersome. It looked like something from an old World War Two movie. I stood in front of the mirror in the bathroom and practised holding it up.

'Just give me my money,' I said, but my voice was trembling. I took a deep breath and focused my mind. 'Just give me my money,' I said again.

I had to be sure my hand wouldn't shake at the critical moment. He had to believe I was completely calm and in control. I wanted to look like someone who was used to handling firearms. If he saw me shaking he'd know I was bluffing. He had to believe I was willing and able to pull the trigger if I didn't get what I wanted. I practised for a while, getting used to the feel of it, waiting for daylight and a time when I knew my contact would be in his garage. I was going to wear a glove on my right hand. It had to be a big glove, so I could slip it on and off my hand easily. I didn't want to draw attention to myself by being seen to be wearing gloves in spring on the way in or out of the garage. The problem was, I could hardly fit my finger round the trigger when I had it on. I practised until I had a technique that worked.

As it grew lighter outside I dressed myself very carefully in a blue suit and shirt. I wanted to look relaxed but smart. I didn't want to look desperate. I went back to the mirror and held the gun up again.

'Just give me my money,' I repeated for the hundredth time. I was surprised by how confident I looked.

I didn't have a holster so I had to work out how to carry it so that it wouldn't be noticed by anyone else and wouldn't fall out. In the end the only place was the inside pocket of my jacket. It was far too big and I had to walk with my arm clenched across my chest to hold it in, but it was the only option.

My target operated from a scruffy little garage, opening on to a South London high street. There were no customers around as I came in, just a mechanic working under the bonnet of one of the cars. As I pushed the door to the office behind me I turned the 'open' sign to 'closed'. There were people passing by outside on their way to work or the shops, unaware of the tense scene going on a few feet away from them. Seeing me, and knowing I'd want to talk business, the owner came out of the office and told the mechanic to close the gates that the cars came in through at the back. I guess he thought we were going to have an argument. Perhaps he even planned to teach me a lesson for being so pushy.

As soon as the gates were shut I pulled out the gun and pointed it at him, turning my back to the window so passers-by wouldn't see anything. He was shocked. I thought my hand was shaking, but if it was, he didn't notice. He backed off immediately, his whole tone changing.

'Just give me my money!' I said.

All the rehearsals had paid off. The words came out with all the controlled menace I'd hoped for. I realized that the man in front of me, who I'd thought of as a real hard nut, was now shitting himself, shaking, backing off and apologizing, trying to make light of the whole situation. If only he'd known just how scared I was inside. If only he'd known the gun was as harmless as a child's toy.

'You,' I said to the mechanic, who was standing, staring with his mouth hanging open, 'fuck off!' And he scurried away.

I knew they weren't going to be calling the police because I could see they still had some of my cars sitting around the premises.

'I just want my money,' I said.

'I haven't got it.' He spread his hands as if helpless to do anything about the situation.

'Either you've got it,' I said, lifting the gun as if taking aim at his head, 'or you're going.'

I needed him to believe I was mad enough to kill someone for five thousand pounds. In fact, if I'd had bullets and he'd refused to pay it's possible I would have shot him. I had nothing to lose by that stage and I might well have turned the gun on myself afterwards.

'Okay, okay, okay!' He held his hands up to slow me down. 'Calm down, calm down.' It looked like I'd convinced him but there was still time for him to double-cross me again.

He walked to the safe, jabbering nervously all the way, and opened it. As the door of the safe swung back I couldn't believe my eyes. I'd never seen so much money in my life. Every deal he ever did must have been for cash and he can't ever have been near a bank. It was crammed with piles of money, all wrapped in neat packages. I was now really angry. If I'd had bullets I might have started firing.

'Why the fuck didn't you pay me?' I shouted, gesturing at the safe with the gun. 'You had all that and you couldn't give me the few thousand you owed!'

'It's just business,' he shrugged. 'Just take the money.'

He must have been able to see how serious I was because he was shaking and sweating uncontrollably. There must have been a hundred thousand or more in the safe and I could have walked out with it all, but I knew that would lead to more trouble. This way he might have lost a bit of face, but he would only have paid me what I was owed. If I'd stolen from him he might have hired someone to come after me. I would always be having to look over my shoulder and that was exactly what I was hoping to get away from by buying into a legitimate business. This way it was a fair deal. I'd already learnt that it was sometimes the smallest people who could cause you the most trouble if you upset them.

'I only want what you owe me,' I said. 'Give me my five thousand and two hundred for collection expenses.'

I didn't see why I should have to pay for the loan of the gun. It didn't occur to me to take any more than I was owed. The rest wasn't my money and I hadn't earned it. I wanted to get a reputation for being someone you didn't cheat, not as someone who went round robbing people.

He pulled the right amount of money out in bundles of twenty pound notes, each bundle worth a thousand pounds. The hardest part was waiting while he counted out the two hundred pounds.

It seemed to take an eternity. Having got my money I put the gun away and turned to leave the premises. Once outside, a smile slowly came to my face as I realized I was on my way to having my own legitimate business. I felt good about having taken charge of the situation and got my money. Now I had to get rid of the gun as soon as possible.

As I drove away a tear ran down my cheek. I guess it was pure happiness, but maybe it was also because of what I'd been reduced to doing just in order to get what was owing to me. Now I could live again.

Once I was back at the house I scrubbed the gun clean of fingerprints, wearing gloves to handle it from then on. I put it in a bin bag, being careful to get no prints on the plastic, then put that bag into another so I could carry it. I burned all the gloves on the bonfire, which I kept at the bottom of the garden. I made a phone call to my contacts to say I was returning the gun to where I'd found it and went out to the car, driving to the same lay-by. When I got to the lamp-post I did the same thing as the man who'd dropped it there, making a big thing about putting the bonnet of the car up, so that I'd have an alibi if anyone happened to spot me. I prayed no police would draw up to ask me what was wrong. I walked casually to the lamp-post and tipped the inner bag out of the outer one, putting the outer one back in the car to take home to burn. I didn't want anyone ever to be able to trace that weapon back to me.

A week later I bought the bar and from that moment I noticed that people looked at me differently wherever I went. I'd suddenly become 'someone', just because I owned a bar. Word gets around quickly about something like that. A lot of people started offering me drinks out of respect, but I never accepted. I didn't want to owe anyone anything.

22. The Bar Business

So 'The Kid' had moved into the bar business. I knew the place already as I'd been going there as a customer, although it wasn't a place I ever did business with when I was selling drink. It was always busy but it had gone downhill and needed a new set of hands at the wheel. I was twenty-two years old and knew nothing about the business, I'd never worked in any bar before and my only contact was that sometimes I supplied other bars and clubs with drink. But none of this bothered me. I was quietly confident in my ability to succeed. I'd managed to get this far against the odds, hadn't I?

On my first evening there I was really nervous but knew I couldn't show it. I needed to show everyone that I was in charge or I would be ripped off left, right and centre. I'd gone in the previous day and been shown the technical ins and outs of the place like how the alarm worked, the safe, the computer system which controlled the tills and stock and how to change a barrel, all the usual things that go on when handing over a business. The one thing I wasn't shown was how to pull a pint. But it didn't matter as I wasn't planning to serve behind the bar on the first night. I kept a close eye on the girls to see how they did it. The evening went well and I began to feel even more confident. Everyone treated me with the respect you would expect of a boss. That night I stayed behind after closing time and practised until I could pour a perfect pint. I was now ready to serve my customers with confidence as well as enthusiasm.

The place had great potential. There were two DJ stands, two bars, and a huge television screen up on the wall but, best of all, I was the youngest man on the premises. I didn't allow anyone in who was under twenty-five years old because I knew it was the older punters who had the money to spend. I didn't want loads of teenagers filling the place up and buying one drink an evening. I wasn't even old enough or experienced enough to hold a licence, so I employed the previous manager to help run it, to be a licensee and be my second man.

I was already known by the staff before I arrived and they seemed as keen as me to make a fresh start and give the place a new lease of life. Everything in my life changed overnight. At first business was slow. We were less than half full and the customers weren't coming in before nine at night to have a drink before they went clubbing. I made a drastic decision and decided to take a gamble. I believed that in order to get people through the door I needed outside help. I was running a cool bar so I decided to have a celebrity DJ on Friday nights. I hired Neil Fox from Capital Radio. He came in once or twice a month and would mention us on his radio show, saying where he was going. We put banners outside the bar and word got round quickly. The first night he came we had queues outside the bar from seven in the evening and we had to call the bouncers to come in early to control them. The bar was back to its former glory in no time and I was sure I had a flair for the business, which would take me right to the top.

Money was pouring into the tills and every night seemed to be party night. On a Friday I'd be standing on the bar tipping tequila down people's throats. Bank holidays would be theme nights with all the staff dressing up, which pleased the lads greatly. I even put in a dental chair, which customers sat in while I poured the tequila into them. The place had a great buzz. Fridays would be club night so the music was modern and got everyone in the mood for a great night out. It was also girls' and lads' night out. On Saturdays it was mostly couples who came into the bar, although they were often the same people who'd been in the night before without their partners. Sunday was 70s and 80s night and was always packed. It felt as if I had finally arrived.

There was never any trouble because the rumour had gone around that I wasn't someone you messed about with. I did nothing to dispel the rumours; none of it served me badly. People knew not to cause trouble in my bar. Me, I was just happy, smiling, joking and really enjoying my job.

Money was rolling in and my first job was to keep up to date with my current mortgage payments. That kept the mortgage company at bay, although they were still after the back payments. I went to court a couple of times because they wanted to repossess the house, but the judge knew I was trying my best and gave me time to get myself on my feet so long as I could keep up the current payments.

Each week I met the previous owner of the bar to go through the accounts and he would get what he was due, but it seemed that each week, as we were making more and more, he also wanted more and more. He didn't get away with it all the time but I could tell he was envious of how I'd brought the bar back from the brink.

A meeting was booked to see the brewery that had supplied the bar before I took over. I thought nothing of it, assuming they were going to show me their beers. The local rep came in and introduced himself. He asked a few questions and I told him that I'd bought the bar, paying a deposit and buying the rest of it through the takings of the business.

'Strange,' he said. 'I can't see how. You see, the man you "bought" it off owes the brewery over £350,000 and we have a charge on this property. We're looking to foreclose on him.'

My mouth must have dropped six inches. I couldn't believe what I was hearing. Because of my inexperience and eagerness and because I was so desperate to get a foothold in a legitimate business,

I'd signed the contract that the previous owner had put in front of me without really reading it. It was my own fault, but I'd let him take advantage of my naivety. I was mad but I knew I had to bide my time if I wanted to salvage anything from the wreckage. My dreams had been shattered once more. I might be enjoying the job, but I wasn't building a business I could do anything with.

I managed to keep the place afloat on cash flow for about nine months and then I realized I couldn't do it any longer. The previous owner had debts everywhere and all I was really being was a glorified manager. I'd been ripped off. I'd poured the money in and taken hardly anything out, but in fact I'd never owned anything worth having. In the end I realized I was out of my depth. There was nothing I could do to straighten the situation out. So I made a conscious decision to leave. I took what money there was in the safe – about three grand – and left the keys with the manager, who I asked to inform the previous owner of my decision.

When he found out he started calling me and issuing threats, saying he wanted the rest of his money, but I took no notice. I had bigger problems than him on my plate.

Once I was out of the bar I had a lot of time on my hands to think over my situation, and I realized just how badly he'd ripped me off with the whole deal. The suppliers were now after me for unpaid bills. Because I'd kept paying them regularly there was only about £13,000 in all. I heard that the bar owner was going around telling people I was a 'nobody' and that he'd 'dealt with me'. After about a week I decided I had to do something about it. I called him.

'I want my original seven grand back,' I told him. I thought that if I got that back I wouldn't feel so bad and could pay some of my creditors off. But also after going to so much trouble to raise the seven grand I felt I deserved to keep it. 'I'm coming round for it.'

He simply laughed and hung up the phone. He fancied himself

as being a bit tough, just because he was in the bar business, but I knew better. I needed help so I put a call in to my former contacts, the ones who had got me the gun, explaining what had happened. They knew I had the bar, having wished me all the best when I started. It was out of their area so they weren't bothered by the competition. They asked me for his telephone number and said they'd give him a call. Half an hour later the bar owner was back on the phone to me, oozing jollity and friendliness and suggesting we meet up to sort things out. It seemed that one phone call from my friends had been enough to change his whole attitude.

'It needs to be a neutral place,' he said, obviously worried about the call he'd just received. 'And we need someone else there.' He suggested the name of a mutual friend who'd first introduced the two of us.

The three of us met in a pub car park a couple of hours later. He was waiting in the back of a car for me. I got in beside him and ignored his outstretched hand of friendship.

'You fucked me over,' I said, 'I ought to pop you here and now.'

He wasn't to know that I never wanted to see another gun as long as I lived. I think the rumours about what I'd done in the past had finally reached him and he seemed to take this threat seriously.

'Of course,' he said, all smiles and reasonableness, 'none of this is personal. It's only business.'

I was sick of hearing that line from people who thought that cheating people was fair as long as it could be called business.

'This is what is going to happen,' I went on. 'You're going to take over the thirteen grand debt and I'm going to keep the money from the safe.'

I knew that doing it this way would completely clear my business debts and I would then be able to focus on what I was going to do next, concentrating my efforts on clearing the personal debts which were still hanging over me since the purchase of the house.

He agreed to take over the debts and I was now free of the bar, but still not free of debt. I had to come up with another way to generate money, quickly, if I wasn't to end up back where I started. Those nine months in the bar had given me a taste for running my own place. I went to see one of the breweries to ask if they would give me somewhere, but I was still too young, only just turning twenty-three, and didn't have enough experience for their tastes.

The one thing I learnt out of the whole experience was how few real friends anyone has. Alan had always told me that you could count your true friends on the fingers of one hand and I could now see that he was right. As long as I was a bar owner I seemed to have hundreds of friends, but when the bar went, so did they. The ones who stuck by me knew me before the bar and were friends because of me, not because of my job.

23. Living on the Edge

The night that I threw up my fish and chips proved not to be an isolated incident. My bulimia was growing worse. Most people think it's a complaint that only strikes women; they're wrong. Because I was so desperate to succeed and keep my head above water I had to bottle up all my worries and nerves in order to appear cool. Whether I was posing as a hard man with a gun, quelling my anxieties about stealing cars, or trying to keep afloat a bar that was already weighed down with debt, the pressures were enormous for someone who had no one to confide in. I was constantly on edge inside my own head. I would eat far too much, just in order to comfort myself and banish all telltale signs of hunger that might remind me of the horrors of my childhood. Feeling guilty and uncomfortable, I would then bring it back up soon after. Perhaps my subconscious always remembered those early years of hunger at home, and warned me to eat as much as possible while I could, because it might end at any moment. Late at night, when all the stresses and worries seemed to pile up, I'd stuff myself on chocolate, going on and on until I felt gorged, and then I'd go into the bathroom and purge myself, wanting to feel clean again. It was a sad and solitary way of existing.

As I sat in the once homely house, which was pulling me further and further into debt, staring at the worn bits of carpet on the floor for hours on end, trying to work out where I kept going wrong, it felt as if I was more or less back where I'd started. The slump in the property market was still going on and the house was now worth less than the mortgage I had on it. If I sold it I'd still be in debt to the building society for the difference. I was still spending Christmases alone, still buying my own birthday presents, still struggling to find a way to get rid of the debts, let alone build some capital to make my dreams come true. All I wanted from life was a chance to get started, to get on the first rung of the ladder, but no one seemed ready to give it to me. People I did business with tried to rip me off and nobody would give me an honest chance to prove my abilities. I felt that I was still trapped in a tiny room with no doors, just as I had been when I was a child. I was tired, tired of the mistakes I'd made, tired of the choices I'd made, tired of the constant struggle since childhood; but most of all I was tired of being alone. I had no more energy for the fight.

24. The End of the Road

I'd never been scared of death, so I decided to end my life. There just didn't seem to be any point in going on.

The process of taking my own life started in the most mundane of ways, with a shopping trip down to the high street. I went to two different chemists' shops and bought two large boxes of paracetamol. I knew if I tried to buy them both at the same place it might arouse the suspicions of the people behind the counter. My favourite drink was Jack Daniel's, so I bought myself a bottle to help wash the tablets down.

I'd weighed up the various possibilities open to me. I'd thought about sitting in the car in the garage with a pipe from the exhaust to the window, but it seemed an unpleasant and dirty way to die. I thought about falling into the Thames, but someone might see me and try to save me. I didn't want to attract attention. I imagined that with tablets I'd just fall asleep and be taken away from here. It seemed the neatest and easiest way to go.

I walked slowly back home with my shopping. There didn't seem to be any reason to hurry, since I only had one thing left to do. I locked the heavy Victorian front door behind me and then deadlocked it. No one else had keys to the house, but I didn't want to take any chances. I'd been shocked by how quickly all the friends I'd had when I was the owner of a popular bar had disappeared the moment I went back to just being myself. I suppose they were all only acquaintances, not real friends.

What I was about to do was not a cry for help; I didn't want to be found until I had gone, this was a decision to end everything. I got myself a glass of water, went up to the bedroom and locked that door from the inside as well.

A guy called Peter had turned up unannounced one day. He'd lived at the house with Margaret when he was a kid and I think he imagined she was still there. I could see he was upset and invited him in. It must have been a shock for him to see the place that once seemed so homely and lived-in looking so desolate. He was in a terrible state. His girlfriend had left him, he'd lost his job and he was deep in debt. He seemed to be close to killing himself. This was before I got the money for the bar and all I had was about a hundred quid in my pocket. I felt so sorry for him, so I gave it to him. I felt really good about being able to do something for someone else. Now I knew how he felt.

I had a small hi-fi in the room and I put on a classical CD which I'd discovered in a shop and which had some of the tunes Colin Smith had recorded for me all those years ago, including 'Ebben? Ne andrò lontana' which had had such an effect on me. Instead of accompanying me on my dream trip to America, as I had once imagined it would, it was going to provide a background for a different sort of journey. The familiar music was soothing and provided me with a little company as I prepared myself for my last few minutes. I left the curtains open, I didn't want the neighbours noticing closed curtains and calling the police.

I sat down on the bed and swallowed a handful of tablets, washed down by swigs of Jack Daniel's. A few minutes later I was in the bathroom, spewing them up. That was obviously not the way to do it. I decided to forget the Jack Daniel's and swallow the rest of the tablets with plain water. I went back into the bedroom and started again, swallowing so many tablets it started to hurt in my chest where the sharp edges had dug in on their way down to my stomach. When the tablets had all gone I lay down on the bed and felt a sleepiness creeping over me as my body finally started to relax and my mind seemed to float away. I was aware that I was falling into a deep sleep. Tears were running silently down my cheeks. It had all been so disappointing, but now I was going and I didn't have to worry or struggle any more. It felt like the most enormous relief.

25. Waking Up

I could see the ceiling of the room moving slowly around above me. I was terribly thirsty. In my confusion I thought I was in a new place but as my mind cleared I realized I'd actually just come round from what was no more than an overdose. I wasn't dead. The tablets hadn't been enough to finish me off, but they'd left me unable to move or even think straight. I lay motionless for what seemed like an eternity, too drowsy and lethargic to make a move, just as I had felt on the way into this big sleep.

I must have slept for a couple of days. I had no idea what day of the week it was when I'd lain down, so I couldn't tell how much time had passed when I woke up. I'd never been a great sleeper; I could never lie in bed in the mornings, right from the days when I used to go out searching the streets for milk floats. Once I was awake I had to get up. But this was different. I guess my body was exhausted and needed the sleep that the tablets allowed. The thirst was becoming unbearable. I was going to have to do something to relieve it. With an enormous effort I pulled my body up into a sitting position. I waited for the room to stop spinning enough to be able to stand without falling and hauled myself off the bed. After a momentary wobble I managed to find my balance and walked slowly to the door, carefully placing each foot in front of the other. It was hard to get my thoughts together enough to unlock the bedroom door. I was still too drugged, lethargic and exhausted to be able to work out how to turn a key. I had virtually no strength left as I plodded downstairs in search of water.

Once I'd satisfied my thirst I crawled back on to the bed and drifted in and out of sleep for a few more hours. During my periods of wakefulness I started to assess the situation. If I wasn't dead, I was going to have to take some very definite steps about getting my life on track. Things suddenly seemed clearer and less hopeless. Perhaps all I'd needed was a complete rest, which I'd given myself by accident. It was time to see things more objectively and positively. Now perhaps I'd be able to find the energy to start the fight all over again, wiping the slate clean and going after the dreams I'd lived for as a child. I lay thinking about America and the ideas I'd had about getting there one day and finding freedom and happiness. I remembered how passionately I'd wanted to be a futures trader and how I'd somehow lost my direction in the hustle and bustle of trying to survive and trying to get together the capital I was still certain would be my passport to success.

'Okay,' I thought to myself. 'You've been given another chance, this time you're not going to waste it.'

I stayed behind that locked front door for about a week, getting my strength together and recovering from the pills. It was a good rest and I began to see things more clearly.

I made a list of my true friends; people who'd stuck by me through the ups and downs. One by one I called them, when my strength had returned, pretending nothing had happened and being my usual upbeat self, seeing how they were getting on and talking like guys do.

I was now ready to restart the upward struggle.

26. Starting Again

The first thing I did was swallow my pride and sign on for unemployment benefit. I'd never wanted to go that route because I'd seen how it had degraded Gloria, and the rest of us through her. I didn't want to be the sort of person who had to rely on the state for support because I wasn't able to stand on my own feet. It had always seemed to me that the weekly Giro had been part of our problem in the past rather than part of the solution. I wanted to be independent of any state assistance. But now it was time to be practical. They would give me some cash so I could eat and get myself back on the road again. To my amazement, when I went in to see them and gave them my details, I discovered they would also pay my mortgage for me. That bought me a little more time.

A few weeks later a friend told me he knew of a couple of guys who wanted to rent a room. Would I be interested? I would have done this before if I hadn't been afraid of the house being repossessed. It hadn't seemed like an option. Also, I was wheeling and dealing at the time and I didn't want other people around the house. I needed privacy and security. It was all nonsense, of course, which I now saw very clearly.

The two guys moved in and within a couple of weeks, with the rent money coming in, I was able to sign off from unemployment benefits. I immediately felt far better. I started to get back into the swing of life. With a bit of cash in my pocket from the rent I was able to put together some better deals, buying and selling again as I had been before the bar business.

One evening, sitting in a club with some acquaintances, I spotted a blonde girl across the other side of the dance floor with a bunch of friends. She was really gorgeous. Our eyes met, like in all the clichés you ever heard about boys meeting girls. It was the sort of scene that happens in pubs and clubs around the world every second of the day, a boy sees a girl across the floor and likes the look of her. It was a cliché, but no less exciting for that. I was still desperately shy around women, particularly after the behaviour I'd seen going on at the bar. But this time I knew I had to pluck up the courage to act. I couldn't take the risk of the evening going by and not having made contact with her. If she left without me getting a phone number I might never see her again. It sounds so corny but even before I'd spoken to her I knew this was someone special.

I watched her from the corner of my eye as I tried to act naturally with my friends. I was trying to pluck up the courage to walk across the room and ask her to dance, but I couldn't face the thought of her saying no. It might be she didn't want to dance, or didn't want to leave the table with her friends, and then I would have blown my chance, and it would be a long walk back across the club floor with my wounded pride. Then I saw her get up and go towards the toilets. She walked past our table and I said something to her. She turned and smiled and said something back, then walked on. With my heart in my mouth I stood up and followed her out. I'd committed myself now. I had to go through with it. At least if she said no out here I wouldn't be humiliated in front of the whole club. We chatted for a while and exchanged phone numbers. We stood talking for some time and, amongst other things, I found out her name was Jackie; she was working as a PA, and wasn't in any steady relationship.

She told me she was going away for the weekend so I didn't phone her until Monday and then made the call and asked her out. She agreed. We had a date and I knew at that moment I'd found my soul mate, a best friend and someone I wanted to share the rest of my life with. What had started out as the cliché of a boy spotting a girl he fancies across a crowded bar had blossomed into another cliché; I had fallen hopelessly in love. I couldn't believe how nice she was; as well as beautiful and sexy she was kind and peaceful. It amazed me that she was so beautiful and natural. When we were together she never asked me difficult questions about my past or my situation, just accepted me for what I was and who I was. As the relationship progressed we remained good friends as well as lovers. I was still suffering from bulimia, but I managed to hide that from her. We laughed all the time we were together. I'd never met anyone like her in my life and she changed everything.

Jackie's family was very different to mine. Although her parents were divorced they were both good, kind people who'd brought her up as they should. They were a million miles from Gloria and Dennis and accepted me without a moment's hesitation. They obviously trusted their daughter's judgement. If I was all right by Jackie, that was enough for them.

Suddenly being in such a serious relationship taught me a lot about myself, even trivial things. I hadn't realized quite how fast and greedily I ate my food until I went out for meals with Jackie and had finished whole courses when she was still on her third mouthful. It must have stemmed from the years when Wayne and I would cram food in as quickly as possible, swallowing it without chewing, terrified that someone would catch us and take it away if we didn't hurry. The way I ate must also have contributed to the bloated and uncomfortable feelings I experienced after every meal, which prompted me to make myself sick.

These sorts of things Jackie could point out to me and we could make a joke of them, but there were other aspects of my behaviour which she found too difficult to discuss with me. Three months into the relationship she rang up and said she didn't want to go out with me any more. I couldn't understand it. It had been going so well. How could she want to end it so suddenly? It was a crushing blow.

'Okay,' I said, not wanting to show how devastated I was by this news, and having no idea how to ask her why she'd made such a drastic decision.

For a week I lived with the agony of thinking I'd lost the one person I really wanted, knowing I'd never meet anyone like that again. The relationship had fulfilled all my worst fears of rejection and disappointment. Yet again I'd been shown just how great life could be, and then had the joy snatched away from me. At the end of the week I realized I couldn't just accept it. I had to find out what had made her make such a terrible decision. I rang and asked what I'd done wrong.

'You never show me any affection,' she explained. 'If we're walking down the street you don't walk with me or hold my hand, you just stride on ahead with me following behind. I've really fallen in love with you, Kevin, but you don't show me any sign that you love me.'

As she told me these things, I realized they were true. It was the way I was and I'd thought nothing about it. Now she pointed it out I knew she was right. This was the first true, adult relationship I'd ever had with anyone. I had no experience to draw on as to how to do it. I'd never seen my parents being affectionate to one another and although Alan and Margaret had a good marriage they were not in the first flush of romantic youth when I met them. I found it impossible to show affection. If a child has been rejected by both his parents I guess some shutters are bound to come down somewhere deep inside his brain, to guard him against pain in the future. I couldn't find any way to lift those shutters, however much I wanted to. I was also unreasonably jealous. I was so terrified of losing Jackie now that I'd found her. If she went out for the night with some of her girlfriends, I'd be imagining the sort of goings-on that I'd witnessed during my time in the bar. Even though I knew she wasn't like that, and I trusted her, I couldn't get the pictures out of my mind. Nothing this good had ever happened to me before and I couldn't bear the thought that I might lose it.

By talking about some of the things I'd always kept hidden inside, although never about my childhood, Jackie freed me and I was able to tell her how much I loved her and how I wanted to spend the rest of my life with her. I couldn't believe I'd nearly lost her through pure ignorance. Whenever people see what I've got now and tell me I'm 'lucky', I always think they're wrong. They don't know what I had to go through to get here. I now believe that you have to make your own luck; you have to work hard and if there is something in your life you don't like you have to change it. But if there is one bit of luck I have had, that I will always be grateful for, it was finding Jackie. As soon as she was in my life everything turned round. It didn't happen immediately, but things just kept on getting better.

I started looking for normal jobs again, so I could get the house a bit straight for Jackie, in the hope that she would move in on a permanent basis. I saw an ad for people to sell photocopiers, an industry I had some experience of, and I went for an interview. The company was based in Bow, in East London. I knew I was good at selling and they wanted to pay commission so they were happy to have anyone who would bring in business. I didn't think I was likely to get a better offer from anyone else for a while, given my track record so far, but I gave them one stipulation before I started.

'I'll work hard for you and I'll make you money,' I said, 'but never fuck me with my wages. If I've earned the commission then pay me; never, never mess me about. If it's owed, it's owed.'

I was back on the road and I was making sales. Bit by bit things started to click into place. I straightened out the mortgage so there was no danger of losing the house. I was able to get the lodgers out so Jackie could move in and we could have a nice first home, which we slowly did up and furnished as we could afford it.

Despite the warning I'd issued at my interview, the company I was working for started messing about with my money, just as they all do; not paying me what I was due. I didn't make a big fuss to start with, just nagged them to pay me whenever there was a chance.

27. The Self-Destruct Button

Once we'd overcome our initial difficulties, my relationship with Jackie was going so well I could hardly believe my luck. We seemed to be perfectly in tune about everything. One of the things we were a hundred per cent in agreement over was that we both wanted to have children. There was no great rush, since we were both still young, but we didn't take any birth control precautions, allowing nature to take its course. I'd always thought I could be a great dad. I'd seen so many examples of how not to do it over the years, I felt sure I would be able to learn from my experiences and give my own children everything I never had, both materially and emotionally. I suspect I was also looking forward to having another chance to experience childhood for myself, properly this time.

When Jackie told me she'd fallen pregnant I was beside myself with excitement and delight, hardly able to bear the long months of waiting before we would actually have the baby in the house. I'd been dreaming of the joy of fatherhood for so long. We were both euphoric and felt that something very special was being given to us. After a couple of months, however, when I actually saw the tiny bump swelling in Jackie's stomach I felt a terrible chill of fear. Demons began to appear in my mind, keeping me awake in the small hours of the morning, pricking me with worries and anxieties I hadn't experienced before, bringing me out in a cold sweat. How would I cope with being a father? Would I turn out to be like my own parents? How would I know how to do the right things when they were never done for me? I'd heard so often about how people who abuse children have nearly always been abused themselves. What if I followed the same pattern and found it impossible to control my temper with the child, or was unable to hold myself back from hitting them? Would I, like my parents, turn into an uncontrollable, spiteful, hateful father? If that happened I wouldn't be able to face it.

Ninety-nine per cent of me wanted a child more than anything else in the world, but one per cent was terrified of what would happen to me if I became a parent. As the days passed the one per cent gained a stronger and stronger hold over my mind. I knew I could be a great father, but the negative thoughts were eating away at me, driving me inside my own head and further from Jackie. I couldn't confide my fears to her because I would never have been able to find the words to explain what had happened to me in the past to make me think that I could become a monster. So I started to withdraw from her, throwing myself into my work and staying out late with friends rather than going home and facing my demons. I was drinking more and more, usually Jack Daniel's. I loved Jackie more than anything or anyone and I hated myself for not being able to explain to her what was wrong, but I knew I couldn't tell her about my past. I wanted to explain everything to her but I was so ashamed I couldn't find the words.

Jackie was obviously puzzled and confused by my behaviour, but if she asked me what was wrong I would just reply 'nothing' and retreat even further inside my scrambled head, becoming ever more distant. Jackie is a totally non-argumentative person so she never forced the issue. She took to going round to her mother's more, rather than being alone in the house, waiting for me to come home. It was getting so that we were only seeing one another at weekends. She was becoming increasingly upset which made me angrier with myself for what I was doing to her. She couldn't understand why I was behaving so oddly when she knew that I wanted a child as much as she did. She could see no reason why our wonderful relationship seemed to be suddenly turning so bad.

The tension was growing all around and my bulimia, which had become less acute since I'd been in the relationship, flared up. I was vomiting after almost every meal, something else I was hiding from Jackie, not wanting to face the truth and see the reaction in her eyes. I kept getting flashbacks from parts of my childhood that I'd been successfully suppressing for years, making the nights even more restless and my fears even more ferocious.

I was becoming more and more distant from Jackie and from life in general. I would never want to hurt any child and the thought that I might do so was driving me insane. I was fighting myself and driving away the one person I loved more than anything, but I didn't seem to be able to do anything about it.

One night, while having drinks with some friends, I must have downed the best part of a bottle of Jack Daniel's. A girl I knew a little showed me some affection and I took the bait. I could make all sorts of excuses, like having drunk too much or being under pressure, but none of them would mean anything. It was the worst thing I had ever done and there was no excuse. There was no one else to blame. I could have said no and I didn't. Alan once joked, 'A truly strong man is one who can walk away from a naked woman.' I'd been weak and I was so ashamed I didn't know what to do with myself.

The moment it was over I thought of Jackie and my stomach felt like a thousand butterflies were trying to escape. I knew I had done something terribly wrong and I was disgusted with myself. I was so filled with self-hate I couldn't even look at my face in a mirror. I'd become the sort of man I most despised.

The guilt landed on me so heavily I knew I would never be able to bear it. My love for Jackie was so great I could never lie to her. I'd been fighting with myself for what seemed like an eternity. We wanted each other so much but my behaviour was unacceptable and I couldn't face up to the demons inside. I felt trapped.

I would have to do something or it would crush us both. I deserved to be punished. I realized that I was going to have to confess to Jackie what I'd done if I wanted our relationship to stand any chance of survival. I couldn't hope to spend the rest of my life with her and bring up children together if I'd lied to her about anything. I knew it was going to be a cruel thing to do, but I'd already done the worst thing possible, and to keep it a secret would only be compounding the crime. I might not have told her about my past, but I'd never lied to her and I knew I never could. I had to take control of the situation and face the consequences, even though I was more frightened of losing her than anything else.

I looked deep inside myself and decided the demons were only a small part of me. I was a better man than this. I could be a good husband and father, but not if I didn't deal with the situation as honestly as possible. I told Jackie what I'd done.

Seeing her tears broke my heart. I loved her so much and I was so desperate to spend my life with her and with our child, and now I'd put the whole thing in jeopardy through sheer stupidity and weakness. She obviously wanted to get away from me and went back to stay with her mother.

I realized completely how badly I'd treated her and how much danger I was in; that I might lose everything and end up without Jackie and my child. I was going to have to do everything possible to convince her that I loved her. I had to make her realize how much I missed her when she wasn't there. I had to overcome my fears about how I might react to the baby. Even though we were living under different roofs, I made sure that I went with her to all the pregnancy and childbirth appointments. I put every ounce of effort I could muster into showing Jackie how much I regretted my stupid mistake and how much I wanted to become the best father in the world and to take care of her and our child. I wanted her to know how hard I was willing to work to make our relationship good once more.

Bit by bit the atmosphere improved. She was incredibly forgiving. I would never have been able to forgive such a betrayal if it had been her who had slipped up. She was the only woman I had ever met that I wasn't nervous of. If she had betrayed me I would never have been able to recover. But she was stronger than me, and as we carefully reconstructed our relationship it actually seemed to move on to another level. The sight of Jackie carrying our unborn child was now bringing us so close that it was as if we were inside each other's souls. Our love and Jackie's forgiveness made me see what an incredible, caring woman she truly was. We came together as if a bulldozer had smashed away some of the emotional blocks within me. I knew that it was only me causing all the problems.

I was still unable to explain to her what had happened to me in my life before meeting her, but I was at least able to indicate that there was something wrong in my childhood, which made me frightened I would be a bad father. I promised that one day I would feel able to tell her everything. Not many people would have been understanding enough to be able to leave it at that. Most people would have demanded to know the whole story; would have felt that after such a betrayal they were owed a full explanation. Jackie was able to see that I wanted to be able to tell her about my demons, but for some reason wasn't able to. She worked as hard to convince me that I would be a great father as I was working to convince her that I loved her and wanted to have a family with her. Her kindness and understanding saved our relationship and retrieved my life from the total mess it could have descended into at that moment. The way she handled herself during those weeks and months made me admire and love her even more than I had before. We grew even closer and more in love. I found I was beginning to dwell less on my worries about how I would cope with the baby. The demons' voices seemed to be growing a little fainter in my head.

She came back home from her mother's and we started to prepare the house for the new arrival. The nursery looked fantastic, with Beatrix Potter pictures all over the walls. She had saved our relationship and our future and saved me from myself.

28. The Happy Ending

The first time Jackie had ever seen me cry was when I was standing beside her in the hospital with my daughter in my arms. I felt so happy. All my life I'd wanted to be someone else. Now I didn't want to be anyone other than myself. I had the most wonderful woman in the world and now I had this perfect baby daughter as well.

She was so tiny and soft, her face so purple after the efforts of nearly twenty-four hours of labour. My uncontrollable weeping was partly joy at holding my baby daughter in my arms, and partly relief because I realized that there was no way in the world I would ever be able to harm a hair on her head. Just as I had known when I met Jackie that I would never be able to hit her or abuse her in any way, I now knew that my daughter was going to be entirely safe in my care. I saw how foolish all my fears had been, how they had become exaggerated in my own mind, and I cried as if I would never stop, my shoulders heaving with the sobs, all inhibitions swept aside on a tide of emotion.

When we got home and started the business of looking after our precious new baby in earnest, I was desperate to do everything right. I wanted to be the exact opposite of my own parents. But as I cradled her in my arms, trying to soothe her to sleep, I realized I didn't know any nursery rhymes. So I made a point of sitting down and learning them. I wanted to be as close to the perfect father as I possibly could be. Despite the enormous effect music has had in my life, and despite the fact that I listen to it at every possible opportunity, I still sing very badly. But neither my daughter nor I cared about that. I just wanted to comfort her and she wanted to be comforted.

I was working hard selling in order to keep the money coming in and I hadn't forgotten my dreams of one day becoming a trader, but I kept having other ideas along the way. One time I put an advertisement into *Estates Gazette*, a British property magazine, asking for £250 million for a property portfolio I wanted to buy. I received between forty and fifty calls from people wanting to know more. Some of them were big companies, some small. I was still only twenty-four years old and I didn't have the knowledge or experience to convince any of them to take it any further, apart from one speculator who suggested we meet in London. He was exactly the sort of man I dreamed of becoming. He reminded me of who I wanted to be and what I should be focusing my energies on. He'd been down a couple of times but got back up and carried on fighting, which I admired more than anything – having the courage to get back up and fight when you're knocked down.

There was a big push on at work over a three-month period to meet the end of the year targets and we managed it, but then they didn't pay me for my extra efforts as agreed. To begin with I remained patient, because money was no longer as tight as it had been and I was not drowning in debt any more, but when I'd been asking them for the money for six months I decided I was being messed about, I'd given them enough chances to pay me. They didn't know about my past, although I had smacked a guy in the mouth for calling me an idiot when we were all out having a drink one night, so they should have guessed I wasn't willing to be jerked around for ever.

I was always in at work by seven in the morning and when the boss came in one morning I asked him where my money was, as I always did.

'Can I talk to you now?' I asked.

'Kevin,' he said, without breaking his stride, 'I'll talk to you about this later.'

It was a put-down and I was no longer willing to take it. I could see he was going to keep this up for ever if I didn't do something.

Once more I rang the friends who'd helped me in the past and two days later there were four guys parked outside the office in a car, waiting for me to call them in to sort things out. I was going to have to pay for their time, but it would be worth it if I got my money. I couldn't believe I still had to resort to these sorts of tactics, just because no one would pay me what they owed me. Yet again they would probably excuse themselves with, 'It's just business, nothing personal', but I was fed up with having to do this sort of business.

I walked into the boss's office.

'Morning, Kevin,' he said.

'I want to talk to you,' I said.

'Not now, Kevin,' he said, going back to his paperwork.

'If you don't talk to me now I've got four guys in a car outside who are going to come in and kick the shit out of you.' I gestured towards the window.

He looked puzzled for a moment, not sure if I was being serious or not. He stood up and walked to the window. Looking out he saw the car and it was easy to see the sort of men who were sitting inside it.

'Why are you doing this?' he asked, in a voice that suggested I was betraying our friendship in some way.

'Because you're having a laugh at my expense,' I replied. 'All these months I've been grafting and you won't pay me what I'm owed.'

'What do you want me to do?' he asked.

'I just want you to pay me what you owe me from the end of the year when we made you all that money.'

Two hours later they gave me five grand and I was able to pay off the guys in the car.

'I don't think you can work for us any more,' the boss said when the business had been done.

'No,' I agreed, 'I don't think I can.'

'Hang on,' his partner interrupted. 'Let's talk about this.'

They knew I was hard-working and had made them money. After a few heated exchanges they offered me a new job.

'Listen,' I said. 'I'm going on holiday with Jackie. When I get back I'll let you know what I've decided.'

I'd never had a proper holiday in my life. Our little girl was eight months old and Jackie's mum was happy to look after her. We both needed a break. We headed down to the Maldives, which must be the most idyllic tropical paradise in the world. There were little wooden cottages on perfect white beaches, blue skies and blue waters; I'd never known peace like it. All my life I'd been dashing about, too hyperactive to be able to sit still for even a few minutes, but there I finally wound down and relaxed. I even read my first ever book (a John Grisham thriller). I was so chuffed with myself for having been able to read it all the way through. I spent hours every day just listening to music and clearing my mind. I felt I was finally ready to start my life properly, putting everything bad behind me. I told Jackie about my vision of becoming financially independent, and as I explained it to her in that perfect, peaceful setting, I realized I was now old enough and experienced and settled enough to start making my vision a reality. Sitting on that desert island, thousands of miles from home, I was able to see clearly that everything could now change – for the first time ever I felt completely relaxed and in love. Despite the perfection of the place we both missed our baby daughter dearly.

When we got back to England from the Maldives I started to study the financial markets and trading practices in earnest. I also read everything I could get hold of which would increase my knowledge on every front. I felt I had twenty-five years of catching up to do, from learning nursery rhymes for my daughter through to complex concepts of financial strategies. Something was still missing. My love for Jackie was the best thing that had ever happened to me. It gave me butterflies in my stomach every time I thought about her. I realized what was missing and proposed. Jackie accepted.

I was determined it would be a big romantic wedding, something that showed the world how much we loved each other and gave us all a day to remember. Jackie's family were all invited and had accepted, but there was a problem on my side. My invitation list included my friends, brothers and sisters, but not Gloria and Dennis. I was ashamed of my past and was nervous about inviting them. Naturally Jackie was curious as to why the invitation list didn't include my parents. She knew some things had gone on in the past, but not of anything that would stop my parents coming to our special day. At that time I didn't feel ready or able to tell her of my past, so it was easier for me to invite them. But also I wanted them to come to show the world I did have a family if only for a day. There was part of me that desperately wanted to have a normal family wedding.

I dreamed of having a perfect wedding day, with supportive parents who loved me, just like the weddings that occur every day all over the world. I dreamt my father was there for me giving me advice and support, and that my mother, future mother-in-law and Jackie would all get together and arrange and organize a magical day. Gloria and Dennis, as well as all my brothers and sisters were invited. Everyone except Robert, as nobody knew where he was. I knew Dennis would be too shy to be able to face such a crowd, but Gloria did come, together with my brother and sisters.

We held the reception in a marquee in the grounds of a beauti-ful old Georgian house. At the wedding Gloria was very quiet and throughout the day stayed close by her children – we rarely spoke. But what made my day, apart from Jackie and my little girl, was that my brother Wayne was by my side. We were true friends. My sisters seemed to enjoy the day too – for them it was an opportunity to escape their laborious life.

Three years after we had my daughter, my baby son came along. I couldn't believe my luck. I now had two perfect children. Holding a little replica of myself in my arms, I realized that I still had demons that needed to be brought out. But that was not the time. I was just too busy trying to secure our future to be able to spend time delving into emotional problems.

I went back to my old photocopying equipment company for a couple of months, just to show that I could, and then I left to set up on my own. I knew now I would never get together the money I needed working for other people. I had to have control of everything, which meant starting my own company.

The telephone and technology boom was in full swing and I decided I'd go into the business of setting up telephone systems for companies. I knew absolutely nothing about telephones, just as I'd known nothing about washing machines or photocopiers or the drinks businesses until I got into them, but I did know how to put in the hours and how to sell. I left my job one day and by the next I'd formed Synex Telecommunications Ltd for one pound and was on the phone selling to the companies that were already in my address book.

I began by just picking up the phone at home and making calls to see if I could find people who needed products. Most of the calls were fruitless, but I was starting to learn about the marketplace. I needed to get a dealership and I had a few thousand pounds saved. I went to see Ericsson to ask if I could represent their products. I could see they thought I was another dreamer who would give up as soon as he heard about the commitment they required for a dealership. They told me exactly what I'd need in the way of premises and trained staff before they would agree to me selling their products. They obviously didn't think they would ever be hearing from me again, but I now had something to aim at. Two months later I'd rented premises on the Purley Way in Croydon and I'd hired engineers. I also knew a few people who wanted to buy systems by then. Ericsson agreed to give me the dealership. Within three years Synex was employing over forty people and turning over just under £2.4 million.

As well as me working hard at the office, Jackie and I had also been doing up Margaret and Alan's old house, making it the best in the street, and eventually, when the property market had taken off again, we sold it for a nice profit and so were able to move, six or seven years after I'd bought it from Margaret. Although it was a beautiful house by the time we'd finished with it, I was keen to move away, to leave all the unhappy memories of my past behind and start somewhere completely fresh. I saw a tiny advertisement for a mock-Georgian house in the paper and went round to see it on my own. It'd been on the market for quite some time but hadn't sold. It was at the end of a cul-de-sac filled with the sort of perfect family homes you see in American movies, with white pillars round the doors and smooth green lawns sloping down to the road. In front of the house stood a forty-foot pine tree and that was what made my mind up. I could just picture how I would cover it with lights at Christmas-time. It would be like a fairy tale. I'd fallen completely in love with the place.

The house itself was in a pretty bad state, having been lived in by an old couple who hadn't done anything to it for years, but I could see through that to what it could be like. Jackie burst into tears when she saw how much work was going to be needed to get it up to the standard of our old house, but by then I was so bewitched by my vision of how it would look at Christmas she couldn't talk me out of it. It was the ideal family house and I worked on convincing her that we could turn it into a paradise.

The only thing I had going for me was my mouth, and I worked it morning, noon and night to bring in the business. Any profits we made I invested back into the business and I kept a tight control of the finances. We were a professional company and a number of high-profile customers trusted us. I made sure I always paid everyone on time. I wanted to get a reputation for being someone who always kept his word. The industry was booming to such an extent there was room for everyone, and I was willing to work harder than anyone else to win the business and to serve clients to my utmost ability. We landed a number of big contracts from well-known companies. I had a team of sales people, but I was making the majority of the sales myself. It was hard work but I was proud of everything I was achieving. I set up another division in the company, which sold call time and line rental.

I had plans to expand across the country but it was hard to get staff because it was a boom time and bigger companies were offering salaries that we could never match. I came across a whole team of sales people who were willing to open up a Birmingham office for me. They were an experienced team from a rival who told me they would be bringing customers with them. I had no reason to disbelieve them and we opened a Birmingham office. The promised sales failed to materialize and our overheads soared. I'd made a fatal error. There was now friction between the London and Birmingham offices. I had been in discussion with a venture capital company about putting money in with the idea of floating it on the stock exchange. They were impressed with our track record but it didn't happen. The market was turning and the boom time was coming to an end. When I saw that we were getting into trouble I decided to take evasive action. I phoned up the chairman of a property company whose business we were tendering for and suggested that they buy us out. They provided serviced offices, with about seven thousand customers, and were planning to put our services into all of them. I was very honest and told him that I wanted to close the Birmingham office to cut my losses and then sell him the London operation.

We had a meeting and he agreed in principle to buy the company at a fair price, but told me to keep the Birmingham office open because their head office was up there. I was so happy. All my dreams were coming true. At last I was going to have the financial independence I'd always craved. I respected the company chairman and didn't feel we needed to employ expensive lawyers. Everything seemed to be working out well. Because Birmingham was still running the money was going out fast and the deal was taking several months to complete. I went to one last meeting to finalize everything and they told me they weren't going to buy the company. By that time I was in a fair amount of debt because I'd kept the Birmingham office open and had been supporting the sales team.

I didn't know what to say. I was now in serious trouble. No one else was going to buy the company now it was carrying so much debt. I'd put all my faith in them, been completely honest, and everything had collapsed.

'Do you want to buy any of the business?' I asked.

'We'll buy the call time and line rental part,' he replied and I realized that was all they had been after from the start. I told him I'd think about it.

On the way home I hit the wheel of my car on a kerb and ended up, stuck in the middle of nowhere, changing a tyre with all my dreams in tatters, when just a few hours before I'd believed I was a free man. To cap it all I couldn't even get the wheel off. I felt desolate.

I didn't sleep at all that night, just paced up and down trying to see a way out. In the end I had to do the deal they wanted. I was so angry with myself. I could see they'd played the game brilliantly, that it was not personal, that it was 'just business' and I had been naïve. I had to close down the rest of the company and call in the liquidators. I felt so bad about the people I was letting down.

In some ways I'd been a good employer, in others I know I wasn't. I was good at giving people a chance, especially people who hadn't been given a chance before, and it nearly always paid off. But I'm not a 'people person'. I suppose I had that beaten out of me at a very early age. If employees rang in sick or came to me with moans, which always seemed very petty to me, I'd have a lot of trouble empathizing with them. Overall I knew I'd be happier working on my own at my own pace, not having to worry about other people's needs or hurt feelings.

Although the eventual outcome of the deal was a fantastic disappointment, I had come out of it with a bit of money and for the first time in my life we had some to spare. We took the children to Disneyworld in Florida for my daughter's sixth birthday and it was as big a treat for me as it was for them. Even this tiny glimpse of one corner of America confirmed all my beliefs about what a wonderful country it was. Part of my payment had been in shares, which I'd been told I could sell at any time. I tried to sell them before we went to America but was told they hadn't been released to be sold. The price then collapsed. When I came back I decided to fight for compensation because I felt I'd been cheated. The stress of dealing with lawyers was enormous but I was determined not to give up. In the end I couldn't stand it any more. I bypassed the lawyers and went directly to the finance director of the company and laid my cards on the table. He convinced me that they hadn't done it on purpose but he did agree to make a settlement. It was a lot less than I'd been expecting when I started into the sale, but it was something, and at least it meant that I could move on and put the past behind me.

Selling the company meant that I finally had some time to sit back and think about where I had got to and what I still needed to do with my life. I'd found that having a son had brought many of the feelings about my own childhood I'd been suppressing for so long bubbling to the surface once more.

Although I had everything I wanted in life and was happier than I'd ever dreamed possible, I became upset because I could see myself as a small child when I looked at him. I realized how helpless and in need of protection I'd been and how badly I'd been betrayed by those who were meant to be looking after me. I'd managed to push my past into a box at the back of my mind and block it off, but now it was impossible not to be reminded of just how bad it had been. When I saw how little and vulnerable my son was, how dependent on us to guard him and look after him and guide him in the right directions, I realized all over again how much I'd missed. When I read about cases of child abuse and murder I understood how close I had come to being one of those children in the papers and it made me angry. I knew I needed to do something about dealing with the demons once and for all.

29. Looking Back Through Other Eyes

In 1993 a large envelope came through my door. It contained a green cardboard folder with a compliments slip from Social Services attached. There was no explanation as to what it was or why I'd been sent it. I glanced at it, but at that time I didn't want to be reminded of my past and it seemed to just contain information from files. It didn't interest me enough to go any further. I put it away, thinking I might look at it later, and then forgot about it.

Several years later I came across it again and looked more closely. I realized it was information the social workers had written after visiting my family. It had been prepared at the time they finally decided to find me a foster home and I was taken to Alan and Margaret. As I read I was transported back into the family house, suddenly seeing us all through someone else's eyes. The picture was horribly vivid and told me things about Gloria and Dennis I'd never known.

Gloria was born in 1941, so she was almost thirty by the time she had me. Dennis was two and a half years younger. At the age of five Dennis was sent to a children's home, his father having been killed in the war and his mother being unable to care for him. Having not seen her for three years, he moved back when an uncle came to live with her. When he was ten he was held responsible for setting fire to a haystack and went back to the children's home, where he remained until he was fourteen.

The social worker wrote that Dennis was of limited intelligence and suffered poor health, having had an operation for cancer of the testes and a vasectomy in 1977, which would explain why they never had any more kids after Brenda. The file explained that he was then diagnosed with epilepsy and retired from British Rail on medical grounds. Apparently, he also suffered from psoriasis when life became too stressful at home.

Then the report turned its attention to Gloria. Apparently she was the eldest of five children and experienced two long separations from her family during childhood and adolescence. She spent a year in hospital when she was eleven after being badly burned and at the age of seventeen was admitted to hospital again under Section 6 of the Mental Deficiency Act. That piece of information certainly made sense. All her behaviour became more understandable in the light of mental problems, if not forgivable. She remained in that hospital for about five years. In 1974, when I was three years old, she was put on probation for two years for defrauding the DHSS. That explained why she was never given a book for her Giro payments, why they always sent them through each week.

'To say the least,' a social worker had written, 'this is a chaotic family in every respect. The parents' limited intelligence and lack of understanding of, and inconsistency in, childcare has resulted in a very turbulent style of life. On a practical level, the family have consistently had problems in handling money and maintaining a clean and hygienic house. When they were living in New Addington their house used to smell of urine and the children had been observed urinating on the floor.

'In terms of management the family's record is poor. The parents' attempts at control have been inconsistent and sometimes out of proportion. Physical hitting has been perceived as the main method of controlling the children. All the children seem to be very active, boisterous, loud and attention seeking. It feels as if they're vying with each other for the parental affection that exists (and to some extent this affection is quite real). The situation has been exacerbated by the parents' tendency to make favourites of certain of the children and scapegoats of others.'

I paused for a moment to get my breath. Scapegoats were certainly what Robert and I had been. All the memories came flooding back. After a while I felt strong enough to continue reading.

'This picture of a noisy, chaotic family, limited parental coping abilities and material deprivation provides the context for numerous reports of suspected child abuse which this department has received since November '74, in respect of all the children, but in particular Kevin.'

So the reports were getting through. They did know what was going on. All the time that I was being beaten black and blue the Social Services knew about it. They knew that my life was in danger, but still they left me there.

The report talked of meetings that had been held and decisions taken to do nothing due to a lack of concrete evidence. It talked of places I was taken to before Yarborough that I don't remember, and of reports that one foster family sent me back because I was aggressive towards their other children, insolent and disobedient. When we moved from New Addington the social worker reported that he was going to try to make our family 'less dependent' on Social Services.

'This was not an easy task,' he reported, 'as Mrs Lewis made great efforts to pull me into the family life. She wanted to use me as a listening ear and was not pleased when it became clear I would not fulfil this function.'

If only there had been someone listening.

'Visiting the Lewis family is neither an easy or pleasant task as one is invariably beset by a scene of chaos. The noise level is quite unbearable as the members of the family communicate by screaming and shouting rather than by talking. Throughout interviews, the children make constant demands on Mrs Lewis' attentions – again in competition with each other. When they don't get the response they want they're very quick to kick up such a fuss that their demands cannot go unnoticed. Thus, it is absolutely impossible to do "family" focused work with them.'

The report went on to describe how Gloria was the main spokesman and Dennis literally hung around in the background, sliding off to the kitchen if anything vaguely awkward was discussed.

'One gets the feeling with him that life and his family are all too much for him – I've never seen him smile; he always looks worn out, ill, harassed and is quick to anger. Mrs Lewis is a loud lady with whom it is very difficult to have a normal conversation in that it is virtually impossible to get her to focus on a specific issue that I might be there to discuss. As my contact has been less than that of her previous social worker, it feels that when I do see her she has to give me a complete run down on everything that's happened to her during the weeks since I'd last seen her.'

They then went on to talk about each of the children, admitting that Robert was one of the scapegoats.

'His school reported that he had a bruise under his eye. Robert said that his mother had hit him, his mother denied it. With no independent witnesses, the truth remains hidden – however, Mrs Lewis is known to lie.'

They confirmed that Brenda was Gloria's favourite and that Wayne was skipping school. It finally got round to me.

'Kevin now says, quite openly, that he has no feelings for his mother, that he hates her. My observations of their interactions suggest that there is little love lost between them and it is certainly fair to say that Kevin is not Mrs Lewis' favourite.

'When Kevin is shown affection he can be a lovely lad. He himself returns any affection shown to him and can be very loving. He can be polite and pleasant, thoughtful and eager to please. He has an uncanny, almost oversophisticated, ability to analyse himself, his needs and his thoughts and verbalize his analysis. On the other side I have seen him purple with rage when in conflict with his mother. He is the recipient of quite severe physical punishment and has now learned to fight back.

'For whatever reasons, there is now little love between Kevin and his parents. Kevin comes across as a child starved of, and desperate for, some affection. He clings to people who show him some care (e.g. his Year Head at school). Kevin himself certainly contributes to the antagonism between himself and his parents, but this does not alter the facts that it is very likely that some of his basic needs are not being met.

'Kevin is at a point where the chaos is over-whelming him and perhaps we need to offer a light at the end of the tunnel.'

I guess that is all that anyone can ask for, a light at the end of the tunnel.

30. Reflection

I had several reasons to write this book. I wanted to tell Jackie my story so she would understand why I am the way I am. I wanted to sort out the thoughts and feelings that watching my son grow up had brought out in me. And I wanted people to know what it is like for those who have nothing and no one when they start out in life, to maybe make them a little more tolerant and understanding of people who are different, and see what has gone into making them that way.

In some ways it was an easy story to tell because I'd lived it and remembered almost every stage with horrible clarity. Some of it I enjoyed writing, but other bits were painful to relive, reminding me of things I had carefully forgotten. The thought of trying to get the book published was even more frightening. I was worried that I was selling my soul and fretted at the thought of the questions that publishers and the public might ask once I'd submitted the manuscript to the world. I thought it would help me to exorcize my demons, and perhaps it will when it's all over, but it has also released others that I had been keeping carefully locked up.

When I look back at my life so far I can see how lucky I've been. Things could so easily have gone differently. When I hear on the news of children who have been abused and murdered I know exactly what they have been through. I know what leads children to turn to crime and prostitution and how poverty destroys their lives and souls. I have escaped from that.

I've always wanted to do what's right and that has driven me on to the next thing each time as I've struggled to get as far away from my childhood as possible. Jackie changed everything for me and for that I owe her my heartfelt thanks. I also owe thanks to Uncle David and the staff at Yarborough for the comfort and security they offered me during my time there, and to Colin Smith whose persistence got me to Alan and Margaret's and introduced me to music. Then there was Gini who gave me respite during some of the most difficult times, Alan who sowed the seeds of ambition, and the friends who stayed with me through thick and thin. Then there are my children, who have brought me so much happiness in ways they will never understand.

I'm grateful to my brother, Wayne, for keeping in contact, and to all the people who don't know that they have helped me in some way, like you have by taking the time to read this book.

I have seen that what goes around comes around and now my parents are getting older and need love, comfort and support, but there is no one there for them. I could never bring myself to treat them as normal grandparents and take the children round for visits, and so they have to go on waiting.

They are both still living alone, deserted by their family and without friends. He spends most of his time in the pub; she sits in the house, desperate for company but unable to make a single friend. None of my brothers and sisters have managed to escape in the way I have. Robert is still with the funfairs, I believe. I hear about him now and then through the others. Wayne lived at home with Gloria until he was thirty, and now he's living with his girl-friend's parents. My three sisters have fifteen children between them. They all live in terrible flats in deprived areas, reliant on the state for every penny. They're trapped now until their children are old enough to stand on their own feet, but they won't have done anything by then, so who's going to employ them? I hope they don't fall even further through the net.

I still miss Alan, even after ten years. I feel my own life is finally beginning and I would have loved to share it with him. I haven't enjoyed it much up till now but at last I have a family to support who support me in return. My head is full of ideas of what I want to do next. Jackie and I have sold our dream house to give ourselves the capital we need to build the next stage of our lives. I don't know exactly what I will do yet, but for the first time ever I have choices. I've enjoyed writing and would like to continue to have the freedom to write. At present I'm writing my second book, this time a novel. I like inventing things, writing trading systems for the financial markets and looking for new opportunities. There are so many things to do that it's hard to choose. It was tough saying goodbye to the house that we all loved so much and which held so many happy memories, but we have to move on. I may not have had anyone to guide me in life at the beginning, but now I have my own experience to look back on and it tells me that you have to keep trying and that you can't stay still.

Today my passion is to learn. I spend hours lost in books, from studies of Leonardo da Vinci to some of the most complex equations the financial markets have to offer, from the stories of great explorers to woodworking and creative structures.

I'm no longer afraid of who I am. After wanting to be someone else for so long I'm finally glad to be me. Music has continued to be an enormously liberating influence and I now sing all the time, very badly I must confess, particularly when I'm alone in the car. It must look a strange sight to other drivers. My musical tastes vary from Rachmaninov to Missy Elliot, from Marilyn Manson to Elvis.

I still have dreams of what else I'd like to achieve. I'd like to have a house with a bit of land round it, so I could be at peace when I wanted to, and I'd like to travel all over America and Canada with Jackie. I'd like a little more financial security to remove the last few worries and I'd like to be able to ring the bell at the New York Stock Exchange; that has always symbolized freedom to me.

I sometimes go for long walks in the local countryside. The wide-open fields help me clear my head and think about the future – I rarely dwell on the past any more.

I know one day I'll have fields of my own and spend days smelling the sweet air and listening to the wind singing through crops I've planted myself. Now it seems as if anything is possible. If I lost it all tomorrow I'd get up the next day and start again because I've learnt that the most precious thing we possess is life itself.

These days I want to try everything that life has to offer. I can't resist any of the extreme sports; maybe I miss the adrenaline that I was brought up on. I also want to learn to paint and I tried learning the piano, but it made my knuckles ache from the damage that was done in the fights. I know my painting's not very good but with each new picture I find I can express myself more freely. I'm passionate about cooking and being able to use fresh produce is something I will never take for granted. I love taking the kids to school and working on ideas for new opportunities.

Today I'm so happy I can't stop bouncing from one thing to another. With all the stress of having to deal with other people gone, I don't even have problems with the bulimia any more. On family occasions like Christmas and birthdays I get even more excited than the children. They tell me Santa comes to the house every year, but I always seem to be out when he calls, or in the garage. The children's favourite time is when Mr Ticklehand comes out to play and the house erupts into laughter and screams of excitement and happiness. When they have birthday parties and all their friends bring them presents I have to hold tightly on to my emotions, in case my happiness for them and my memories of what birthdays can be like overflow. Sometimes, after we've switched the lights out at night, I turn my head away from Jackie so she won't see the tears in my eyes. But now they're tears of happiness.

I'm now going to sit down and raise a large glass of red wine to everyone who helped me through the first thirty years of my life. And to thank you for reading this book – you have made it all worthwhile. Now it's time to get on with fulfilling my dreams.

The Kid Moves On

Contents

Preface

One of the reasons I wrote *The Kid* was to try to exorcize my past. I believed that if I wrote it all down and shared it with my wife, Jackie, I would be able to face the demons that lurked inside my head, clear out all the stuff that I had been suppressing for so long, and we could get on with our lives together.

But I was to have no idea how difficult it would be to deal with and accept the memories that came bubbling to the surface during the writing process. Nor did I have any idea how hard it would be to relive the story over and over again for the press and television, and to suddenly find the eyes of the world upon me. Imagine going out into the street each day and feeling that everyone else knows all your most shameful secrets, while you don't even know their names.

All the time, however, I was able to console myself with the thought that by writing about the past I would be able to make the future better – for us as a family and perhaps even for other people reading the book. So when I discovered that history was repeating itself in the Lewis family, and that Gloria was still behaving towards children in the same way she had behaved towards me, I was at first devastated, then angry and ashamed, and finally determined to do something about it.

But at the same time as dealing with all these overpowering emotions, I was having a ball. Writing a book that was a bestseller was like the icing on the cake of our happy family life. I suddenly had the ability to make my dreams come true. The question was, what were my real dreams? And was that all they were, or could they be turned into reality? As life always shows, nothing is ever as easy as you think.

1. Telling Jackie

The manuscript of *The Kid* was finally ready, but I was apprehensive about giving it to Jackie to read, even though that was the main reason I had written it. Writing an honest account of my life had been a deeply personal and upsetting experience, and there were bits of the story that had proved to be almost unbearably emotional for me to write down and relive. The thought of now showing the manuscript to someone else, even my wife, was making me anxious to say the least. Once she knew the truth there would be no going back. I had heard the phrase 'baring one's soul' but I had never realized how difficult that would be. Now that everything was on paper I must admit I felt naked and vulnerable, and I was nervous about the emotions that were awakening inside me. Seeing my past laid out so vividly in black and white made it harder to deal with.

I wasn't sure how Jackie would react to some of the things that I had revealed. In the process of telling my story I'd found I was stirring up feelings I hadn't experienced before. I suppose that was why I'd been so careful never to think about them. I'd been telling myself that I didn't need to think about the past because dwelling on it wouldn't help me or my family, now or in the future. Some of the memories I believe I had deliberately avoided experiencing for fear that I wouldn't be able to cope with them. And some of the revelations from my childhood were just plain embarrassing to admit to myself, let alone Jackie: things like wetting the bed and living in a room where the walls were smeared with excrement.

So many of the memories had been locked away for so many years because I'd never wanted to think about them, never wanted to look back at painful, unhappy times. I always preferred looking to the future, making plans and getting on with life in order to escape as far away from my past as possible. I wanted to spend my time thinking about things that I might be able to enjoy, rather than things that I could no longer do anything about. It was as though my subconscious knew those memories would hold me back in the past and so had hidden them away deep inside my head. I've always told myself there is nothing you can do to change the past; what's done is done. But now those memories had resurfaced with the birth of my children and the sight of them growing up brought it all to the front of my mind. This was another reason why I had decided to put it on paper in an attempt to make sense of it all.

Jackie has always accepted me for who I am today and never worried about what might have happened in the past, but I felt I owed it to her to explain why I am the way I am. I wanted her to know everything about me, including things that I would have been unable to find the words to say out loud to her. It was easier just to write it all down and hand it to her. That way I could explain it to her without sounding as if I was feeling sorry for myself. Self-pity is an emotion I firmly believe to be a sign of weakness and something I am always keen to avoid.

The urge to explain things about my past had been becoming stronger as I saw my son growing up and found myself unable to resist thinking about my own childhood when I was his age. Flash-backs to scenes that I had succeeded in putting out of my mind for years had resurfaced as I watched him develop as a child. I did have some flashbacks before he was born and as my daughter was growing up, but they tended to be memories of my sisters and of some of the things that had happened to them and my self-doubts concerning being a father. They were troubling thoughts and hard to ignore, and I believed that writing them down would help me to clear them from my mind, so I wouldn't have to think about them again. It was a bit like preparing a 'things to do' list; once I'd committed my memories to paper I hoped I wouldn't have to remember them any more and would be able to move on and think about other things, good things about my life, my family and my career, knowing that the past was safely recorded somewhere else, somewhere outside my head. Finally my whole life was in the manuscript as I watched it emerge from the printer, the ink still wet, the pages warm and pristine.

The reason I'd decided to write my life story in the first place was because I had made a promise to Jackie a few years before that one day I would explain my past. I knew so much about the person I love, but she knew very little about where I came from. I also wanted her to know everything that had happened to me in the years before I met her, so that she could understand better what was going on in my head as an adult. I'd poured my whole heart into the manuscript, dredging up memories that had been buried for years, to make sure everything was explained and I believed that by doing this I might be able to get it out of my head once and for all and move on.

There were parts of the book that I found very hard to write, and I found myself feeling confused as each door in my memory led to another and then another; taking me on a journey deeper and deeper into my past; uncovering horrors I had wanted to forget. I had very few happy memories before I met Jackie but it was no good pretending my life had started on the day she came into my life.

It was when trying to tackle these emotional scenes from my childhood and adolescence that I realized I needed help from someone who could look at the story in a clear and objective way. I decided to enlist the help of Andrew, a writer. We worked together on the most difficult parts, breaking them down one by one and then placing them in chronological order to ensure they made complete sense by the time Jackie came to read them.

She'd known all along that I was writing it, and that it was going to be about my life before I met her, but she didn't pester me to let her read it. Every so often she would ask how it was going and I would reply 'nearly there', and she would just smile encouragingly.

Once the manuscript was finished and ready for Jackie, Andrew said he thought it read very well and asked if I'd ever considered showing it to a literary agent or a publisher with a view to having it published.

'No,' was my instant reply. At that stage there was no way I could even contemplate seeing my life published as a book. It was going to be hard enough to reveal my past to Jackie, let alone to someone I had never met. Andrew saw I wasn't ready and so didn't push the matter any further, apart from saying that if I did change my mind he knew a literary agent by the name of Barbara Levy who might want to take a look at it. Not knowing anything about the publishing industry, the name meant nothing to me, and I put the whole idea out of my head. Anyway, I told myself, Jackie hadn't read it yet and I wanted her reaction to the material before I even thought about showing it to anyone else. I needed her approval and to know that she would still see me as the normal bubbly person I had been since meeting her.

Jackie knows I've never been good at showing my emotions except with my children and has never tried to force me to explain or ask me difficult questions, which is just one of the hundreds of reasons why I love her as much as I do. She instinctively knew there was something very wrong in my relationship with my parents because of the lack of communication between us, but she didn't pry as to why that might be.

On the odd occasions when Gloria, my mother, would ring I would know instantly who it was through her distinct loud tones and I would hand the phone straight to Jackie, with no explanation and barely a hello to Gloria. Jackie would handle the conversation politely and discreetly, never questioning me afterwards as to why I might not want to speak to my own mother. As far as I know Gloria never wanted to talk to me on these calls anyway, apparently relieved when I passed her straight to Jackie. If Jackie picked up the phone first she would whisper who it was and I would shake my head, not wanting to talk to her. I don't think Gloria believed I remembered any of my childhood. Maybe she had forgotten most of it herself or chose not to remember. Gloria would then talk to Jackie as though everything was fine between me and Gloria, and that we had a caring, normal mother and son relationship. Sometimes I wanted to grab the phone and say, 'Stop pretending you've been this wonderful mother. You're so full of self-pity, don't you see what you've done?' But if I did that I'd have had to reveal my past.

I hadn't wanted to give the manuscript to Jackie until I was sure it was as good as it could be, but once it was ready I still sat on it for around a week. I would keep looking at it neatly stacked on the shelf waiting for the right moment, until one evening I thought 'what the hell', picked it up and walked into the kitchen where Jackie was busy clearing up for the night. She saw me coming in, manuscript held tightly under my arm. We looked at each other, and she immediately saw what I was holding and gave me a reassuring look.

'Here it is,' I said, placing it on the work surface then walking off quickly before she could say anything. There it lay – my whole life on a hundred pages of neatly printed white paper. It didn't look much, but it was my story. Some bits I was proud of, like helping Chris in the frozen lake and Kimberley in Yarborough – and later standing up for myself and saving the house from repossession. But it also contained my secrets. I had no idea how she was going to react to what she was about to read, especially my detailed account of my indiscretion with another woman. So many times I had put it in then taken it back out again. Eventually I thought it best to leave it in because I felt if I'd left it out, she might sense I wasn't being completely honest with her, and it was very important to me to tell her the truth. I owed it to Jackie, so she might understand me better.

Because it was late and Jackie was tired she didn't read it that night. She tucked it away in a drawer just in case the children saw it as she knew that would lead to one hundred and one questions that neither of us were prepared to answer. It was the following evening, once the children had had their bedtime stories and were fast asleep, that she picked up the manuscript and brought it into the lounge. I was sprawled out on the sofa watching television and, as we exchanged smiles, I saw the pages in her hand. I realized she was ready to settle down to read it, and I knew I couldn't be in the same room as her.

'I'm just going to get some petrol for the car,' I said, clambering off the sofa.

I'm sure she knew it was an excuse and that I just wanted to be out of the way. But she seemed less taken aback by my leaving than that I willingly handed her the remote control! As I went out of the room I saw her switch off the television, swing her legs up on to the sofa and open the first page. The house was silent and there was an air of anticipation and an atmosphere I can't describe. I got the car keys and quietly closed the door behind me. I drove to the petrol station, filled up and then drove around the countryside for at least an hour and a half, singing along to the music on the car stereo, trying to imagine what Jackie might be thinking as she discovered who her husband truly was and what had really happened to him. I drove until I was tired of the music and my eyes felt heavy. When I got back home I walked round to the front door and I saw the lamp in the lounge was still on and, through the window, Jackie sitting frozen on the sofa – it was as though she hadn't moved in all the time I had been out. I quietly opened the front door, kicked my trainers off and popped my head round the door. The first thing I noticed was the manuscript lying open on the coffee table. As my eyes focused in the dimly lit room I saw my wife, her eyes red and blotchy. The television was still switched off and she seemed to be a hundred miles away. It was obvious she was upset, but when our eyes met neither of us knew what to say to each other. I didn't want to talk about it or hug her, for fear of the emotions that would be unleashed. She looked stunned and neither of us knew what to do. So I thought it best to leave it and pretend nothing out of the ordinary was going on. I took a deep breath and smiled.

'Hi,' I said, cheerfully. 'I'm going up to bed.'

She looked up at me with a sweet, strained smile.

'Cheer up,' I said, 'it's not that bad.' I didn't know what else to say.

She smiled again, but the effort seemed even harder for her and I saw her bottom lip shaking. I went upstairs and got ready for bed.

It took Jackie a long time to come upstairs that evening. As I lay awake in bed she stayed downstairs on the sofa, lost in her own thoughts. I really wanted to go back down, put my arms around her and comfort her, but I think she just wanted to be alone, too stunned and angry to know how to react. When she eventually came up it took us ages to go to sleep. Neither of us knew what to say to each other, and so again we didn't say anything. At first we lay back to back. I knew she was upset and so I made the first move by touching her leg with my foot and stroking it gently. She stroked back with her other leg on mine and I rolled on to my back. Jackie rolled on to hers and then turned and rested her head on my chest. I put my arm lovingly around her. I felt a warm tear fall on to my chest and I hugged her tightly, comforting her until she finally fell asleep.

For the next few evenings, after we'd put the children to bed, she would sit down with the manuscript and take in a few more chapters. I still couldn't stay in the same room while she was reading because every so often she would glance up at me and I couldn't bear to look her in the face, so I would find myself something else to do in another part of the house, or I would go out on some fictitious errand or other. Actually, I told myself, this is a bloody good time to sort out the garage.

I think she knew what was going on and also I think she wanted to be left alone to absorb everything without having to worry about my feelings. We didn't speak about the manuscript at all while she was reading; we just carried on with life as normal, as if nothing out of the ordinary was happening. It was a bit quieter than usual around the house, but the kids always made sure that didn't last for long. Being observant of their parents' moods, like most children, they sometimes asked if anything was wrong, especially with Mummy. We would both just smile and carry on having fun and enjoying family life in what was generally a very happy home. As Jackie was coming to the end of the book I noticed she was becoming a lot more cheerful and back to her usual self. I wondered what she would say and how she would behave towards me now that she knew so much.

Finally the silence about the book that had hung between us throughout those one hundred pages was broken. She came out to the dining room where I was sitting late one evening, trying to keep busy. Putting the manuscript down at one end of the table, she walked up behind me and wrapped her arms tightly around me.

'Everything makes sense now,' she said. 'I'm so proud of you.'

'Are you all right with it?' I asked, my hand holding hers.

'Kevin,' she replied, 'I married you for who you are now, no matter what happened in the past.'

We smiled at each other and I realized I'd done the right thing; she now knew who I was before we met. Showing her so much of myself had brought us even closer together than we were before. She could understand so many things that must have puzzled her about the way I behaved sometimes; how I was so ambitious and determined to succeed and the way I sometimes became over-protective of the children, and how I would jump in to help my brothers and sisters at a moment's notice. She would understand why I didn't let the children see their grandparents and so many other decisions that must have seemed puzzling in the past.

'It's all behind me now,' I said. 'I don't want to dwell on it any more. I want us to get on with our lives together and look to the future.' I knew she understood and that she wouldn't be referring to any of the incidents she'd read about again unless I brought the subject up first, which I had no intention of doing.

She just smiled. 'Don't forget to enjoy now,' she said and kissed me on the cheek. I knew she was right. It would be all too easy to become so wrapped up in the future that I let the present slip past.

'I'm never going to talk to Gloria or Dennis again,' she said, looking down at the table.

I stood up and we held on to each other tightly for ages before going into the lounge to watch some television together. We began to play and joke about who should have the remote control and then something funny came on and it wasn't long before we were laughing again.

Later that evening I told her what Andrew had said about show-ing the book to an agent, and that I wasn't sure about letting other people look at it because it was so personal, and because I wasn't certain whether there would be any legal comeback for any of the misdemeanours I'd admitted to. We talked about it and eventually agreed there was no harm in at least showing it to this agent to see what she thought. It might be that she wouldn't think it was good enough to publish anyway and that would be the end of it. It could then be boxed up and put away for ever. If she did like it we could cross that bridge when we came to it. I called Andrew the next day and told him to let the agent, Barbara Levy, take a look at it.

2. Finding an Agent

During the writing process, especially at the beginning when I was thinking about my early years, old childhood habits had started to surface and I couldn't shake them off, even after the manuscript was finished. It was as if stirring up the mud at the bottom of my memory had allowed these long-buried habits to float to the surface from their hiding places in my subconscious. Jackie noticed that I wasn't as cheerful and bubbly as usual. I seemed to be stuck in my own quiet world and incapable of spending much time in any one room, feeling that I had to keep moving around. She kept asking me if I was all right.

'I'm fine,' I would say with an exaggerated grin, not sure whether I was or not. She asked me so often that it began to annoy me.

I also started to become anxious very easily and when this happened I would stand in a certain way, my right hand rubbing nervously down my leg, shuffling my feet, as I did as a child when I was about to be attacked. My eating habits and table manners started to change. At the dinner table I would clean my cutlery obsessively, licking it and then furiously rubbing it on my clothing until it gleamed in the light. It was already sparkly clean but that didn't make any difference. During each meal I would repeatedly brush the tablecloth with my hands, desperate for any crumbs to be wiped away leaving everything clean. If we went out to dinner, as soon as I finished a course I would hold up my plate for it to be collected by the waiter or move it away from me to the other side of the table. I'd wipe the tablecloth clean of breadcrumbs with my serviette, and only then feel able to rest happily and watch Jackie eat.

I was eating faster and faster, stuffing food into my mouth and sometimes swallowing without even chewing, then placing my hand over my mouth so no one could see what I was doing. As a child I had always covered my mouth after cramming as much as I could into it in order to stop it being taken out again, or just to hide the fact that I was eating at all. It was happening again and I would finish my meal before Jackie and the kids had even taken their third mouthful. I also took to sniffing everything, like a suspicious dog, whether it was my food or my clothes or just passing scents in the air. I was becoming more and more aware of the world around me; sights and sounds as well as smells, just as I had been as a child. Some smells reminded me vividly of my past: the smell of freshly polished wooden floors would take me back to the many schools I was sent to that I never fitted in at; or the smell of the rubbish as I emptied the bins would remind me of the tin house and the house in Norbury which we moved to later on. But there were also good smells – I always found taking in deep breaths of fresh air and the scent of flowers uplifting and it made me feel happy. So to overcome the problem of the smells I took to buying Jackie fresh flowers regularly. I loved the fact it brought a smile to her face, especially because I wasn't doing it to apologize for something.

My sleeping became even lighter than usual; the slightest movement from the children's rooms would have me leaping out of bed to check they were OK. When I got to their bedrooms there they would be, sleeping peacefully, and I would return to bed, ready to listen again. Any night-time sounds made me tense, whether it was the children mumbling in their dreams, air bubbles whispering through the heating system or the boiler sparking into life. The nights were becoming long and tiring.

The children noticed that I was becoming more withdrawn and this made me feel even worse about what I had written, frustrated that I couldn't get back to my cheerful self. I'd always enjoyed a glass of red wine and I began drinking more. This started when I began the book and soon I was consuming a bottle a night.

Worst of all, I could hear myself saying 'sorry' the whole time; sorry for this, sorry for that, sometimes sorry for the sake of saying sorry. I was really starting to annoy myself. It got to the point where the children started doing the same, apologizing for no reason, and it sounded terrible to me. It was obvious where they were catching the habit from.

'Never say sorry unless you've done something wrong and you mean it. Don't just say it for the sake of it,' I told them sternly, although I was speaking to myself as much as to them. Discovering I was behaving like this shook me. I realized I had to look at what was happening to me.

It was then, as I stood outside myself and watched the way in which I had been behaving lately, that I worked out what was happening. I had locked my past away so tightly for so long, never wanting or needing to deal with it, that now I had written it down it was like opening a can of particularly poisonous worms, allowing the imprisoned memories to burst out of their hiding places. I was also beginning to feel emotions I had never experienced before – emotions I had always studiously avoided feeling – and now I had opened up that can of worms I didn't know how to deal with the issues I was facing. Or how to keep them from overwhelming me and more importantly my family.

I'd written the book in order to release myself from the past, but it seemed to have made things worse; this wasn't supposed to happen, I kept telling myself over and over again. I found that I got emotional every time I thought about anything to do with my childhood. Mental pictures were coming back with shocking clarity. I could vividly see the room that I was forced to spend so much time in, even smell it sometimes. I could visualize clearly my childish scribbles on the filthy walls. These scribbles depicted a life outside the house, and had helped me escape from the reality of what was going on all around me; but they were cries for help that no one would see until it was too late to do anything.

By facing up to my past I had removed the mental barriers I'd erected over the years and had released the floodgates; and I had no idea how to handle these difficult emotions. I was in danger of drowning and was clinging to my bad habits like liferafts, or like a small child might cling to a comforter or sucking their thumb.

A few days later Andrew heard back from Barbara that she liked what she had read and wanted to meet me face to face. It was arranged that I would go to see her at her office in London a few days later. This was good news as far as the book went, but unnerving news for me. I was afraid the unfamiliar emotions that were welling up inside were going to overwhelm me and make the meeting difficult. In business meetings I could always be strong and hold my own because there was nothing personal involved. It was just a transaction between two companies. But this was different. This was all about me and my life. It was a different kind of meeting and I didn't know how to handle it. The more I thought about what might happen when this unknown woman began asking me intimate questions about my past, the more apprehensive I became.

The night before I was due to go I was unable to sleep, tossing and turning all night, wondering how this stranger would react to me and how I would react to her. During those long hours of darkness I thought about everything I'd written. Was I just feeling sorry for myself? Or had I never accepted my past for what it was? This manuscript was supposed to release me from my past so I could move on, but it was making things worse. Had it all been a terrible mistake? I didn't feel how I had expected to feel. If I had known it was going to be like this I would never have written it down on paper in the first place. But I had written it, and now I was being offered some choices as to what I might do. It would be foolish not to at least listen to the possibilities open to me.

This unknown woman I was going to meet was the only person in the world who'd read the manuscript apart from Jackie and Andrew. She was the first stranger who would know all about my past before even meeting me. She would know about the things that had been done to me and the things I had done to other people. Almost all my secrets had been laid bare and I felt sure she would be judging me as a result.

She'd already said she liked the book, which was good, and meant I didn't have to worry about retelling the story to her, or about convincing her that it would make a good book; but how would I behave with her and what questions would she ask me? Would I be able to control the emotions, which felt so new and raw, when I talked about my past to her? She was bound to ask me questions about the difficult times. I didn't want her to feel sorry for me; that was the last thing I had ever wanted. I never wanted pity when I was a child and I certainly didn't want it now. I thought other people's pity was insulting, and would always hold me back. Only the weak, I believed, feel sorry for themselves. But I knew at the same time I had to get control of all these new emotions if I was going to find any mental tranquillity again.

I got up early the next morning, bored of lying in bed, my brain wide awake but my eyes feeling heavy from lack of sleep, and set off for London. I didn't put any music on during the trip; I wanted it to be quiet so I could reflect on all the thoughts I'd had the night before. I reached the offices three quarters of an hour early for the appointment. I preferred it that way. The last thing I wanted was to be arriving late and flustered. I needed to have time to gather my thoughts. I parked the car and sat, composing myself. As the minutes ticked past agonizingly slowly, I tried to picture what would be happening over the following hour or two. It was as if I was in a trance, thinking about what would happen next, working on automatic pilot. My head was hurting from all the questions that were circling around it, finding answers to none of them. In the end I clapped my hands together as if to snap myself out of my thoughts.

'Just keep cool,' I reassured my reflection in the rearview mirror. I turned on the car stereo as a distraction, playing some Red Hot Chili Peppers and Marilyn Manson, laughing at my own foolishness as I tried to sing along.

When the moment to go in finally arrived I made my way to her office with my rucksack on my back. It contained the green file with all the evidence from Social Services to prove my story in case Barbara challenged it, and the big black sketchbook that I use for all my ideas and inventions. I rang the bell and was buzzed into the impressive-looking building. Her secretary greeted me with a friendly smile and led me into a small reception area. She offered me a seat while we waited for Barbara to finish whatever she was doing, but I chose to stand, not yet ready to settle.

My eyes scanned over the massive bookshelf that covered one whole wall, studying row upon row of books. It was peaceful inside the office, comfortably furnished, and a thousand miles from the traffic and bustle of the streets outside. It was a calm environment and I immediately began to feel less intimidated. I had seen a closed door as I came in and guessed that the woman I was coming to meet, the woman who knew everything about me, was sitting behind it.

'Are these all clients of the agency?' I asked, trying to break the silence that very quickly settled between us.

'Yes,' the receptionist smiled encouragingly, 'they're all Barbara's clients.'

As I got to the end of the rows I heard the door to the other office open and I turned round. Suddenly Barbara was there, an elegant woman with a voice so calm and soft it took me by surprise. Never having been used to soft voices in my childhood, they have a particularly soothing effect on me. Jackie has the same air of tranquillity about her, which is one of the reasons I fell in love with her.

'Kevin, hi, I'm Barbara,' she said as I put out my hand and she shook it gently. I returned her smile with my head down.

She led me through to her office, which was pleasantly furnished with yet more bookcases filled with neatly aligned books. She invited me to sit on the sofa, and offered me a drink.

'Water, please,' I replied, my voice a little hesitant.

As she went to fetch it my eyes wandered along the lines of books and over the manuscripts, which were on the floor in piles. It was a very comfortable room, everything neat and tidy and in its place, with a vase of fresh flowers on the table. The room smelled less like an office and more like a home. Barbara was back with my glass of water and offered to take my jacket.

'No thank you,' I said abruptly.

She must have seen that I looked nervous and uncomfortable as she calmly sat on a chair opposite me. If I'd had butterflies before, they were now doubling their efforts to escape from inside my stomach.

'I thoroughly enjoyed reading the book,' she said. 'Has Jackie read it?'

'Yes.'

'What does she think about you coming here today?'

'She's fine with it,' I said, keeping my answers controlled and to the point in case I got tongue-tied.

My palms were sweaty as I clenched and unclenched my fingers, and I began nervously rubbing my hand up and down my leg. My discomfort must have been obvious because she kept the meeting short and to the point, which I appreciated greatly. As this lady tried to put me at my ease I could feel tears welling up inside me even before I started to talk. I wasn't sure I was going to be able to get the words out and so I remained quiet and listened to what she had to say. 'Don't get upset,' I told myself, 'just keep it together. Don't be a fool.'

She explained how she would go about marketing the book if I was happy to work with her; how she would send the manuscript out to four publishers she thought might be interested and invite them to make offers, and what was likely to happen after that. She was talking about contracts and percentages and I was only really hearing half of what she was saying because my own thoughts and feelings were rushing in so fast.

Fighting back the emotions that threatened to break through, I told her of my reservations about publishing – and how I wasn't sure that I was ready to cope with the world knowing my secrets. The meeting was coming to an end and I was beginning to breathe more easily.

'So where do we go from here?' I asked, as I stood up to leave about an hour after arriving. 'If we decide to go ahead, do I ask you to work for me, or is it the other way round?'

We decided that if I went ahead it would be more a question of working together.

'Cool for cats,' I said, and we both smiled at each other. I was feeling more relaxed now, knowing that the meeting was coming to an end, and I said I would discuss it with Jackie before making a final decision.

I also now felt able to tell her what was on my mind. 'The book is so personal,' I admitted. 'There are parts I'm ashamed of and bits that were only meant for Jackie.'

'Kevin,' she said, gently but firmly, 'you have nothing to be ashamed of.'

I could understand that in her eyes I might not have anything to be ashamed of, but in mine things looked different and I couldn't change the way I felt.

'Kevin,' she went on, 'if you had written it to be published would you have been so forthcoming and truthful about your life?'

Almost certainly not, I thought to myself, but I didn't say anything, simply shaking my head.

We shook hands and as the office door closed behind me I gave a huge sigh of relief; partly relieved because I had managed not to get upset about my past and partly because I hadn't been asked to prove anything. To have to prove to a stranger what had happened, recalling the beatings and tortures all over again and justifying the actions of others was something I couldn't have faced. As I stood outside the door I held my hands out just to see how much they were shaking. I walked towards the stairs and wiped away a tear that had rolled down my cheek. I could see that this was all going to be much harder than I had anticipated.

Even in that initial, brief meeting Barbara had explained a great deal about the industry I was on the verge of being catapulted into. I felt that if I chose to take the plunge I would now have in Barbara an ally I could trust, someone who would always have my interests at heart. At the back of my mind, however, a little warning voice was still telling me not to get too excited, that no one, as I had learned many times before, can be trusted until they have proved themselves to be trustworthy.

That evening, over yet another bottle of wine, Jackie and I talked it through and decided that we would take the plunge and let Barbara try to sell the book. It didn't have to be an absolutely final decision yet, we could always change our minds again later, but we might as well find out if publishers were interested at all. If they weren't then we could forget about the whole thing and get on with the rest of our lives, having lost nothing. I rang Barbara the next day to tell her of our decision and she promised to get back to me as soon as she'd had some reactions from publishers.

3. Feeling Naked

Once Jackie and I had decided that we would see if the book could be published, Barbara sent it to the four publishers she had in mind, telling them that she would like to hear their reactions within a fortnight. I decided to put the whole thing out of my mind, that way I wouldn't be disappointed if no one liked it. If anything came of it, I was sure Barbara would be ringing me very quickly.

In the meantime the flashbacks were coming thick and fast. It seemed endless. When I was alone at home I would sit down and think of the past, seeing myself with my legs up in the air, kicking my own mother just to get her off me, or trying to wriggle away from Dennis while the stick or buckle was coming down on me. I would look down and catch myself anxiously rubbing my legs, as if I was trying to soothe the pain away. The worst thoughts were when I remembered some of the times that I couldn't get away and I would simply bury my head in a cushion and cry. I felt so stupid to be getting upset about something that I never wanted to think about again, but I couldn't seem to stop the memories from surfacing.

Within a week Barbara had called to tell me that three of the publishers had made offers for roughly the same amount, and that the editorial team at Michael Joseph, one of the publishing houses owned by the Penguin Group, had asked for a meeting with me the following day, a Friday. It felt good that they liked what I'd written, but at the same time I could feel the uncomfortable swirl of emotions that I had experienced when I went to meet Barbara for the first time.

Barbara went to great lengths to explain to me who would be in the room at the meeting and assured me that they were very interested to chat to me. A time was set, just before lunch, and she and I agreed to meet in the company's lobby area before going up to their offices. I was glad when she said she was coming with me as I certainly didn't want to go alone.

When I told Jackie the news, she thought it was great that such well-known publishers should be showing an interest. I knew she was right and the fact that one of them wanted to meet me was even more promising, but it meant I was going to have to put myself through another meeting with strangers who would know everything about my life, including all the most humiliating details.

That night, just like the night before I was first due to meet Barbara, I didn't sleep a single wink. My mind was churning as I wondered how I would behave with these people and what would happen when I got there. I was trying to picture the scene so that I wouldn't be taken completely unawares, but I couldn't imagine what a publisher's office would look like. All evening I'd been trying to hypnotize myself not to get upset when they asked me about incidents in the book, remembering how I'd felt talking to Barbara for the first time. The last thing I wanted to do was to burst into tears in front of a bunch of strangers.

The next morning, after a restless night, my eyes heavy once again and my head aching with all the same questions as before, I headed back up to London. Before leaving I packed my rucksack once more with the green folder from Social Services, just in case they wanted proof that I was telling the truth, and my big black book in case they wanted to see other things I had done. I also packed a notepad, which was something I had always done when I was attending business meetings. I took it so I could make notes if I needed to, but also, more importantly, so I could persuade myself it was a business meeting, thereby making it seem less personal.

Although I knew it was possible that nothing in my life would be the same again after that Friday morning, which was one of the many reasons I was feeling so nervous, I had no idea just how much everything would change as I made my way into London with my rucksack firmly on my shoulders.

It was late morning when Barbara and I met in the lobby of the Penguin headquarters in the Strand and I was relieved to see a familiar face, someone who was comfortable in an environment where I was feeling completely out of my depth. I felt like a little boy again, stepping out into a grown-up world for the first time. It reminded me of an occasion when I was small when I'd dressed as Worzel Gummidge for a school play and walked out on to the stage in front of a silent audience. Our family was well-known in the neighbourhood and I felt they were just waiting to see how someone from the Lewis family with our reputation would behave. Like then I was unsure what was expected of me. I felt under pressure. I wanted to do my best, but was anxious I'd let myself down.

The lobby was impersonal and the anonymous surroundings gave no clues as to what might lie ahead as we registered our arrival with reception.

'Are you ready, Kevin?' Barbara asked as we sat down to wait.

'Yep,' I replied. She could see I was anxious. Sweat was starting to trickle down the side of my face.

'It will be OK, Kevin. Just be yourself,' she said with a reassuring smile. I took a deep breath and smiled back.

Then with the ping of the lift coming to our floor the doors opened and Lindsey Jordan, an editorial director from Michael Joseph, came down to collect us and take us up to their boardroom. Barbara stood up to greet her. I followed her lead and found myself stepping back behind Barbara, wanting her to do the talking on my behalf. It was as though I was standing behind a teacher as I was introduced to yet another new class. The two women obviously knew one another and greeted each other warmly. For them I guess it was just business as usual. Then Lindsey came round to me.

'You must be Kevin,' she said with a wide, friendly smile. I couldn't find any words so I just shook her proffered hand and smiled back, my throat too tight to speak.

The greetings dealt with, she led us to the lifts and she and Barbara made small talk as we ascended. They tried to include me in the conversation with polite questions, to which my answers were brief and quiet. I could think of nothing to say as I fought to control the mixture of excitement and panic that was gripping me as we rose further and further from the streets outside, where only a few minutes before I had been just another anonymous person who passers-by knew nothing about. All I could think of was that I wished Jackie was by my side. So that's what I did and, as I turned to look in the lift mirror, there she was, standing beside me behind Barbara and Lindsey, like my own personal genie. A grin spread across my face as I turned to look at her beautiful face and encouraging smile.

Jackie disappeared when the lift doors opened to send us on our journey. As we entered the offices Barbara and Lindsey walked ahead and I followed on behind, gazing around in wide-eyed wonder. The first thing I noticed, and what took me aback, was how quiet it was. It was more like a library than any office I'd ever been in before. As my eyes wandered around I couldn't get over how many books there were everywhere. I don't know why I was surprised to see books lining a publisher's walls, but I was. It was like entering a different world. Even though I'd started to read books as an adult, I'd never lived in a bookish environment. So many words telling so many stories and describing so many different lives, reminding me how many things there were that I knew nothing about; it was hard to imagine how the modest story of my childhood and my struggle to find a place in the world would fit in amongst them.

As we walked through the large offices the hush would occasionally be broken by background voices or the hum of a photocopier going backwards and forwards. I felt I should be walking on tiptoe for fear of disturbing people's concentration or earning their disapproval. It was then that I started to wonder just how many of the people I was passing had read what I had written. I knew this was a dream come true and I had to keep reminding myself that I'd actually written a book and that these people wanted to publish it. I was grateful, I really was, and it was a great compliment. But I now knew why I kept getting so upset; it was because I felt naked, stark bollock naked. When people glanced up from their desks as I walked past I wondered if they'd read what I'd written. Did they know all about me; my past, my present and all my future dreams? I felt I had nothing left for myself. It was as if I was parading past them with just my rucksack on my back. Was I selling my soul? Yes, I rather thought I was. I kept my head down trying not to make eye contact, and speeded up to catch up with Barbara and Lindsey, narrowly missing a filing cabinet on the way.

As we reached a large, internal, glass-walled office I noticed a man and two women inside, standing talking to each other. As we drew closer they turned and were watching us, their eyes fixed on the three of us as we went through the office door. I didn't like being the centre of attention. As I passed through the glass door I was faced with a line of people who definitely knew all about me because they had read the manuscript closely enough to want to publish it. I didn't know whether to run away or just cover my private parts. I was feeling humiliated by all the attention. I remembered Gloria and the many things she did to humiliate me so many times over the years. I tried to tell myself this was different. This was not me standing naked as a child while Gloria rained blows and abuse down on me.

As we came into the office Barbara and Lindsey moved to one side giving the three people room to come directly to me, even before greeting Barbara, hands outstretched and broad smiles. They each introduced themselves to me. There was Tom Weldon, the managing director of Penguin General Division, Louise Moore, publishing director from Michael Joseph, and Grainne Ashton, the marketing director. Barbara had already told me who I was meeting and what their functions were, but the feelings of nakedness and worries about how I was going to handle the situation were now preoccupying my mind and I was feeling extremely vulnerable.

All eyes in the room came to rest on me again as we settled down to business. The spacious office had a desk in one corner and a large oval table in the other, which was where we were all to be seated once our refreshments had been organized and the formalities attended to. I reached into my rucksack and took out the notepad and pen and placed them carefully on the table in order not to make too much noise. I then placed the rucksack between my legs. They were all smiling and being so polite, as you would expect, but still I was anxious about the way I was feeling and had visions of Gloria being in the room with me.

Their eyes remained fixed on me, even when Tom opened the meeting by saying how much they liked the book. They then went to great lengths to convince me that they would love to publish my story and explained what they would like to do and how they wouldn't put me through anything I didn't want to do. They were all being so kind and so complimentary about the book that I found it hard to take in. It seemed strange that only a few weeks before I was struggling to convince anyone of what I could do. I tried to avoid their eyes and distract myself from my feelings. I glanced around at all the books on the walls. It must have seemed as though

I wasn't interested in what they were saying, but I couldn't help it. I kept seeing Gloria and some of the things she did. I started fiddling nervously with my hands in my lap, like I might have done twenty years before when I was called into the headmaster's study to be told off for some misdemeanour or when I got home and Gloria and Dennis were fighting in another room and I would huddle away in a corner trying to keep out of the way, but knowing that at any moment they would burst in and use me as a punch bag to release their frustrations.

I didn't know what else to do with myself and was becoming agitated. I was anxious to get a grip and so I tried to prove to them that everything I'd written was true and began fumbling nervously around in the ruck-sack, trying to get out the green folder. I was looking down, grateful to escape their eyes and all I could hear was my own voice saying, 'It's true. It's all true.' But they assured me it wasn't necessary to prove anything, that they believed me.

'We know what you've written is true,' one of the women said.

I stopped fumbling and sat back up, taking a deep breath as I tried to compose myself. I looked up and they were all still looking at me. I noticed there were tears in some of the women's eyes. I looked away again quickly, swallowing back my own emotions.

I didn't have to prove anything because they were all totally on my side but the feeling of nakedness was almost overwhelming, encouraging my emotions and visions of the past to bubble dangerously close to the surface again.

I looked up once more and realized that all the women had tears in their eyes now and my heart sank. If they all started crying I didn't think I would be able to control myself for much longer. I had no idea how to react to this sort of display of emotion. My life had always gone at such a fast pace I'd never had much of a chance to dwell on the past until I wrote the book, let alone discuss it with other people. Now, at last, I was being afforded that luxury and I wasn't sure how to handle it. Barbara smiled at me across the table and I tried to smile back. We got on to a conversation about my children and I couldn't control the rush of emotion any longer. I swung my chair round to look at the bookshelves behind me so that my face was hidden from them as I fought to compose myself. My jaw was hurting from trying to stop myself crying, but I couldn't hold the tears back any more. My eyes filled with water.

'Oh, bollocks!' I said to myself.

I could hear their words as they talked about the book and how they worked together as a team and a family, and how they would like me to join them. I think they carried on talking about the book because they didn't know what else to say, but what else could they say? What's happened has happened. I tried to concentrate on what they were saying in order to distract myself from the emotions that their tears were stirring inside me and to allow me time to compose myself. When I felt able to turn back to face them they asked me a few questions, but I had a feeling they'd already decided what they wanted to do, even before they met me, and that they'd just wanted to check I didn't have two heads before committing themselves to publishing my book.

I was determined to answer a question they had asked about the children, but while answering I think my voice must have cracked and they all began wiping their eyes again and passing around the tissues. I felt desperate to get out of the building and into the fresh air, to be on my own with no one looking at me or knowing anything about me or feeling sorry for me. The panic was growing inside me and I wanted to gather my thoughts. Did I really want to publish this book if it was going to make me feel like this?

'Kevin is still a little unsure that he wants to do this,' Barbara warned them, as if reading my thoughts, and they immediately started reassuring me again that they would look after me and would never make me do anything I didn't feel comfortable with. They were such a nice bunch of people I could quite believe that they would do their best, but could anyone protect me from the feelings and visions that were constantly struggling to escape from inside? If I felt this emotional in a meeting of half a dozen people, how would I feel when the world was able to read the story of my life? I couldn't answer that question, nor all the others that were spinning around in my head. I stared down at my hands, picking at the skin nervously.

The effort of holding everything in was making my head hurt and suddenly, while Barbara was talking, I said, 'I want to go home now,' very abruptly.

Barbara could see that I'd had as much as I could handle and called a halt to the meeting. It felt very strange to have an agent looking after my interests; very strange but also very satisfying. We all stood up and said our goodbyes. I distracted myself again by looking at the rows and rows of books on the walls as they all made a bit more small talk before we left. But every time I looked at a book, they would give it to me. I kept protesting that they didn't have to give me things, but they insisted. As we left the building I took a huge gulp of fresh air. The gentle breeze quickly dried my eyes and cooled my face. I placed the rucksack on my back. It was now so full of books that I thought my shoulders would break, but I must admit it felt good to be given the gifts.

After saying goodbye to Barbara outside the building I felt relieved that it was all over, but my mind was already busy with questions about how I was going to be able to handle having everyone know about my life. I was excited by what was happening, but it was hard to focus on any one thought when there were so many jostling for space in my head. Would I be able to cope with interviews if this book was published? Would I be able to accept my friends and relatives knowing everything about me after having kept the secrets for so long? What if the book was a failure, how would I feel then?

It seemed like a giant leap into the unknown, partly exhilarating and partly terrifying, and if I hadn't had Jackie and Barbara on my side I don't know if I would have had the nerve to go through with it. I think without them the manuscript would have gone into a box in the attic, collecting dust, never to come out again. The emotions would have been sealed up inside me once more and I would have got on with my life doing something else.

As the meeting was held on a Friday, we now had the weekend to think about what we were doing. I imagined the people at Michael Joseph were thinking as much about whether I would be able to pull off the necessary promotional work for the book as I was. After the meeting Barbara had been as gentle as always, telling me not to worry and just to enjoy the weekend and wait to see what happened. She told me she'd never before been to an editorial meeting where everyone had tears in their eyes and she thought that must be a good sign.

Bizarre, I thought to myself.

I took the long route home to give myself time to sort out my thoughts. How was I going to deal with the feelings of nakedness? How would people react to the book? Most importantly of all, how would my brothers and sisters, and Gloria and Dennis react? I knew I had to tell my brothers and sisters what I'd written. I hadn't thought about it previously but the prospect now filled me with anxiety. What would happen if they didn't want the history of the Lewis family to be out in the open?

Jackie had picked up the children from school by the time I got back and I tried to put it all out of my mind until Monday, hoping that by then it would become obvious what should happen and how Jackie and I would deal with it.

'How did it go?' Jackie asked eagerly as soon as I came through the door.

'Really cool,' I said, 'but at one point I got a bit upset.'

She put her arms around me and hugged me tightly. My arms stayed at my side because I was still having visions of Gloria. We then got on with playing with the kids and planning what to do for the weekend. But all that was about to change.

4. The Offer

We were in the kitchen a couple of hours later, giving the kids their tea, when the phone rang. It must have been just after six o'clock, a time when you might have imagined everyone was leaving their offices for the weekend.

'Hi, Kevin, it's Barbara.' By now I instantly recognized Barbara's familiar soft voice. 'I have some fantastic news.' Even her reserved manner couldn't disguise her excitement.

'Oh, yes?' I replied, a little hesitantly.

'Michael Joseph have quadrupled their offer if we agree not to talk to any other publishers.'

'Oh,' I said, not able to take in what she was saying. 'OK.'

Her voice rose just a little, as if she realized she was going to have to explain herself more clearly. 'Kevin,' she repeated, 'this is fantastic news.'

'Cool,' I said.

She was obviously unsure how to take my lack of excitement at such an extraordinary turn of events, and was a little disappointed that I wasn't jumping around with joy. 'Well,' she said, 'think about it over the weekend and let me know what you decide on Monday.'

I put the phone down and calmly told Jackie what I'd just heard. Jackie understood the importance of the call immediately and let out an hysterical shriek of delight. She didn't need any time to let the news sink in. As she jumped about and hugged me I could see that something amazing had happened, but I still couldn't quite believe it. I was shocked and my arms were still down at my sides as I tried to work out what was going on in my

head. I was beginning to smile and I could feel goosebumps travelling up my arms and down my back.

I phoned Barbara back a few minutes later, not quite sure what
to say.

'Are you sure?' I asked calmly.

'Definitely,' she replied.

'That's pretty cool, isn't it?'

'Yes, Kevin,' she said, obviously relieved that the penny was
finally dropping, 'it's very cool indeed. It's absolutely brilliant.'

'OK, thank you,' I said, and hung up once more.

A few minutes later I rang again. As the news was filtering a little
further into my brain I was becoming more and more excited.

'This is bloody brilliant!' I said, a huge smile on my face and
tingles running all over my body.

'Yes, Kevin,' she laughed, 'it is brilliant.'

Now, the anxieties and doubts I'd been experiencing, and all
thoughts of how I was going to deal with what I had written were
suddenly driven out of my head, replaced by a lovely new feeling
of lightness, something I had never experienced before. It was as if
a huge weight had been lifted from my shoulders and a feeling of
security had settled in its place. Maybe, I thought, everything was
going to be all right after all. As I thought about it more, and once
the reality of what had happened had finally sunk in, my grin
stretched from one end of the room to the other. Not only was my
story being believed, and not only were people showing an interest
in what had happened to my life before meeting Jackie, but now
we had no more money worries, at least for a while. I will never
forget that feeling. It was nothing short of spectacular. No more
getting up each morning in order to fight just to survive, not for
the foreseeable future anyway. We intended to enjoy every moment
of this new-found feeling of financial security. As a family we could
now plan what we wanted to do in the future to help ensure our

happiness and security. I'd always wanted to be given a chance in life, now I had it and I was going to grab it with both hands.

That evening Jackie, the children and I were dancing round the kitchen we were so happy. I lifted the children into my arms as we danced to Elton John's 'Are you ready for love?' which is my daughter's and my favourite song. The kids had known that I was writing a book, although I'd told them they couldn't read it until they were at least twelve. I didn't want them to be exposed to the sort of life their dad had led until they were mature enough to handle it. Ideally, I would prefer them not to read it until considerably later, but I doubt if they will wait that long.

We spent the rest of the evening listening to Elton John and Barry White tracks blaring from the kitchen while playing around the house, chasing each other through the rooms, until we eventually wore ourselves out. That evening I lay in bed with a huge, relaxed smile on my face. Life, I decided, was bloody brilliant.

I've never been any good at lying-in, especially lately with my past making my nights so restless, but now I got up early because I didn't want to waste any of my fantastic new life. Over breakfast the next day we decided we would each buy ourselves a treat to celebrate the good news and headed off to Bluewater shopping centre. The kids both chose a toy and Jackie, much to the relief of the rest of us, said that she'd come back on her own another day to buy herself some clothes. She wanted to take her time and knew that the kids and I would be getting impatient within a few minutes.

Having sorted out the children it was my turn to decide what I was going to buy for myself and I knew straight away what I wanted. I'd always fancied an electric toothbrush. It's one of those frivolous items I could have bought many times over the years, but never got around to doing. So I decided now would be a good time to indulge myself. I went into the shop and picked up the biggest box with an all-singing, all-dancing electric toothbrush

– flosser, accessories, you name it, it had it. The fact that every time I brushed my teeth with it my nose tickled and I would be continuously scratching was of course beside the point.

After we'd finished shopping we headed for the cinema, splashing out on posh seats in the sofa section and taking in giant buckets of popcorn and packets of sweets. After the film we went out to dinner and later that evening we headed home. As soon as the kids got into the car they fell into an exhausted sleep with their hats still on their heads. We drove silently home that evening, Jackie and I smiling all the way, with her hand resting reassuringly on my leg. That night I enjoyed the deepest sleep I can ever remember. Life, I decided as I drifted off, was very good indeed.

5. The Big Wait

Because the manuscript was in a finished state when it was sent to the publishers, there was very little for me to do once they'd accepted it. They wanted to make hardly any changes at all, which I was very pleased about. It would have been awful to have had to justify every scene, or to have to go back and re-write chunks of it. It made me think that perhaps I would be able to put it all behind me. But now that the project that had been filling my thoughts and my time for several months had temporarily disappeared from my life, it had left a disconcerting vacuum in its place.

The editorial staff at Michael Joseph had taken the book over and were doing whatever they had to do to prepare it for the market in seven or eight months' time. They were designing covers and briefing sales people, arranging advertising and dealing with printers – all the things that they were expert in and I knew nothing about. So there I was, sitting at home thinking of those people silently going about their business, working on my life in order to make it as pleasing as possible to the general public. It was a good feeling, a confident feeling. I would sit at home and think of all these people working on what would be called *The Kid* and a pleasant smile would spread across my face.

Occasionally I would receive a phone call or an invitation for lunch, or I would be sent something to look at, but mostly they got on with their jobs and I was left to wait until publication, which was scheduled for the following June.

The best thing about it all was that I now had the freedom to plan what I wanted to do with my future. The first thing I noticed was that, now I had the time to sit back and think properly about my choices, I began changing my ideas about what I wanted to achieve. Things I'd thought about doing, like trading in the futures markets, or working in telecommunications, believing they would get me as far away from my past as possible, no longer seemed so appealing. Now, for the first time in my life, I was actually able to choose what direction to go in, and with my past still so vivid in my memory it wasn't long before I was thinking differently about my future. I had enjoyed certain aspects of writing the book and the creativity involved in coming up with new inventions and I wanted to take both skills to the next stage.

I remembered how, as a child, I used to go to my room to try to escape the rows and the beatings, usually in vain, and would spend hours locked away, sometimes too frightened to come out. Or there would be the times when my body would feel simply too painful to move and I would stay out of the way just to give myself time to recover from whatever had happened earlier. There I would be in a dishevelled state, my clothes worn and smelling, passing the time by drawing pictures on the cold, damp, grimy walls. I used anything that would leave a mark: a nail, a piece of chalk I found on the streets or in the woods or a pencil or felt tip I'd stolen from school. Anything that would make a mark without making a sound that would tell anyone else in the house what I was up to, scribble after scribble. I would draw a life far away from where I was, a life I would dream of after watching television programmes about far-away places. The pictures would depict stories of a fantasy life that would allow my mind to escape from the stifling reality around me. Even if my body was hurting from some punishment or other, my mind was still free to wander. Because the house was in such a terrible state, with dirt and excrement and half-torn wallpaper on the walls, and because the things I drew were recognizable only to me, no one noticed or cared what I was doing. Our house was always chaotic. On the occasions that Gloria did catch me she would immediately start mocking me, screaming abuse an inch away from my face. I would try to ignore her, but this would only infuriate her further and she would then punch and kick me, knocking me on to the floor while she carried on regardless. Once she was exhausted and satisfied she would break up or throw away whatever I had been drawing with and I would have to find something new. Sometimes late at night with the small train and music I had smuggled in and hidden inside the mattress, I would listen and play on my own and continue my dreams on the wall. During the days I could see my ideas clearly amidst the mess, and at night, despite having no light, I could still picture them clearly in my head with no more illumination than the moonlight coming into the room through the uncurtained windows. Inside my mind I could always see those scribbles of a life far, far away which helped to make those walls slightly more pleasant to look at. Thinking back now I realized that what I'd been doing all those years was trying to create my own stories like the ones I saw on television.

The television screen had been my only means of escape from the reality of life with Gloria and Dennis. The programmes were often American, and the plots full of straightforward heroes and villains, people winning wars single-handed, beating the bad guys to a pulp. As I thought about those daydreams I realized that that was what I really wanted to do; I wanted to put my ideas and stories on to screens, like I had in my mind so many times as a child, lying on my bed, trying to lose myself inside my own daydreams, escaping from the violence and torture all around. Now I had the choice I naturally knew what it was I wanted to do. It was clearer than anything I had ever seen; I wanted to write and dream up stories as I did as a child. Things that had once helped me escape into a world of peace and tranquillity, today would help me escape from the visions of my past that were still haunting me. Then I wanted to put them on the big screen, just as I saw them in my head. I wanted to direct films. Knowing that was what I wanted to do was one thing, but I also had to be realistic. Could I actually do it? I wanted to convert my scribbles on the bedroom wall into film scripts. I wanted to make use of my past and turn it into something positive. The question was, how was I going to go about making that happen? It's easy enough to say that you want to be a script-writer or a film director; it's not so easy to make it a reality.

I also knew that I wanted to write more books and continue sketching ideas for inventions, something I had always done when ideas came to me. That would be a great life, I thought to myself. These, I knew, were long-term plans, but I had to start somewhere and I couldn't see any reason why I shouldn't start straight away. So I wrote them down in big letters in my black book – *write, direct, invent* – and underlined each one.

For the first few weeks after the deal with Michael Joseph I spun into a whirlwind of activity, my head suddenly cleared by the rush of excitement of knowing what I wanted to achieve. After dropping the kids off at school I would go to a local café for coffee and eggs. I would sit at a corner table out of the way of the other customers, jotting my ideas down in my big black book – ideas for more books and films, and designs for wild inventions. Sometimes Jackie would join me, sitting peacefully beside me as I doodled away. I might then go for a drive, listening to whatever took my fancy, clearing my head from all the ideas whirling around inside it. On returning home I would work more, sometimes taking a break in the after-noon to watch a film which I now looked at differently, studying each scene carefully, believing that one day I would write and direct those big movies myself. I would go back to work until the children came home from school, than I'd be eager to close the book and spend time with them.

I was constantly trying to force thoughts of Gloria and my past from my mind and sometimes I could manage it for quite long stretches of time, which was a big step forward. I'd embarked on writing the book in the hope that I would clear out some of the emotional baggage that had been cluttering up my subconscious for so long, but initially I'd actually found the opposite happening. I appeared to have started a chain reaction. Every door I opened in my memory seemed to lead to several more forgotten ones. In the past I wouldn't have been able to cope with some of the emotions these memories evoked, and they were still hard to cope with, but now I hoped I wouldn't have to think about any of it again for months, not until the book was published and I had to fulfil my end of the bargain by talking to journalists and whatever else the publicity people at Michael Joseph might ask of me. For a while I could work without the baggage of the past affecting me. It was like being suspended in a strange limbo. Everything in my life had always seemed so urgent up till then, and now nothing was urgent any more. We didn't even have any money problems thanks to Michael Joseph's generous advance. It was a wonderful, heady feeling and every idea I came up with seemed to me to be dazzlingly brilliant.

Sometimes, in the midst of this frenzied creative activity, I would be troubled with self-doubts; was I aiming too high and expecting too much of myself with all these dreams of becoming a novelist, film director and inventor? Could I succeed at any one of these demanding vocations, let alone all three? Was I in danger of spending the rest of my life just dreaming and hoping and never bringing anything else to fruition? The determination to prove that I was a doer and not a dreamer spurred me on to even more furious bursts of energy, sometimes working late into the night. It would be at this time that I would think most of that room where I used to be scribbling on the walls and Gloria would be there. Now, however, it was as if we were separated by thick glass so that she could see what I was doing but I couldn't hear her. She would be smashing against the glass screaming and shouting to break it down and get to me, but she couldn't. I would slowly turn towards her and she would stop and I would stare straight at her, my eyes looking at her defiantly and then turn back slowly and carry on while she erupted into another attack trying to break the glass down.

At the end of the fourth week I gave Barbara a list of things I wanted to write about and told her all about my future plans. It was then that reality bit me hard on the backside.

'Kevin,' she said, her quiet but direct tone of voice halting me in mid flow as I pitched yet another stream of ideas, 'you've got to slow down. We must at least wait and see how the first book is received before you can start selling other ideas on the strength of it. Relax and enjoy life for a bit.'

I put the phone down feeling disheartened and frustrated with myself. I realized she was right. I did have to slow down. How stupid I had been, I thought to myself. I no longer had to be paddling at full speed all the time just to stay afloat, as I'd had to do when trying to establish myself in business, and when simply trying to survive before that. Rather than grabbing every idea that came into my head and running headlong towards the goal with it, I should take some time to reflect and think things through before acting, build solid foundation blocks and take things one step at a time instead of rushing on just to get away from something in the past. Time suddenly seemed to grind to an almost unbearably slow pace; a pace that I had never been used to. The sudden freedom meant I needed even more self-control than when I was struggling.

The need to fight had gone and whereas a few weeks before that had seemed like a relief, and I had revelled in the freedom, now that Barbara had slowed me down I missed the adrenalin of constantly moving forward. I needed a channel for my get-up-and-go, and I missed the daily challenge of struggling to achieve a nice future and of getting as far away from my past as possible. I started to look back through my black book with frustration, scribbling angrily over the writing and tearing pages out. Worst of all I had visions of Gloria and Dennis laughing over my shoulder.

After my conversation with Barbara my days still started with taking the children to school; seeing them run in happily invariably brought a smile to my face. Then I would sit in the coffee shop with my black book, but it no longer mattered what I had achieved by the end of the day because none of it was going anywhere, not for a while anyhow. Success felt so close I could touch it, but I just had to wait for things to take their natural course. I truly knew what direction I wanted to take. I knew that it would take time if I was going to do things correctly, but I was still impatient. It was a complete lifestyle change, and although the result was something I had always wanted, I was finding it hard to adapt to. Then there was another feeling that I hadn't experienced before: I began to feel that I didn't deserve the advance; I hadn't worked hard enough for it; I hadn't proved I could do anything – I had just taken it and that made me feel useless. The heady feeling of freedom was slowly evolving into one of frustration and boredom. Changing speeds from a hundred miles an hour to virtual standstill was very hard to get used to and the pace was beginning to drive me insane.

I also began to feel that I had become an outsider in my own life story. Whenever someone from Michael Joseph called with a question or a request for information I jumped at the chance just to get involved again, but it never lasted for long. The call would end and I would be back on the outside of the process once more.

The days passed into weeks and the boredom and frustration grew deeper and deeper as I sat at home feeling useless. It annoyed me every time I would waste a day because it was something that went completely against everything I believed in.

As I slumped in front of the television watching DVDs I would be constantly snacking on packets of chocolate biscuits, crisps, sweets or any other stodgy food that would feel sweet and comforting as my brain went numb and I lay lifeless on the sofa, only ever moving to reach for something else to eat or for the remote control. Eventually I would feel so bloated, guilty and annoyed with myself that I would drink a pint of water straight down, wait for it to hit my stomach and then go upstairs and purge myself in the bathroom. I would then sit on the cold bathroom floor, filled with even more guilt and annoyance for what I had just done, telling myself to get a grip, that I was better than this. It was a pattern of behaviour from my past that I had thought I would never be repeating, but I didn't seem to be able to stop myself. I couldn't see any way out of the pattern I was falling into.

Ever since writing about my life I began to drink more and it wasn't long before I was consuming a bottle of red wine a night. It helped take away the visions of the past that I was so desperate to leave behind. But now I began to drink earlier in the day too. I would open up a bottle of wine just as the children came home from school, as if in reaching the end of another day I needed to reward myself for my fruitless hours, finishing it during dinner. Once the kids were safely in bed, having had their bedtime stories, I'd then open another bottle and settle back down on the sofa in front of the television, sipping, pouring and staring stupidly at the screen until I fell asleep.

I enjoyed my wine, and began to relish going out in the day to choose what I was going to drink, picking bottles that to me were tasteful and enjoyable, taking my time over making my selection. My behaviour wasn't affecting the children in any way, because if I drank too early in the day I would take vitamin C and guzzle down a pint of water. But Jackie soon noticed that I was watching a lot of television and not achieving much else with my days. I'd also started to let my appearance go, only bothering to shave once a week and wearing my scruffiest old clothes all the time because I didn't feel there was anything to dress up for. Some days I looked twenty years older than my age. Jackie's comments on my appearance and behaviour were becoming more and more frequent, but whenever she suggested I might be drinking too much I would dismiss her fears out of hand. I tried to cut down the amount I drank but when that happened vivid scenes of me aged five or six would return, and I'd watch myself as the beatings rained down on me and I tried in vain to protect myself. I never seemed able to clear them from my head. My brain was dead, my stomach bloated and I was spiralling into a cycle of self-pity and guilt, which made me drink and eat more and more. I wanted to get back up and fight, but there was nothing and no one to pick a fight with.

The fact that I was drinking so much and convincing myself that I was not getting drunk made it even worse, because what was to stop me going on to open more bottles? If I got to finish two in a day, which I occasionally did, without any ill effects, then what would be enough? Where would it end? My affection for Jackie and the kids never changed and we still laughed and joked together as we always had, but underneath the surface I felt completely useless as I watched her getting on with the job of being a wife and a mother. I knew I was getting under her feet because she would just have tidied the lounge and a few minutes later there I would be, bottle open and food on the coffee table. All week I looked forward to the weekends, when the cycle would be broken, the kids would be at home so we would be doing things together all day and my drinking and eating would go back to normal.

It wasn't long before I started opening the first wine bottle at lunchtime, instead of waiting for the end of school, and spending the afternoon in front of the television as well as the evening, one movie after another after another sliding past my brain, hardly touching the sides. My eyes and head would hurt as I attempted to supress the constant battling with the visions by the glare of the television.

I have never been a great sleeper, but this new lifestyle made things even worse. After dozing all afternoon on the couch I found I was waking up at midnight, thirsty from my daytime bingeing and feeling angry with myself for wasting another precious day, but not knowing what I could do the next day to avoid it happening again. I felt useless and imagined that I was turning into Dennis, my father. There he would be, standing with his arms out on the kitchen work surface, cigarette in one hand, glass filled with gin in the other, spending the evening steadily drinking and getting more and more angry at anyone or anything. I never got angry when I drank and in the back of my mind that made me believe I was different from him.

Then one afternoon, having drunk a whole bottle of wine within an hour, I pictured Dennis coming home from work and standing alone in the kitchen with a bottle of gin and his Elvis Presley tapes playing in the background, trying to escape Gloria's shrieking and the other stresses of his life and the chaos that reigned in the house, but this time as he turned his stocky body round to face me I saw my head was on the body of my father. I sat bolt upright spilling my drink over my clothes. My throat was sore and my teeth felt like they were covered in a layer of grit from my usual purge of lunchtime stodge and wine. My eyes were forced wide open and a tear slid down my face as a chill ran down my spine. I went straight upstairs and had a sobering shower. I had less cause to be drinking than him, I told myself, because I had a beautiful, supportive wife, not someone like Gloria shouting and screaming at me every time I turned round. My health was good, which his wasn't, and I had worked hard to achieve the freedom I had wanted for so long. There was, in other words, no excuse for messing it all up. I had to get a grip of my life. I got dressed and went downstairs.

That picture of my face on Dennis's body made me realize that I could easily be sliding down the same slippery path and that shocked me. What had happened to all the dreams I'd been nursing for so long? I was finally in a position to make them come true and I was doing the exact opposite. I was being offered an opportunity to do things that I would be able to look back on with pride at the end of my life and I was letting them all slip away. I realized I had to straighten myself out and, as always, decided the best way to do that would be to write down what my problems were so that I could see them more clearly.

'Right,' I said, deadly sober although swaying a little from the sudden movement, and I went to fetch myself a piece of paper and a pen. I sat up straight and drew a line down the middle of the pad. On one side I wrote the heading 'what I want to do' and on the other 'what I don't want to do'. I underlined both of them in thick black ink. The babble of the television started to annoy me and I switched it off so I could concentrate. The silence felt good, and I opened the window to let in some fresh air. Things were starting to clear in my head and it wasn't hard to identify the things that were wrong; I was drinking too much, eating too many of the wrong things and watching rubbish television to fill the time and to distract myself from the tedium, all of which were making the situation far worse. In a nutshell, I was bored, and this was pushing forward visions from my past. I knew I was drinking to clear them, but that was the wrong way to go about it. What I needed was something to do – a fact which I wrote in big letters at the end of the 'what I don't want to do' list.

So, what did I want to do? This wasn't hard either once I'd focused my mind. I wanted to write and direct films and continue with my scribbles and inventions, but in order to do that I needed to feel fit and well again so I could pursue my dreams effectively.

I decided to write down what I was going to do about the immediate problem of getting myself motivated and back into shape again. I considered starting by giving up the drinking and dealing with the eating disorders, but felt that would be attacking the results of my problems rather than the causes. I needed to tackle the question of what I wanted to do with my life first. Once that was sorted out it would be easier to tackle the drinking. But I knew that I couldn't go from a sofa coma back to full speed overnight. Before that could happen my mind and body needed to be fit enough to cope with the task ahead. I drank another pint of water. I was alert and sobering up fast.

The moment I had something to focus my mind on I found I was able to contemplate the idea of filling my days more constructively and consequently cut out the drinking. I formed a plan; since one of my favourite drinks is ice-cold water, I made sure that during the day the wine glass I always used had iced water in it instead of wine. I decided that I would allow myself a couple of glasses of wine in the evening if I had achieved something during the day. If I hadn't achieved anything, then I wasn't allowed to drink. I realized that up till then I had largely been drinking because I hadn't achieved anything, which I could see was the wrong way to be going about things.

I tried to stick to three meals a day, which was hard in the afternoons when I was used to gorging myself. Instead of sweets, biscuits, chocolate, pie and every other sort of junk food, I started making myself salads. I'd go to the fridge and throw together rocket, tuna, sweetcorn, cubed tomatoes and cucumber in a bowl with salad cream. I found my appetite just as easily satisfied, my stomach not as bloated and my brain not dead, so I could carry on working and thinking through the afternoons without falling into a sofa coma. If I found myself starting to fancy a drink in the afternoon I would get out of the house, going for a walk or for a drive and taking a bottle of water and my music with me, distracting myself from the idea of drink.

The most important thing was to get back into a routine and so I got up at six thirty every weekday morning and shaved every other day. My beard isn't heavy enough to have to do it every day, so there was no point in making my skin sorer than it needed to be, but I wanted to look smart and fresh again. After dropping the kids at school I only allowed myself to go for coffee every other day. Afterwards I would do some exercise so that by ten thirty the blood was pumping and I was ready for work.

I began by going for walks each morning along a route I already knew and liked, and then I started running part of the way. Each day I ran a bit more of the route, building my stamina and fitness gradually. At first, believing I would find running boring, I tried taking music with me, but I found it annoyed me. It interrupted my thoughts, which seemed to flow faster and faster as I ran, my heart racing.

Although I had joined a gym to use the treadmill, I found I preferred being outside, filling my lungs with fresh air, looking at the scenery, feeling the blood pumping through my veins and clearing my head, making my thoughts more fluid.

As my mind became more stimulated my body no longer seemed to need any wine. My mind and body were telling me they didn't want it and so I only drank water. My sleeping patterns improved, making me feel more alert during the day. I also found that I was now better able to get on top of my emotions. I was no longer getting upset about my past, and the old childhood habits – like stuffing my food in too fast and fussing about with my cutlery – were retreating back into their boxes once more. My subconscious was begging me to rebuild the barriers that had helped me through the early years of my life. The visions and feelings of my childhood started to float away and Gloria wasn't around me any more. I would sometimes think of her while running and it would just spur me on to run faster. The faster I ran the quicker I pictured her turning away and disappearing.

Now that I was getting back in control of my life I could see that I had the sort of successful family life that most people could only dream of, which gave me an even firmer springboard from which to have a successful career. I was very honest with myself and admitted that my biggest flaw was that I would always rush into things. Now I didn't have to do that any more. I decided I would take my time, plan my future correctly and not dash around as if I still had to make enough money every day to feed us and pay the rent. This time I was planning for my family as well as for myself.

Just shaving wasn't going to be enough to smarten me up; I was going to have to tackle the way I dressed too. Taking a roll of black bin sacks with me one afternoon I headed for my wardrobe, starting with a favourite old green jacket, which I knew Jackie particularly disliked.

'What are you doing?' Jackie asked, having got home with the kids from school to find me pushing clothes into bags.

'Moving on,' I told her and she walked up behind me, stroked my back, smiled at the sight of the green jacket in the bag and went back downstairs, leaving me to it.

I then made a more detailed list of what I should do next. I wanted to write scripts, but first I needed to establish that I could create the right framework for the kind of films that I enjoyed. I made a promise that I would be brutally frank with myself. If something I wrote was a load of rubbish, then I had to admit it and move on to something else. My main criteria for judging my work was, would it be a film that I would want to watch or not? If I didn't want to watch it myself, how could I expect other people to?

My black sketchbook was filling up with story-lines and I was happy to be replacing the ones I had torn out in anger. Now plot after plot was growing and expanding as I worked harder and faster, the blood pounding round my head after the running. I would punctuate my efforts on the scripts with drawings and descriptions of inventions; everything from ways to power a house to DNA missiles, from bringing G3 bandwidth together to install in offices to a device that would go on the front of trains in order to scan the tracks ahead for abnormalities. I have always found that my mind is coming up with possible solutions to problems I come across in daily life or triggered by something I might read in the papers. I didn't always know what I wanted to do with the inventions, but I believed it was important to record them, so that I would remember them later. My brain was alive and buzzing once more. I was able to move on.

My mind and body were fit once more and I felt it was time for me to embark on the successful career I had always wanted. I sketched out my career plan on paper, breaking it down bit by bit so that I could see exactly what I needed to do. I would need training in how to write the scripts properly and in the skills needed to become a film director. I started to enquire at colleges, universities and film schools, asking them to send their prospectuses. A few days later I would be waiting impatiently for the post. These glossy and informative brochures looked slick and professional and I would take them with me on the school run and on to the café, poring over them as I had my coffee and eggs, trying to see how they could help me realize my dream. In every brochure, however, there was always a paragraph that would puncture my bubble. They all said they needed a certain level of education; GCSEs, A levels, degrees, or experience in the industry, none of which I had. No one wanted to attract students who had left school with no qualifications at all. I wasn't going to give up at the first hurdle, however, and so I called each of them in turn to see if there was any possibility that I could do one of their courses anyway. I knew I had the necessary ability. I love learning and I knew this was what I wanted to do more than anything. But they were having none of it. I simply couldn't get on these courses unless I had the relevant qualifications or experience. When I asked them how I was to get experience without the training their answers were always evasive. But having been rejected several times still didn't dissuade me, and the recurring image of me painstakingly scratching away on the walls as a child made my resolve stronger. 'I'll show them,' I said to myself. 'I'll bloody show them.'

While I was searching for a college that would accept me, I kept up my self-educating activities. I love movies about heroes; the sort of people who I remember seeing as a child; people who overcame evil and fought for what was right; the sort of characters and plots that I had been scribbling about on the bedroom walls all those years ago. I made a list of the films I'd liked over the years and found out who the directors were. I searched out their scripts on the Internet, printing them out continuously for two days, only going out of the house in order to buy more paper and ink. Then I began to study their work, deconstructing the scripts as closely as any undergraduate film student. I watched the films on the screen at the same time as reading the scripts, to see how the directors had translated the words from the page into moving images. I became fascinated by what was on the page, each scene broken down, every word and every camera angle: internal, external, wide angle, mid shot, close-up, extreme close-up. A whole new world was opening up to me and it made me hungry for more.

The first script I read was *Raiders of the Lost Ark*; a film that meant an enormous amount to me in my teenage years. I also pored over the scripts of the films *Titanic, Gladiator, Swordfish, Dog Day Afternoon, Black Hawk Down, Pulp Fiction, Devil's Advocate, Ronin* and *Austin Powers*; and on and on it went. I researched all the film-makers who were successful in the areas that interested me, directors like Ridley Scott, Steven Spielberg, George Lucas, John Frankenheimer and Quentin Tarantino.

I needed to be realistic about what I could and couldn't do. I was never going to be great at writing comedy, for instance, or romance. What I knew I wanted to do was make action thrillers, in both my novels and scripts, and the only way I would be able to prove I could write would be to just get on with it. So that was what I did, slowly building the blocks to story-lines that I hoped would later be transformed into novels and film scripts. Every so often I would remember what all those people at the colleges had told me over the phone. Was I really aiming too high? Was I dreaming? But every time I thought that way it would spur me on further to prove them wrong.

After the confused feelings and visions of the previous eighteen months and the adjustment of one minute trying to do a hundred things at once and the next sitting in front of the television and just waiting for the book to come out, it seemed that I was now back in control of my life again. The way I looked at it was if *The Kid* was a hit that would be a bonus, but I was still going to be busy and successful even if it sank without a trace. Barbara had made sure I understood what a risky business publishing is and how many books never earn enough to even pay back the advances that the publishers hand out. Although everyone at Michael Joseph was being incredibly optimistic, I knew there was a chance it wouldn't work and I would never earn another penny from it. I needed to get on with my life as if I hadn't written the book at all. That way I would be able to put my past behind me.

During this period we were living in rented accommodation. This was a situation that always made me feel a little insecure and so I began to keep a lookout for a house that might be suitable for us. I knew I couldn't afford the farm I'd always dreamed of, but I still wanted us to own our own home. Jackie and I discussed it and we both decided that we wanted something that needed some attention so that we could put our own mark on it, just as we had eventually done in Coulsdon. Finding a good-sized house in need of refurbishment, though, was not easy. It never is, because everyone else is after the same thing. A property developer had once told me that the only way to be successful in residential property was to be able to move faster than everyone else when the right property came on the market. That meant going round the estate agents regularly so they got to know your face, grew to like you and to know that you were serious about buying – building a rapport so that you would be one of the first calls they would make when a new property came on to their books. I had been keeping my eye out for a good property, and as we had nothing to sell we were in a position to move very fast if the right one came up.

That advice and our persistence paid off because after a few months of chasing the agents one rang to say that he'd just been instructed on a four-bedroom, nineteen-thirties detached house in exactly the right condition. A proposed sale had just fallen through after the buyer pulled out at the last moment. It was occupied by an older woman who'd been there for forty or so years and now wanted to move to something smaller and more manageable. He told me I could be the first to see it if I went round immediately. The call was pure music to my ears. I jumped into the car and went to see it straight away. As soon as I drove past the property I knew it would be right. I went in to meet the seller, who was living there with her grandson. It was obvious that the house was now too big for her and she was anxious to move. She told me she'd been messed about by a previous buyer and, as soon as she'd showed me around, I gave her my word that I would buy it from her before Christmas for the price we agreed that day. I'd always made a point of keeping my word on deals, believing it pays to be trustworthy. In the past my word had been all I had to trade with in business since I had no track record and no qualifications. The deal went ahead from there with no hitches, so I knew the house would be waiting for us to start work on as soon as Christmas was over.

I was feeling very positive about life at every level, and my confidence grew stronger each day as my past faded further away. I decided that once the festive season was over I would tell my brothers and my sisters what I had written. I didn't want to leave it too close to publication date, in case they had any problems with it. I had no idea how they would react to having all our dirty washing aired in public, and I had even less idea how Gloria and Dennis would react. Was I doing the right thing by raking it up again after all these years? I was finding it hard to cope with it myself let alone the thought of telling the perpetrators of my childhood pain and suffering.

In the weeks before Christmas, however, things would happen which would change my perceptions of everything once again.

6. Voices from the Past

My mobile must ring a dozen times a day as I chat to Jackie, Barbara and all the other people who make up my daily life. It's a great tool – I love it – but now and then it brings unpleasant surprises.

It had already rung a couple of times that evening, but the caller had hung up as soon as I answered as if they'd lost their nerve at the last moment. I didn't take much notice, assuming they would either pluck up the courage to eventually speak, or else the call would not be important enough to worry about. When it rang again while I was putting the children to bed, I answered it with my usual breeziness and was shocked to hear Dennis's subdued tones. I recognized his shy, muffled voice immediately, even though I hadn't heard it for several years. I was completely unprepared for receiving a call from him, especially as not so long before I had been shaken by the image of myself turning into him. My first reaction was, had he heard about the book already? How could he have done, I thought, dismissing the idea.

I couldn't picture him using a phone at all, least of all for him to make a call to me. It turned out he'd got my number from one of my sisters, all of whom I kept in contact with on a fairly regular basis.

Listening to him I was suddenly transported back again to my childhood. The memories of how hard he would hit me – just as if he was fighting another man – sent a chill through my whole body. I tried to put all other thoughts out of my mind by concentrating on his words, which were almost too quiet and subdued for me to be able to catch them. He told me that my younger brother, Robert, who I had seen only a few times since I left home, had turned up in his life. On the odd occasions that I had spoken to my other brother Wayne, or my sisters, they'd told me that Robert would sometimes just arrive back in their lives out of the blue, regaling them with tales of all his recent adventures. They had described to me how he often seemed to be wrapped up in a world of his own, unbothered by anyone or anything beyond his own immediate needs, and how he fantasized about things. He'd always been inclined to embroider the truth somewhat in the telling of tales, even as a child, which I guess was his way of escaping from the harsh realities of his life, both past and present. Quite often, the others complained, he seemed only to have made contact with them in order to ask for money for food or a bed for the night.

Although none of them had any money to spare, they would try to help him in any way they could. He would always promise to repay them but never managed to do it, living as he did from hand to mouth. Being in such a vulnerable position apparently didn't appear to bother him. Robert's philosophy always seemed to be that if you ignored a problem for long enough it would eventually go away. Sometimes, of course, that approach works, but most of the time it merely allows the problem to grow, or turns it into someone else's. But from what I could make of it all, he seemed pretty harmless, and more like a lost child than anything else. I tried to listen carefully to what Dennis was saying about him and put my reservations aside.

Gloria had always hated Robert with much the same ferocity that she had hated me and, once I was out of the way, having finally been removed by social services from the house, he had been left to face the brunt of her anger and violence. That gave us some sort of bond and I must admit to having a soft spot for Robert even though we hadn't seen each other for so long. After I was taken into care I used to visit home at weekends and noticed that he had disappeared from the house. I paid little attention to his absence at the time, being more concerned about my own problems and knowing that it was those who were left behind at the house who had the most to worry about.

I knew from my sisters that as a young man he'd been drifting aimlessly through life, working for funfairs, jumping from job to job, unable to settle anywhere for long and sometimes living on the streets, but they were unsure how much of what he told them was fact and how much was fantasy – or at least exaggerated fact.

Since all the information about Robert had come to me second-hand I didn't want to form any judgements, but it seemed likely that he was dealing with the demons of our childhood in a very different way from me. Having not seen him for so many years I was keen to hear some firsthand news of my baby brother, particularly as his reappearance in my life coincided with me thinking about our past so much.

Dennis told me that Robert had recently been living out on the streets and in hostels and had been in and out of hospital over the previous few weeks due to an old injury on his arm. His explanations were a bit slurred and confused. It was obvious he had been drinking and I couldn't quite work out what had happened, but it seemed that he was telling me the doctors had had to take a plate from a previous injury out of Robert's arm but, because he was living rough on the London streets, the resulting wound kept going septic and wouldn't heal.

'He's been asking if you could help him,' Dennis told me. 'Christmas is coming and he hasn't got any money, but he can't sign on because he's in hospital . . .'

Robert and I had been through a lot together when we were little and I'd always felt it was my job to protect him, particularly on the occasion that he fell into the clutches of a paedophile when he was too young to know what to do about it, so there was no way I would turn my back on a direct plea for help from him now.

I told Dennis I would go to the hospital the following day to see him, feeling very unsure what I would find when I got there. We said our goodbyes and I must admit my hands and legs were shaking as I put the phone down. I remembered so much of what he did to me as a child that it seemed strange to be talking to him about helping my brother, as if everything was normal between us. That night I thought a lot about how this quiet, shy man would burst into black rages, his anger fuelled by drink and aggravated by the uncontrollable chaos which filled the house.

The following day, as I travelled into London to see Robert, I felt a lot of conflicting emotions. Pictures of him as a child kept coming into my mind. The last time I had seen him was over five years ago, when he was in his early twenties. I was looking forward to seeing him again, although at the same time I bore in mind the warnings from my other brother and sisters. I felt excited but wary about how he might have changed in the intervening years.

From the moment he left home Robert had been living from one moment to the next, never thinking beyond the next few minutes, never able to make a plan or see a way to improve his lot in life. If he'd had a meal or a drink or a few pounds in his pocket then that was all he needed until that little bit of money ran out or his hunger or thirst returned. He had no idea how to support himself or move past the damage that had been inflicted on him at the beginning of his life. I was hoping that now we were back in contact I would be able to help him change this dangerous pattern of behaviour; help him make plans and look to the future. I found so much comfort in looking forward rather than backwards and I wanted him to be able to do the same. I believed that if he could do that then he would be able to see the possibility of a more comfortable and satisfying life, just as I had done as a young man, and that that would drive him forward to make more of an effort to get some stability in his life.

I felt increasingly nervous once I arrived in the alien, sterile environment of the hospital, trying to find my way around the endless corridors with their confusing signs. When I finally reached the door of his room I opened it slowly, unsure what I would discover on the other side. The first thing I saw was this fragile young man lying in the hospital bed. His vulnerability shocked me, knocking the wind out of my chest as I walked into the room. I tried to act casually, as if my visit was the most natural thing in the world. I took a deep breath and smiled, unable to think what to say. Even though he was twenty-seven years old he looked like a little lost boy, as if all strength and life had been drained from him and he had no fight left.

When he saw me a weak smile almost lit up his face and I felt a genuine glow of pleasure at the sight of someone who had come from the same place as me, who understood what it felt like to live as we had lived, who shared so many experiences and feelings, memories and fears. I loved him, as I did my other brother and sisters, and when I looked at him lying in the bed, attached to a drip, too exhausted to cope any more, I could see myself as I might have been if things had turned out differently. My emotions were still dangerously raw from revisiting all my childhood experiences and the sight of this sick, damaged, exhausted boy brought them painfully back to the surface. During that first hospital visit the conversation was slow and sometimes awkward. There were long silences between us as we both stared at the television, desperately trying to think of things to say to each other. Although it was uncomfortable, we were both happy to be in each other's company and that was enough for now.

I visited him regularly in the coming days and he seemed to be growing stronger and happier with each visit, a bit of colour creeping back into his cheeks as he chatted up the nurses. We started talking about his recent adventures, his girlfriend, his time working on the funfairs and about a bit of trouble he'd had with the law. It seemed he'd never stayed anywhere for long, and never managed to organize himself to get a permanent place to live, even when the alternative would be a night spent in a cold shop doorway.

'Why don't you stay with Dennis?' I asked.

'I do sometimes,' he said, 'but it isn't easy.'

He told me how things between them would be fine during the early parts of the day, but the more Dennis drank the angrier and more aggressive he became, kicking and swearing at Robert and venting all of his pent-up emotions and frustrations, just like when we were children and he had to live with Gloria.

'Why don't you defend yourself against him?' I wanted to know. 'You're a man now; you're stronger than him. You don't have to take that sort of thing any more.'

'He might chuck me out of the flat and I wouldn't have anywhere else to go,' he admitted. I could see how hard he found it to stick up for himself in any situation.

I wasn't surprised to hear how Dennis had behaved towards him because I'd heard from the others that he still drank. We all knew how emotional and angry he could become when drunk, although I had hoped time might have mellowed him. At the back of my mind, however, the warnings the others had given me about Robert's tendency to exaggerate kept nagging away. As I listened to him talking about Dennis I wanted to believe Robert was overstating the facts and that Dennis was not still the miserable, vicious drunk he had been during our childhood, but I had no way of judging. Later that day, once I had returned home, I spoke to one of my sisters on the phone, asking if Robert's stories were likely to be true.

'It may be that Dennis did get angry with him on a couple of occasions,' she replied, 'but only because Robert kept using the flat as if it was his, never making any effort to get a place of his own. Dennis would get fed up with it.'

It seemed there might be two sides to these stories. Robert, I realized, was no longer a helpless child and couldn't automatically expect his father's protection against the world. On top of that, Dennis was the wrong sort of person for anyone to look to for protection. On the other hand, caring for Robert could have given Dennis some opportunity to make up for the terrible childhood he had given us all.

Arriving at the hospital one afternoon for my regular visit, I could see Robert had been badly shaken by something.

'Gloria's been in,' he said.

'Is she still here?' I wanted to know, immediately feeling myself starting to shake at the possibility of bumping into her. I thought about the room in my visions with the glass panel separating us and imagined her smashing it down to get to me.

'No, she came earlier.'

'What did she want?'

'Money. She told me she was in here visiting a friend, so she thought she'd see if I had any money. I could hear her coming from miles away. She was shouting and yelling and swearing down the corridors. I tried to get into the bathroom to hide, but I couldn't make it in time because of this.' He gestured at the drip that he was still having to waddle around with wherever he went. We both laughed at the image of Robert in his hospital nightie, stumbling around as he tried to hide from the terrible roar of his approaching mother.

'You didn't give her anything, did you?' I asked sternly.

'No,' he shook his head vehemently.

Even though we were laughing I could see that he was hurt to think his own mother would only come to see him in hospital in order to cadge money off him. Everyone would like to think that whatever else, at least they're loved by their mothers. It was a luxury he would never experience. That lack of love didn't bother me any more. I never treated her like a mother anyway. I had Jackie and the kids to love me and to love in return. Robert, I realized, was still searching for someone to fill that void and, deep down, I could sense that he still missed a mother figure.

Jackie had told me in the past, after speaking to Gloria on the odd occasion, that she had always had something bad to say about Robert. She was still putting him down. Even after all these years she couldn't leave him alone. Knowing how the filth was always pouring out of her mouth, I hadn't attached much importance to it, but her continuing hatred and contempt for her youngest son after so many years seemed all the more poignant now that I was with him and could see how vulnerable he was. Although Jackie had always been polite to Gloria, until she read the book and found out the truth, she had also tried to steer her away from talking Robert down. She didn't like to hear any mother bad-mouthing her own children, but Gloria was unperturbed. Unkindness came too easily to her, even now when she apparently needed and wanted contact with her children and grandchildren more than ever.

'I spoke to Dennis on the phone and he says he'll put you up when you come out,' I told him. 'But behave yourself.'

'What do you mean?' he wanted to know.

'Just behave yourself,' I said again, and I think he understood what I meant, even if he didn't want to admit it. I then told him that as soon as he got out of hospital we'd organize some more permanent accommodation for him. I also suggested that while he was in hospital he should write a plan of what he wanted to do with himself, both in the short term when he was discharged, as well as in the medium term over the next year or two, and finally in the long term.

'Just be free to write whatever you want,' I told him, jotting the words 'short, medium and long term' on a piece of paper and leaving it on his cabinet.

I was already hatching a plan myself that might take care of his short-term problems. As the house I was buying needed some improvements and modernization, the work would require another pair of hands, and I thought Robert would be the ideal person to help me. It would also give him somewhere to live while he sorted out what he wanted to do next. It seemed the perfect fit.

'I'm going to be buying a house which will need doing up,' I told him. 'Fancy coming to help after Christmas? It's a nice house, just a bit tired, perfectly liveable in though. You could stay there and help me work on it if you like.'

'Yeah,' he said, his eyes brightening. He seemed genuinely excited at the prospect of us doing something as brothers, and I began to think that perhaps together we could find a way to extricate him from the poverty trap that he seemed unable to get out of on his own.

During the time that I was visiting the hospital, Dennis started ringing me regularly on the pretext of discussing Robert's situation. I could tell that he wanted to talk to me about more personal things, but I couldn't bring myself to go beyond the cold, practical details of arrangements and plans. I remained firm and to the point, unable to open myself up to anything sensitive or emotional with him. With no encouragement from me he was too shy to say what he was thinking. As long as we were discussing Robert's welfare there was a reason for us to be speaking. Without that reason I would have been unable to do it. I could never simply have phoned him to find out how he was or chat about the past. It would have been unthinkable, raising far too many of the uncomfortable memories that I had been trying to lock back up.

Did he feel bad about the past or did he even think he did anything wrong? I wasn't sure and, to be honest, I didn't want to find out.

I knew from Robert that Dennis seldom went out any more, not even to the pub. He spent his days alone in his flat, drinking, becoming progressively more confused, slurred and angry as the hours slipped by. Eventually he would slip into unconsciousness, waking sober the next morning and starting the whole destructive cycle all over again. If we spoke early in the day his voice was almost normal, but if he phoned me later his tongue would be clumsy from the alcohol. I felt irritated by this reminder of why, as a young man, he had so often been unable to put right what went wrong in our family life. In our conversations on the phone the drink would make him upset and very emotional, and he would often cry, wallowing so deeply in self-pity it would be hard to follow the rambling course of his speech. I would end the calls as quickly as possible, not knowing how to respond to these slurred emotional outpourings. It reminded me of how emotional he would get in the kitchen. We were so used to it as kids that we didn't take any notice and, annoyed that we wouldn't feel sorry for him, he would lash out.

It was impossible for me to deal with his demons when I was still trying to cope with the ones that had been stirred up inside my own head. The last thing I wanted was to have to listen to a drunken Dennis crying down the phone to me. It was too soon to be dealing with such emotive, personal issues when we had only just started communicating again. During our conversations I made a point of hardly mentioning Jackie and the children, fearful of driving him into an even more emotional state. Listening to his moaning made me angry, which in turn made me feel guilty for being unsympathetic. But it was the only way I could handle this onslaught of emotion from a man who had often beaten me so badly that I would be in pain for days. If Jackie or the children became emotional about things I knew how to handle it, hopefully providing them with the love and support they needed. But this was a grown man who had never given a thought in the past to how his actions were damaging the lives of the six children who were forced to live with him in that little tin house.

Thinking back now, it's possible he had been giving some thought to the damage he had done, and that realization was part of the reason why he was becoming so upset now. Was this what made him drink so much? I don't know. He'd been a heavy drinker ever since I could remember. Whatever the reason, I didn't feel ready to find out; I just wanted to distance myself from him again. His barrage of emotions pushed me away. After his calls I always had trouble sleeping as my mind chewed over every word he had said, wondering if I was doing the right thing in writing about him. But then the memories would come back and I would remember when I was at home and he would burst in to the room after he and Gloria had had a fight. Spurred on by Gloria, who would have told him something bad about me out of pure hatred, he would head straight for me. The blood would drain from my face before the first blow even fell, defeated by sheer fear. Knowing what was coming I would curl up in a ball on the cold, dirty floor to try to protect myself, but he would straighten me out as easily as unfolding a piece of paper and then lay into me with punches, kicks, and lashes with his belt buckle or anything else that came to hand. I would be screaming with pain and limp. My brothers and sisters would be all around screaming for him to stop while Gloria towered behind them, fag in mouth, smiling.

Although I only called him in the mornings when he was more likely to be sober enough to control his emotions, I couldn't always block his calls to me later in the day. There was one evening when I couldn't avoid taking his call. Knowing that he would have been drinking for several hours by then, eager to get back to reading the children their bedtime stories and resenting the intrusion into our private time together, I struggled to keep the conversation matter-of-fact. It was near the end of Robert's stay in hospital, and I was trying to explain to Dennis what would happen, when he suddenly said something I'd never heard him say before.

'I love you.'

His voice was muffled, but the words were quite pronounced.

I didn't know what to do. It took me aback, shocked me and a host of butterflies took flight in my stomach. I put the phone down, quite unable to think of anything to say in response. I finished reading to the children, my mind a million miles away from the story, and kissed them goodnight. There had been so many years that I'd longed to hear those words from him or Gloria, especially after school or during the long miserable, frightening nights, when the pain would seem overwhelming and I would be desperate for help and some sign of hope. I'd built so many barriers over the years that when the words finally did arrive I had no way of dealing with them. Once I was downstairs I stood staring at the phone, the butterflies having returned again, as I tried to work out what I should do. Should I call him back and respond to the words? Should I just leave it?

I left it. It was just too hard to deal with. So many contradictory thoughts and emotions were swirling around my head that it was safer that way. How could I respond after so many painful, desperate years, so many blows raining down on me, one after another after another, my screams and pleas for mercy making no difference to the ferocity of his attacks? How could three little words possibly wipe out all the years of memories? I'd always believed I was his favourite from little looks he had given me and the odd reassuring pat on the back when things were going badly. He seemed to show some favouritism towards me when it came to taking one of us to the pub with him. I liked those outings when it was just him. I would wait anxiously while he got ready to go and if I didn't think he was going to take me I would scream to be taken, to get away from Gloria. Although he took me more than the others, he mostly went on his own, leaving me with her. Once he was gone I would stop screaming, knowing what was going to happen next. She would immediately be shouting at me, her face within an inch of mine.

'Daddy's fucking little boy, are you? Fucking queer,' she would mock me as she got herself into such a frenzy mainly because she knew I didn't want to be with her. Then she would lay into me. I'm sure Dennis could hear the screams of pain as he walked away from the house.

Knowing I was his favourite made her hate me all the more ferociously. It was a catch-22, because it made her work even harder in her attempts to turn him against me when he was drunk and feeling angry at the whole world. The moment he got home she would start telling him all the things I'd done wrong.

'Do you want to know what *your* fucking cunt of a son has done now?'

Even though Dennis had never had any idea how to show his affection properly or how to protect me, Gloria knew he was fond of me, so she would egg him on to attack me. Despite knowing all this, it was still a shock to hear him say something so personal. I was assailed by doubts as to whether or not I was being fair in writing the book and exposing this sad, sick old man's shortcomings as a father. Was I doing the right thing? Had he been doing his best all those years? Had beating me into submission been the only way he could cope?

By showing concern for Robert, and trying to help him, it looked as if Dennis was finally attempting to make amends for all the times when he didn't help us as children, but then he was still attacking Robert when he had had too much to drink, just as he always had with all his children. During my hospital conversations with Robert I found out that Dennis had suffered three strokes, which had muffled his voice and personality even further than in his youth, but did his failing health mean he should be forgiven for everything he had done, or failed to do, in the past? I truly didn't know the answers to any of these questions and so there was nothing to stop them spinning round and round in my head, keeping me awake at night and distracting me during the day. What made it worse was that when I did talk to him a tidal wave of emotions far too big for me to handle came rushing in. Robert and Dennis, I decided, would just have to sort things out between themselves over the Christmas period. Despite all their problems, I suspect they were both grateful for one another's company over the festive season.

I still hadn't told anyone in the Lewis family about the book, but I knew that sooner or later I was going to have to come clean if I didn't want them to feel betrayed when it appeared in the shops and they had to hear about it at the same time as the rest of the world. I was nervous about introducing the subject to anyone, friend or relative.

'I've written a book,' I imagined myself saying.

'Really,' they would say politely. 'What's it about?'

'Oh, it's about my abused childhood,' I would have to reply, and the conversation would then grind to an embarrassed and embarrassing halt. But I knew I would have to tell them after Christmas.

Christmas was wonderful. As always I was even more excited than the children as we traced Father Christmas's footsteps around the house, opened presents, played games and did all the silly things you do at that time of the year. I left Dennis and Robert to look after one another. I knew it wasn't the ideal situation, but I also knew that I'd done all I could for the moment and once the holiday season was over we could concentrate on trying to get Robert settled somewhere permanently.

7. Bringing Us Closer Together

After Christmas I felt refreshed and eager to start work on the renovation of the house and was looking forward to spending time with Robert. I was hugely enjoying all the reading, writing and studying involved in learning about films and working on my own storyboards and inventions, but I felt it would be the best of all possible worlds if I could break the bouts of intense concentration up with sessions of manual labour, working on the house myself alongside Robert and other tradesmen. The rush of physical labour would get the blood pumping through me and stimulate my thoughts even further.

The house had had nothing done to it for years and needed some tender loving care to bring it back to its original condition. It was still perfectly habitable and would be a home for Robert while it was being refurbished, which would hopefully help him get on his feet and out of Dennis's way. It would also give us time to find him a home of some sort so that he could get himself off the streets and out of the night hostels once and for all. I liked the idea of finding him somewhere close to us so we could spend time together, which was something we'd never been able to do before. I was also looking forward to helping him move on, showing him that he could have a better life if he wanted one. Little did I know how hard that would actually be.

A few days after the festive season Robert had moved into the house and we set to work. The man I had put in charge of the project was a friend of mine, who I called 'Little Mark'. I'd worked with him on our other house and knew he was a really good builder and an incredibly hard worker.

We started by gutting the building completely. Within a week we'd filled five skips with rubbish, having brought the house back to its bare walls. From there we worked together putting in a new kitchen and bathrooms, plastering, electrics, staircase, everything that brought life back to this family home. For four months Mark and I worked solidly from eight in the morning to four in the afternoon. I no longer had to worry about going for runs because now I was getting more than enough exercise mixing cement, plastering and plumbing.

In the evenings, once the kids were in bed, I would spend a few hours working on the film scripts and continuing my efforts to find somewhere I would be accepted to train to become a film director. My brain was clear from all the physical activity of the day, which in turn helped me sleep better at night. It was a great feeling. During this time I realized that I actually enjoyed pressure. When it had been taken away by the success of the book deal I had missed it. Now I was able to reapply it with my own self-imposed budgets and deadlines, setting myself targets to get the house completed on time and searching for a place for me to study film making.

My relationship with Robert over this period, however, was to be turbulent to say the least.

8. Brotherly Love

During the months we were working on the house Robert would come and go. To begin with our relationship went well, the three of us laughing and joking all the time, with Robert and Mark exchanging jokes and taking the mickey out of one another's taste in radio stations. When one wasn't looking the other would change stations, which would inevitably lead to a water fight or some other act of revenge. I was looked upon as the serious one and they would try to involve me in their playful banter. I became persuaded to start laying booby traps for one or other of them, like buckets of water placed precariously on top of ajar doors, drenching the victim and ending up with me being chased around the house with whatever weapon they had in their hands at the time. I did get my come-uppance now and then, since they were never convinced by my threats of non-payment. It was a good time. We worked hard and we had fun in a way Robert and I had not been able to do when we were growing up. All three of us were bonding well and the house was steaming ahead at full speed, which was just how I liked it.

When Robert was there we both enjoyed working together and getting to know one another better. We never talked about the past at all. It seemed as though nothing had ever happened. This made me hesitant to bring up the subject of what I had written.

Within three weeks of being in the house, however, I was clearly seeing the other side of Robert's character. Whenever he had a little money in his pocket I knew he wouldn't want to work the next day. He'd always lived that way. It annoyed me to start with and I tried to make him realize that to give himself a future he had to start thinking ahead and that this was a great opportunity for him to get his life in order. But I soon realized I wasn't going to change him. I either accepted the way he was or I didn't. There was no other choice. The idea of listing his goals, for instance, was too alien for him to grasp. When I asked him if he had done it he just responded with a sullen silence.

There were bound to be days when our different approaches to life would cause us to fall out. Sometimes, for instance, Robert would pretend he could do something that he couldn't, and would end up making a complete mess of a job which we would then have to spend days putting right. He didn't mean any harm by it, but what was getting to me was that my brother just didn't want to look ahead. If he did, it would be to dream up some huge, grand plan of how he was going to travel around Australia, which was great, but if I then asked him how he was going to pay for it and whether he planned to get a permanent job and save for his dream, he would just go quiet and retreat inside himself. By asking practical questions I had pricked his bubble. It reminded me of times in my room as a child when the dreams and stories that I been creating inside my own bubble would be burst with a loud bang whenever Gloria or Dennis came into the room and attacked me. Afterwards I would lie there in pain, knowing they could never actually stop the dreams flowing inside my head. With Robert it was like dealing with a kid who has no idea about the realities of life, but still wants to believe that his dreams will come true, which is what has always helped me. I saw that the main difference between us was that, although I also had my dreams of writing and becoming a film director, which might seem far-fetched to some people, I was breaking them down bit by bit and then building the blocks to my goals. Robert didn't want to look at the practicalities of how to achieve his dreams.

On one occasion when he completely messed up a room, I really lost my temper, yelling at him that he should stand up straight and face the world. I told him to accept responsibility for his actions and sort his life out. All my tirade did though was make him turn even deeper inwards and walk off the site. I immediately felt bad for attacking him and becoming annoyed because he wouldn't change rather than accepting him and being supportive and encouraging. I'd always known we were different, but I hadn't realized quite how wide the gulf between us was until that point. I love all my brothers and sisters and I knew Robert was dealing with his past in the best way he could. I desperately wanted to help him get on and to see that there is a better life if you work hard at it, but I couldn't do it on my own. He needed to want that better life himself; he needed to help himself before anyone else could do anything. I knew that he wanted to achieve something in life, as we all do, but he wanted to do it in his own way, not mine. We always made up shortly after our squabbles and I soon realized that he couldn't do things any differently, any more than I could. Seeing how his lack of ambition was holding him back, however, just spurred me on to work harder and harder myself, both on the house, on my family and on my own future career.

When he arrived back on site later that afternoon we sat on a brick wall and I began apologizing for getting annoyed with him because I knew I'd been wrong to lose my temper. I was trying to explain that he could have a better life if only he chose to work at it, that success in any part of life is always hard work and that the rewards are there if you aim for them, but then my mouth suddenly overtook my mind and I blurted out the news that I had been unsuccessfully trying to find a way to introduce into the conversation for weeks.

'I've written a book,' I told him, my head down to avoid eye contact. 'It's going to be published in a few months' time.'

'Yeah?' He was obviously surprised and I could see his mind working as I looked up to gauge his reaction. 'What's it about then?'

'It's about my childhood mainly, and about the way Gloria and Dennis treated us,' I went on. 'I haven't said much about the rest of you, but I have put in a scene about that time you were in the bedroom with that man and I came in.'

I was nervous about whether he would want the whole world knowing about the man who had abused him as a child, even though it wasn't his fault. I could see he was concentrating on what I was saying, taking it all in.

'I've just said that you were sitting on the bed together and he had your trousers down.'

I was unsure, especially not having seen him for so long, how he would react to me writing about such a personal incident. I'd kept putting off telling all of them about the book because I didn't know what I would do if any of my family objected strongly to my story being published at this late stage in the process.

'You could have written a hell of a lot more,' he said eventually, and I heaved a sigh of relief.

'I know I could,' I said, 'but I think readers will get the message.'

'No, I mean you could have written so much more about Gloria as well.'

'I could have, but I didn't want to be a neg-head. I've tried to make the book uplifting.'

As we sat on the wall in the sun, listening to Mark working away inside on his own, we became thoughtful. Both our minds were going back fifteen years or more.

'The trouble is though,' I said, 'I'm having real problems with visions, scenes and smells from the past. I sometimes wake at night in a cold sweat or just think about them during the day. I can't seem to get the past out of my head. They did some sick shit.'

'Why do you think I've been in hospital?' he asked, breaking the silence as our feet swayed off the ground like two small boys.

'I don't know what you mean.'

He rolled his sleeve up and unwrapped the surgical dressing to show me the scar where the plate had recently been taken out.

'I had to have the plate put in because Gloria pushed me off a bike and I fell under a car,' he said. 'After that I was taken into care, and because of other stuff Gloria was banned from coming within a mile of me.'

I listened as he talked about his memories of childhood, which still seemed raw and painful for him. I realized now why he hadn't been there when I'd gone back for family visits during my time in the children's home. He'd been sent away to a care home in Wales, but no one ever told me any details. It seemed normal in our family.

'Social Services looked after me in care homes and foster homes until I was twenty-one,' he explained. 'Then I had to fend for myself, but I didn't know what to do.'

As he talked I realized why Robert was holding himself back in life. He knew the system had let him down; he knew that they should have done more for him and he was able to blame them for everything that subsequently went wrong in his life. It was then that I saw the biggest difference between us. I believed that if I sat at home and blamed all those people who had let me down in the past, I would be letting them win and I would never be able to move on. Instead I'd chosen to say, 'Fuck 'em! They're not going to ruin the rest of my life like they did the beginning. I'm not going to let them drag me down.'

I understood how he felt, especially with regard to Gloria and Dennis still haunting me – it was sometimes as though they were standing over me – but I was determined to put it behind me. He wasn't choosing to do that and I could see this was the biggest thing holding him back. He couldn't stop blaming the authorities for letting him down. He was bitter and angry about the past and how he had been treated. His fantasies and exaggerations were just his way of living his dreams and escaping his past. The difference was I wanted to turn my dreams into reality and was making plans to move on and forget the past.

'Robert,' I said, 'you can't keep blaming everyone else and think-ing of the past. I don't see Gloria as my mother; I just think of her as someone I knew, but not very well. Maybe that makes me seem cold, but I refuse to let any of them – Gloria, Dennis, the Social Services and the others – ruin my life. I only have one life. It's short enough as it is and I'm not going to waste any more of it.'

Robert went on to explain that after coming out of care with no idea how to look after himself, it wasn't long before he found himself on the streets, with no way of getting his life together. I remembered that feeling very well from when I left school and my foster parents and tried to make my way in an adult world that didn't seem to want to give me a break, having no food, no rent money or any way of getting on to the ladder. At one stage he'd got himself a flat, but then he'd let it go, through carelessness as much as anything. It seemed he wanted to be free of all ties and responsibilities. He didn't seem equipped or to even want to take on any of the pres-sures of normal life, like paying a bill or making a plan or saving money. It was easy to see how he might have got like that with only the examples of Gloria and Dennis to learn from. Listening to him I saw how my life could have easily gone the same way as his if I'd been just a little different or had fewer lucky breaks. But I made my breaks happen through sheer hard work and having the balls to take some risks and move on. I really wanted him to understand that he could do the same if he chose to. But I knew, as I did with my other brother and sisters, that I have always been different from them. At a very early age I used to get out the house to work, beg or just steal some food for them to eat. It came to me naturally. I don't know how, it just did.

I turned to face him and could see that he was getting upset by our conversation. I put my arm round his shoulders in an attempt to comfort him. It was clear from the way he sat, cold and rigid, that he wasn't used to the affection and didn't know how to react. There was nothing I could say to make the painful memories go away for him. We went back into the house a short while afterwards and carried on working, which seemed like a better thing to do than wallowing in the past. That night the three of us went out for a curry and got completely plastered, avoiding all mention of our parents or our childhoods. It was clear both Robert and I didn't like talking about our past, preferring to lock the painful memories away. After that brief moment of discovering how similar our experiences had been, and how differently we had reacted to them, it was time to move forward again on our separate paths.

When the house was nearly finished I helped Robert fill out some forms to apply for a council flat, but something else came up in his life and it wasn't long before he was back on the road again, searching for love or friendship or whatever it was he craved, living the sort of life he didn't seem to be able to give up. I was coming to the realization that he was probably too much of a free spirit to ever be able to put down roots. I know he'll turn up in our lives again one day, when he feels like it, and I will always be pleased to see him. We've come a long way together, even though we've been apart for almost all our lives. I was sad to see him go, but there was nothing I could do to stop him.

Having told Robert about the book I knew I had to tell the others quickly, in case they heard from someone else and thought that I was deliberately holding out on them. I know how nervous I would be feeling if I heard that one of them was writing a book about the family. I would definitely want to be told what was going to be said. I talked to my sisters first, knowing that my brother, Wayne, was still in touch with Gloria and feeling unsure about how either of them would react to the news that the world was going to be told about the suffering she inflicted on her children. It wasn't that I cared about confronting her with my stories of what she did to me as a child; it was just that I wanted my other brother and sisters to know first.

The grapevine worked quicker than I could, twisting the news like a game of Chinese whispers and Wayne heard that I'd said something derogatory about him in the story before I had a chance to talk to him, which I certainly hadn't, and he phoned me up in anger. When I explained exactly what I had said he calmed down. I promised to send him an advance copy as soon as I had one, so he could see for himself what I'd written.

When two of my sisters heard what I was doing, it opened the floodgates of their own memories and they started telling me things that they had been so careful to avoid thinking about for so many years. Like Robert, two of them came out with horror stories of their own about other attacks they'd suffered, some of which I had witnessed as a child and many of which I'd known nothing about because they'd happened at times when I was away from home. They told me of beatings with sticks and belt buckles, and of crockery being thrown at their heads. By then it was too late to add anything else to the book, and I didn't want to anyway. The readers were going to get enough of an idea of what life in the Lewis family was like from what I had told them. They didn't need to know every dreadful detail of what went on in that house during those years. All three of the girls said they had no objections to my story being told.

'Do you know,' the third one told me, wistfully, 'I don't remember anything before my thirteenth birthday.'

It seemed that her mind's way of coping with it all was to block it away completely. Whereas I had subconsciously built barriers against the pain for many years, her brain had simply chosen not to remember any of it, and now she could find no way in to the lost memories. We had all discovered different ways to put the past behind us and get on with our lives. With the exception of the sister who had lost her memories, once we started talking the rest of us remembered everything vividly, as if it had all happened yesterday, and as if the wounds still stung and the fear still chilled us. But we soon decided we didn't really want to talk about the past. We never had before and didn't really want to start bringing it all up now. The way we all dealt with it was to not think about it and just get on with life. They wished me all the best and it made me feel much better that they were supportive of the book. But as publication day drew nearer the past was about to repeat itself in the most sinister of ways.

9. History Repeating Itself

It was early one evening, soon after breaking the news of the forth-coming book to the family, that I received an hysterical phone call from one of my sisters. At first the shouting was so loud it could have been mistaken for Gloria, and I had to pull the phone away from my ear. I always experienced a terrible feeling of dread when I heard shouting voices, particularly women's. To me it was a reminder of the chaos of my past, hovering in the background, trying to engulf my new, happy, orderly life and destroy it, pulling me back to where I had started from. I kept quiet and listened intensely, waving at the children to go and play as I got up to find a more private room.

I couldn't make out what she was trying to say at first through the crying and raging. Eventually I managed to calm her down enough to make sense of the story she was telling me. My sister is a single mum with five kids and she had wanted to go out for the night with her friends. Having no one else to turn to she had asked Gloria to look after the children for that one night, and now they had come home with tales of how their grandmother had been hitting them. She said they had bruises to prove that their stories were true.

The news made me feel sick, as I was transported back once again through the years and imagined the nightmare the children must have been put through in those hours they were trapped with their screaming and violent grandmother. One of them told my sister that Gloria had beaten him with a wet towel. So many memo-ries came rushing back. I could clearly picture the times I had seen my brothers and sisters being beaten until they collapsed. I remembered it happening to me and how terrifying it felt.

I would lose my breath while the blows rained down, struggling against the panic and pain, and then I would go limp, just like I had seen my brothers and sisters do. My head would feel light and I would collapse, my feet going from under me, trying to inhale but unable to do so out of sheer fright. Finally, with my face as white as chalk and my lips purple, some natural instinct would take over and I would draw huge amounts of air into my lungs. Then an almighty scream would roar out of me, driven by a mixture of pain and relief. But even then I wouldn't be able to convince Gloria that I was innocent of whatever the imagined crime might be and that I didn't deserve a beating. Witnessing my brothers and sisters being beaten was almost as frightening; watching their faces change colour, and their lips turn purple was always one of the most horrifying sights, especially if it happened to the girls. Sometimes I would shout out to stick up for them and be dragged into their place to take the punishment that Gloria had been intending for them. I still remembered times when I couldn't help them because of the agony I was in. It will always be painful for me to remember, to think of watching the beatings raining down and listening to their pleas for help, knowing I was too weak to protect them.

Now I pictured the same thing happening all over again to my nephews and nieces when they thought they had just been left for the evening with their grandmother, this woman who had constantly been in my thoughts ever since writing the book. Thoughts of what she had done in the past and what she was doing today made me boil with anger.

My first thought was to go straight round to her flat and to show her what it felt like to be picked on by someone stronger than her, but reason prevailed, mainly because Jackie managed to calm me down before I did anything stupid. It was true that if I did something to Gloria that would merely have brought me down to her level, as if I had never learnt anything in all those years and would be perpetuating the violence even further. But I knew I had to do something.

'Give me her number,' I said to my sister, my legs shaking and my mind unable to believe that history could be repeating itself in this way. Hadn't this woman mellowed with age at all? I wondered. How could she do this? She must know what she was doing. My sister gave me the number of Gloria's mobile. 'A mobile?' I thought. 'Fuck me, she can't be living in the Dark Ages any more then.'

I dialled it straight away, my fingers trembling with fury. I knew that if she had been with me at that moment I would most probably have flown into an uncontrollable rage. I don't think anything would have stopped me and I don't know how it would have ended. I was even angrier to find myself talking about her as a woman when I didn't believe she deserved to be classed as one.

I didn't want time to think about what to say and I wasn't prepared to wait to let it settle. I was going to say whatever came out of my mouth without even thinking. It would be the first time I had spoken to Gloria since she came to our wedding several years before. She'd tried to make contact with us once or twice and I'd been told by the others that she still wanted to be part of our lives, but there was no way that would ever happen.

The phone only rang once before she picked it up, apparently excited to be receiving a call.

'It's Kevin,' I said in a stern voice that seemed to come naturally from the anger.

'All right, Kev?' she whimpered in a silly, girlish whine, immediately launching into a babbling diatribe about every problem in her life and every detail of her failing health.

'Listen!' I cut her short, speaking through gritted teeth. 'Why have you been smacking your own grandchildren?'

There was a long silence.

'I haven't,' she said eventually, without conviction. Her voice now quiet and submissive.

'Yes you have. I know you have. I've just been told. They've all got fucking bruises on them. What the fuck are you doing?'

My voice must have sounded venomous. I couldn't control it. So much hatred and anger was struggling to get out past the barriers of self-control.

There was another long silence, which I was determined not to break. My breathing was heavy and turning into panting under the stress of challenging Gloria. I pictured again the room with glass between us, but this time I was smashing it down to confront her instead of the other way round. All I could hear down the phone was the background sound of the television as she gathered her thoughts. I kept silent, trying to calm my breathing. I wasn't going to let her off the hook of answering. I was expecting the line to go dead but it didn't. If it had I would have gone round in person to have it out with her. I was so furious. The thought of history repeating itself was the final straw. Then a quiet little voice came back on the line, like an apologetic child trying to get back into favour after being told off.

'I only tapped them.'

'I know what your "taps" are like,' I said, my teeth still gritted. 'Leave them alone.' I spoke in a slow, pronounced way, wanting every word to sink into her head. She didn't reply and I had a feeling she genuinely thought she'd done nothing wrong. She actually believed that it was normal for adults to beat children up if they annoyed them.

It felt as if she was startled into silence at the discovery that I remembered the things she had done to me as a child. Maybe she thought that all children forget what has happened to them, as my sister had. Maybe she thought we all had fond memories of life with her and Dennis. Or maybe she knew exactly what she had done and what scars I was carrying because of her.

I'd heard rumours now and then that she was still up to her old tricks, but it was never spoken about openly. None of my sisters had ever come to me to explain exactly what was going on; they would just make generalized complaints about what had or hadn't happened. Because I was always keen to distance myself from anything to do with her, I had never pressed them for details. For the first time someone had now told me exactly what had taken place. She couldn't lie her way out of this one, or pretend not to know what I was talking about. I could no longer kid myself that everything was all right and in the past, that she was a spent force and no longer a danger to anyone. I had finally got to hear what she was up to. It was as if I'd caught her unawares by producing evidence of her crimes, crimes that she professed to believe she hadn't committed. When actually confronted she had nothing else to say and no reason she could put forward to justify her actions.

As I slammed the phone down I was still shaking, every memory of what it had felt like to be at her mercy coming rushing back. I couldn't believe that she was still picking on people weaker than herself, like the playground bully who just can't resist taking one more punch at a victim who can't defend themselves. It amazed me that this woman was still so filled with anger and spite. Hearing that she was still hurting children banished any concerns I might have had about how she would feel when *The Kid* was published. There was no longer a shred of doubt in my mind; the world needed to know what she was like. She hadn't changed or mended any of her ways with the years. She was as violent and dangerous to children as she had always been and I was the only one with the power to stop her. It felt good to finally be able to stand up to her. I had tried so many times as a child to defend my brothers and sisters, or most of the time to defend myself. The difference now though was that I was bigger and stronger than her and she knew it. Like any bully she was reluctant to pick a fight she might lose.

A couple of minutes later the phone rang again and I picked it up with a trembling hand, taking a deep breath, still trying to recover from the anger that had exploded in my head and the verbal tirade that had poured from my mouth, leaving my whole body shaking. Gloria's voice came screeching down the line; before I'd even put the phone to my ear she was crying and yelling, swearing about how she was going to kill herself and a hundred other things about herself and the harm she was going to do. She'd had time to gather her thoughts and every one of them was bitter, angry and self-pitying. This was the Gloria I remembered and I had to hold the phone away from my ear once more, allowing the terrible voice out into the air. She'd recovered from the shock of having her bluff called and was now back on her old fighting form.

'Nobody loves me,' she wailed. 'Nobody wants to know what I'm doing. I'm just going to kill myself.'

She eventually fell quiet, as if she had exhausted herself, waiting for my reaction to what was supposed to be shocking news; no doubt frustrated at not being able to get a hold of me as she did when I was a child and shake me, bite me or beat me. Over the background sound of the television I could hear her constantly puffing away, all her frustrations being taken out on her fag.

My voice, when it eventually came must have sounded cold, as if every emotion had finally been drained from me. 'Why don't you?' I said.

She stayed silent for a moment longer.

'All right then,' she snarled, once she realized I wasn't going to retract my words, 'I fucking will.'

The phone line went dead. I look a lungful of air, trying to clear my head and contemplating what I had just said to my own mother.

I kept the phone near me just in case she called again. I didn't want Jackie or the children picking up her call.

Any feelings of guilt I'd been harbouring about writing the book had vanished. Nothing had changed. Gloria had not mended her ways. Just because she was older now did not mean that the past should be buried. She was behaving in exactly the same ways she always had and she had to be stopped. People had to know the truth so that children would not be allowed near her.

Even months later I did not regret those terrible words. Whether it was a child or a puppy she would treat it the same, beating it into submission and breaking its spirit just for the pleasure of bending it to her will. When I spoke to my other two sisters about what had happened they both confessed that they had stopped taking their children to visit Gloria in the past, when she was abusive to them. They must have been dropping hints to me all the time and I had been choosing to ignore them, not feeling able to cope with the thought of confronting Gloria. Writing the book, however, had cleared up a lot of things in my mind and I was no longer willing to let her intimidate me in any way. I was now strong enough to lay down the law. I had to be or the cycle was never going to be broken.

My sisters also told me that if they saw Gloria in Croydon she would simply ignore them, only making contact when she was on the scrounge. It didn't seem as if she was doing anything to redeem herself with any of her children. She wanted their company, but only on her terms and only if they gave her money for fags or treats, like a child that needed to be bribed in order to be good.

People in authority might try to convince themselves that the bad old days of child abuse have gone and that the sort of things that happened to me would never be allowed to happen to a child these days, but they're kidding themselves. The same things were still happening with the same people in the same family. I couldn't bear the thought that history was repeating itself. I had really intended my warning to shock Gloria into realizing that what she had done was wrong, but the indignant hysteria of her response suggested that I still hadn't got through to her. I called my sister back and told her I'd spoken to our mother and if she needed any more help in future to just give me a call.

Later that evening, once the kids were in bed, I told Jackie what had happened. She knew something was wrong, having heard me shouting down the phone, and tried to calm me down as a quietness fell over the house once I'd hung up. Having just read about Gloria and what she did to her children, Jackie wasn't that surprised by the news that she was doing the same to her grandchildren. Once I'd had time to calm down and think about it, I have to admit I wasn't that surprised either. I suppose I was just hoping that she'd got better with the years. I cried that night, asking myself over and over again why she was still able to torment me so. Little did I know that things were about to become far worse.

10. Going to Extremes

Whatever monsters might be re-emerging from my past, I was still determined that my family life with Jackie and the kids would continue to be as good as we could possibly make it. Having worked so hard to get the house into a good condition, and at the same time working late into the night on my film script, outlining my first novel and trying to find a way to get into the film business, it was time to have some treats. Moving back into a home of our own, after more than a year in rented accommodation, felt great. We felt we were safe and secure once more as a family.

Jackie knows that I've always loved the odd adrenalin rush. Perhaps it's a hangover from my childhood when high, constant doses of adrenalin were the norm, brought on by the stresses of family relationships rather than the experience of extreme sports. As anyone who has read *The Kid* will know, I'm always tempted to try anything that gives me that familiar tingling of excitement and danger. So, as a birthday present, Jackie gave me a couple of vouchers. The first was for a flight on a jet aircraft. It was something I had always wanted to do and I'd told Jackie of my dream one evening when we were watching Jeremy Clarkson together on television. Clarkson was lucky enough to be passenger in an F14 fighter jet while it was being taken through its paces in America. The other voucher was for an introductory day playing polo.

My interest in polo had been triggered completely accidentally one day when I was driving along a country lane on the way to visit friends and saw a brightly coloured helmet and stick bobbing up and down behind a hedge. Always curious about new things I pulled the car over and got out to watch. There in the field were three or four people galloping around on horses, practising their polo. They looked so alive and so elegant; their horses (or, as I soon learned to say, polo ponies) were so controlled as their riders dribbled the ball and then took a full swing at it. The ball, which was only about three inches in diameter, was then struck squarely and would fly halfway up the field. The whole scene was so beautiful, like a snapshot that stays in your memory for ever. I'd heard of polo of course, but to see it happening in front of my own eyes transfixed me.

'Now that,' I thought as I watched them charging around, turning at the last minute and stroking the ball, which seemed to then fly for ever, 'is a bit of me.'

I stood there watching for what seemed like ages before getting back in the car and continuing my journey. All day I couldn't get the image of those men and their ponies out of my head. From that tiny taste I was as hooked as any junkie could be and I knew then that this was a game for me.

When I got home that evening I was still bubbling with enthusiasm about the idea of playing polo and followed Jackie around the house like a small child, excitedly telling her every detail of what I'd seen and explaining how much I wanted to try it for myself.

'Just one problem,' she said, when I eventually let her get a word in.

'What's that?' I demanded, unable to see a single reason why I couldn't become an instant polo player.

'You can't ride.'

Bollocks to that, I thought, but said nothing.

It was true that I'd only ever sat on a horse once in my life, and on that occasion I hadn't done anything more than plod gently along on top of an old nag which had frankly seen better days. But I was sure I would be able to find my way round what I thought was such a minor obstacle. I brushed it aside as a mere detail that could quickly be rectified. I don't know if Jackie had as much faith in my abilities to learn a new skill overnight as I did, or whether she just wanted to show me the error of my ways, but it was soon after that that she bought me the day out at polo.

We decided, or should I say I decided, that we would take a weekend together to use both these vouchers. Jackie's mum agreed to look after the kids for the weekend and I booked to do the flight on a Dolphin L29 fighter jet on the Saturday and the polo on the Sunday. As compensation to Jackie for having to sit around watching me as I indulged myself, I agreed to go with her to Bluewater shopping centre after the flight. Even though I admit I'm a selfish shopper and find trailing around after Jackie as she wanders back and forth deliberating over every single purchase almost unbearable, I could see that I was still getting the best of the deal by a long way.

I was looking forward to my weekend full of adventure with mounting excitement as it approached and on the day of the flight I leapt out of bed eager with anticipation. I got up, dressed, and was ready to get out of the door within half an hour, hurrying poor Jackie along all the way out the house and into the car. I think her eyes eventually opened as I slammed the car door and headed down to Manston Airport in Kent. It was a beautiful sunny morning and the air was crisp and fresh, with only a scattering of clouds in the sky. A perfect day for flying, I thought, as if I spent my life in the air and knew all about it. Jackie packed the video camera so that every second of my airborne adventure would be captured for posterity.

'I hope you enjoy this,' she said as we drove down. 'I hope you don't get sick.'

I suddenly remembered watching Jeremy Clarkson being thrown about on the F14 fighter jet, and the internal cameras filming him being ill over and over again. Wimp, I had thought. It had never occurred to me that such a thing would happen to me and I was confident nothing was going to spoil my day.

We arrived in plenty of time, with Jackie repeatedly pointing out that she could have had an extra hour in bed, and I was introduced to my pilot, Gary, who owned the Dolphin L29 two-seater jet plane and who made his living by providing thrills for adrenalin junkies like me. He was all kitted out in his flying gear and looking the business. My pulse was beginning to thump as I was taken to change into my co-pilot's gear, a green flying suit and helmet, and I could feel the tension of excitement building in my stomach. The pilot's wife was handling all the administration details and there were forms for me to sign and procedures to go through, listing minor details like, 'If you have to eject that's not our responsibility' – you know the kind of stuff.

'Well, enjoy your flight, Kevin,' she said, once the forms were signed. 'Don't forget, if you feel ill there's a sick bag on the right-hand side of the cockpit.'

I ignored the idea once again. It wasn't even going to enter my mind. I wanted to get on and enjoy this rush of adrenalin and I definitely wasn't going to do a 'Jeremy'. But she carried on, 'If you throw up in the plane, you'll have to clean it up yourself and there'll be a fifty-pound fine, so please use the bag.' No way was I going to do anything so pathetic. I'll leave that for Clarkson, I thought.

Gary then came back in to escort me to the plane and we both strode out on to the tarmac. The plane looked huge and I was getting more and more excited as we got closer and closer to this magnificent beast. I momentarily forgot who I was as we drew close to the jet, having visions of Tom Cruise in *Top Gun*, but I managed to get a grip and come back to reality before calling my pilot 'Iceman'. It was a great feeling; I was finally doing something I'd always dreamed of.

Gary walked me around the single-engine jet explaining things to me as he did his pre-flight checks.

'So, Kevin,' he said, 'what would you like to do? We could do some acrobatics or some low-level flying.'

'Oh, you know,' I replied, trying to sound casual, 'let's just get up there and throw it about a bit.'

It didn't occur to me that this might be the worst thing imaginable to say to a pilot who wants nothing more than to relieve the boredom of normal flying with a bit of extra daredevilry. I'd just given him permission to do whatever he liked – a huge mistake!

I climbed into my seat behind his with my back to the engine and he strapped me in tightly, showing me how the ejector seat worked and telling me the commands he would give in an emergency. He then pointed over my right shoulder to the sick bags at the side of the cockpit, in case they were needed. Looking back now I have to admit he did have a slightly sinister smile on his face. I just grinned confidently back, much like a turkey enjoying a pre-Christmas pep talk from Bernard Matthews.

Once in the plane Gary gunned the engine with a mighty roar that throbbed through my whole body, making every hair on my skin rise with anticipation and my legs tingle with excitement. Jackie was filming every moment, and I waved from behind the pilot with a grin that could have lifted the plane on its own.

As we taxied off I looked around the cockpit. There were buttons and knobs everywhere in front of me and down the sides. All of them must have had a purpose, but not for me. The only thing I had to decide was where to rest my arms and hands to be sure I didn't touch anything by mistake. I decided to put them on my legs. This was something I'd wanted to do for so long and I was loving every moment. That was of course until we got into the air.

Gary, my trusted pilot, gave me a few instructions over the headphones as we taxied out on to the runway, his voice surrounded with static, just like in the movies. While he communicated with the tower we remained stationary, waiting for our moment to take off. Then the engine erupted and roared into action. It grew louder and louder, making my whole body tingle with excitement. Gary must have let go of the brakes because we raced along the runway and, with another huge roar, we took off. We were up above the sea within seconds, looking down on a cargo ship below, the water as still as a millpond, reflecting the dazzling sun.

As we climbed high up into a safe position we made smalltalk over the radio. Then Gary's tone changed and he said in a serious voice, 'OK, Kevin, first we need to see if you can take some Gs.'

Before I could answer he'd flipped the plane over to the right and we plummeted through the skies, soaring up at the last moment to complete a full loop.

'Fuuuuuuuuuuuuuuuuuuuck!' Suddenly it felt like my arse was being sucked out the back of the plane. My hands were all over the place and I grabbed on to the seat belt, clinging on as if my life depended on it. He then brought the jet back to its original position before flipping it and doing a loop to the left, with the same result. My neck was so tense from fighting with the G-forces that I had to rest it on the back of the seat.

Oh, shit, I thought, as he kept throwing the jet about like a child running around the house with a toy plane. Where did they say those sick bags were?

I wasn't going to ask Gary, who seemed to be relishing the freedom I'd given him to hurl his plane around the skies. My eyes were frantically scanning the cockpit. I looked down and there they were, three wax paper bags. I grabbed one and was instantly sick. 'Oh, bollocks,' I said to myself, my eyes beginning to feel as giddy as a drunk and my stomach heaving.

'You all right, Kevin?' he asked, but didn't wait for an answer before heading off into a series of different manoeuvres, each one more stomach-churning than the last. We went up in a vertical line, the jet blasting us through the sky, resting at the top for a few seconds before heading straight down with such force that the smile was put back on my face by the G-force. Gary then banked it to the right then the left – you name it he did it. Had you been listening in all you would have heard coming from the back of the jet was 'fuck', 'shit', 'bollocks', 'fuck'.

My main concern now was how not to spill the contents of the sick bag and what to do if it split as I went back to use it again and again. I couldn't believe that I'd been ill within only a few minutes of being up in the air and I still had another painful twenty-eight minutes to endure. I couldn't reach for a new bag because I now didn't know where to put the full one.

'Are you OK, Kevin?' he asked again.

'Bastard!' I replied, and he just laughed. Sadist, I thought to myself.

Eventually he took mercy on me. 'Kevin, would you like to take control? It'll help you focus your mind.' He obviously knew I'd been ill. 'Also, try looking ahead.' He could have told me that at the beginning, I thought.

As I tried to focus on what was outside the plane rather than on what was inside my stomach, I wondered what to look at. I could barely see out of the cockpit as I grasped the flight stick, holding the sick bag in my other hand as I took control.

'I have control,' I said, like I knew what I was doing.

'You have control,' he confirmed, and there I was, flying a jet.

'Move the stick about a bit,' Gary told me, but I had no idea how responsive the jet would be.

I pushed it forward and we dropped so hard and fast that all I said was, 'You have control.' In fact I think I might have screamed it rather than said it, sounding a bit like Jackie when she comes across a spider unexpectedly.

Gary instantly took over. 'Have you had enough acrobatics?' he said.

'I'd say so.'

I admitted that I couldn't take any more, but was determined not to go back early. We then came down to do some low-level flying between the cargo ships, which had looked so close together from high up in the skies, but now seemed miles apart as we sped over the calm, sparkling waters of the open sea that looked to be no more than a hundred feet below our wings.

By this time I felt so ill and weak I couldn't even respond when he spoke to me. Returning to the airport he performed one last loop before coming in to land and then threw open the canopy so I could take some welcome gulps of fresh air. I could see Jackie and the pilot's wife coming over towards us, with Jackie filming as she walked, and there was nothing else I could do but hold my unbroken sick bag triumphantly in the air like a trophy. I got out and fell to the ground, knackered, tired and feeling very queasy. The tarmac was moving uncomfortably beneath my feet.

'Full respect to Jeremy Clarkson,' I murmured weakly.

'What?' the three of them said.

'Nothing,' I replied, not having the energy to explain.

Gary gave me a pat on the back and strode inside as Jackie knelt down beside me.

'Are you all right?' she asked. Her voice sounded concerned, but I was sure I could detect a smirk on her face.

That afternoon I did my very best to keep my side of the bargain with Jackie, trailing along behind her at the shopping centre from one noisy, stuffy, overcrowded shop to the next with my insides wobbling precariously around, wondering if I would ever be able to face the sight of food and drink again. Eventually I couldn't take another step, my face was pale and all I could think to myself was, serves you right. By four o'clock I was back home lying on the sofa, still feeling green, and our plan for going out to dinner that evening had to be scrapped.

It's great to have an opportunity to live out your childhood dreams because I now know that I never want to go near a jet fighter ever again, even if I live to be a hundred. I went to bed early that evening in order to get a good night's rest before my next adventure. At least all I'd have to do there was hit a ball, I thought.

I was still feeling rough when I woke up the following morning and set off for my day's polo experience. I'd been looking forward to the flying but having discovered what that involved I had become quietly confident that I would enjoy the polo more. As we arrived, however, the reality of the situation began to dawn on me, reminding me that I'd never actually ridden a hourse properly before. I pushed my doubts to the back of my mind, telling myself that anything must be possible after that jet ride.

Even as the day got under way I wasn't sure if I was in the right place. The men I'd watched playing in the field by the roadside had impressed me with their speed and ferocity and the control they had over their ponies. It seemed a long way from standing on a milk crate on a Sunday morning in the middle of winter, in a line with nine other novices, swiping at a ball with a mallet. After a couple of hours of standing on the milk crates they then explained the basics of the game and it was time to get on to my first polo pony.

When the instructors brought the ponies out they looked extremely bored, nothing like the energetic animals I'd watched that day over the hedge. I realized that no one in their right mind would allow a bunch of beginners to use their finest string of polo ponies and that this might be a good place to start. An old grey pony was brought up to me. It remained stationary and quiet and seemed well behaved – just what I needed. I stood on top of the milk crate and clambered on to the pony as it stood, solid and patient. No problem. I then tried to get it started. I could almost feel it sighing with resignation beneath me as I flipped my arms like a chicken and my legs pumped back and forth as if I was pedal-ling a pushbike.

This animal was obviously so used to dealing with inexperienced idiots like me it knew that all it had to do was walk to where the ball was, stop and wait for me to hit it and I would be happy. So there I was in the arena, swinging the mallet, missing the ball and now and then hitting the pony's legs, then looking round to see if anyone had seen me do it. I caught Jackie's eye and we exchanged grins. On the odd occasion that I did hit the ball the little grey would stroll on to wherever it had landed and wait patiently until I managed to repeat the exercise.

It was a pleasant way to spend a day, but hardly enough to get the adrenalin pumping through the veins. I knew I wanted more. After my group lesson and being told my day had come to an end, I got off the pony feeling as though I was walking like a frog. I hopped out of the arena and Jackie and I stayed to watch the game that was on after us. The riders suddenly became competitive and I felt the same rush of excitement as when I first saw the men practising in the field. I loved the atmosphere of the place, the pounding of the hoofs and the scent of the horses. I couldn't wait to get out on to the field and try it out for myself on a pony that was actually willing to move. But first I had to learn to play the game properly.

Nothing that happened that day had put me off trying the game, in fact it cemented in my mind the idea that this was something I really wanted to do, although I could see that I would have to get a lot more training before I could even think about going out to play properly. There was also no getting away from the fact that I was going to have to learn to ride as well. It wasn't that I was afraid of horses, exactly, I just didn't know what to expect from them and consequently wasn't confident around them. They seemed to be a lot bigger than me and somewhat unpredictable, especially with my chicken arms and bicycle legs.

All the way home I was still brimming with enthusiasm. My first taste of polo had whetted my appetite and I wanted more. The next day I rang the polo club and asked about going to the next stage. They advised having some individual coaching with one of their professionals. They booked me in for lessons the following week with a professional polo player by the name of Martin.

'So,' he said when I turned up on the first day, 'how many times have you ridden?'

'Oh,' I searched the air for an appropriate number, as if there had been so many times it was hard to remember, anxious not to be given the same donkey they'd put me on before, but also not wanting something that would be way out of my league. 'Twelve, fifteen times,' I said, guessing that this figure would at least get me off the starting block.

Martin nodded as if that was enough information for him. He lent me some polo boots, a polo stick, a whip and, most importantly, a helmet and we headed over to the arena once more where a suitable pony for my fabricated experience was awaiting my arrival. As I got closer I could see that it was a lot leaner, younger and more powerful than the grey I first tried. I strode over to mount it in what I hoped would seem like an experienced manner, both to Martin and to the pony itself. I knew it was important to show the animal who was boss from the start. It was only when I took hold of the saddle and slotted one foot into a stirrup that I realized I couldn't get on. I didn't appear to have any of the necessary muscles to simultaneously jump and throw my leg over in the casual way the professionals did. I might be fit enough to refurbish a house or run a few miles, but I still couldn't make my limbs perform this simple task. I scanned the area for the milk crate I'd used previously but it was nowhere to be found. I couldn't allow myself to be beaten at this early stage and eventually, with a great deal of huffing and puffing, I managed to hoist myself on board with Martin holding the saddle firmly down on the other side to counter-balance me. I thought at one point that the pony was going to fall on top of me as I struggled to get on. Eventually, there I was on top of this beautiful-looking polo pony, feeling proud of myself simply to have mounted it; but it was now far too late to convince the animal that I was master of the situation.

I don't know what I did to indicate to him that he should take off at full speed the moment I was on top of him, but he did, and before I knew it I was back on the ground again, exactly where I'd started, except this time I was on my backside. Martin patiently told me what I had done wrong.

'You kicked into his belly and let the reins loosen at the same time,' he said. 'Settle into the saddle, keep your legs away from his belly. Think of him as a Ferrari. He's very powerful and very responsive and you must handle him with care, as you would the car, otherwise you may be giving him signals without even knowing it.'

'Let's try that again,' he suggested politely as I stood up, swearing under my breath as I dusted myself off.

Any hope of recovering my dignity vanished when exactly the same thing happened a second time and Martin realized he was going to have to change the pony and give me a few tips just to keep me mounted long enough to learn something about the game. Eventually I had to admit that I might have got my calculations wrong and perhaps I hadn't ridden quite as many times as I'd first thought.

'I think I may have forgotten quite a lot of what I was taught,' I blathered. 'It was so long ago.'

I got the impression he knew what I was saying and didn't seem surprised, just chuckling as if he had known all along.

The pony, who I dare say was also still chuckling to himself at having called my bluff so easily, was taken away and another one was brought out. My heart sank as I recognized the same animal I'd had on the first day, but I was hardly in a position to protest and actually I was quite looking forward to not falling off for a while. Martin patiently explained once more:

'Keep your legs away from its belly. Just grip on with your knees.'

I'd never used these inner-leg muscles before and it wasn't long before my legs were burning from the strain of trying to grip with my knees and inner thighs. The pain didn't last long and I was soon sitting comfortably, walking and slowly cantering around the arena. My bottom bumping out of sequence with the pony made my whole body shake. But when I did manage to hit the ball from time to time a smile would spread across my face just long enough to register my delight before my body was bouncing around the arena once more.

The more I learnt about the game the more I realized how much skill was needed in order to succeed. I was determined to become good at it, but I knew that wouldn't happen overnight, especially with my lack of riding skills. Hitting a ball with a mallet in your right hand while controlling a horse with your left is not easy. I realized that this was going to be a very dangerous sport if I didn't learn to ride properly and so, to begin with, my lessons consisted mainly of riding, with the last twenty minutes being stick and ball skills around the arena. From there I began playing in 'practice chukkas'.

Just to explain to those of you who aren't familiar with the game, polo teams are made up of four players and a game consists of either four, five or six seven-minute periods, depending on the level of polo being played. Each period of play is called a 'chukka'. At the end of a chukka the first bell rings and an additional thirty seconds is given until the ball goes out of play or a foul is committed. Once the second bell has rung the players stop play immediately and there is a three-minute interval during which the players leave the ground and the ponies are changed. Each player is handicapped annually and a handicap can range from minus two to ten. The figures refer to the player's value to the team. Being a beginner I was a 'minus-two' player and at the other end of the scale there are only a handful of ten-goal players in the world. Each team is built from scratch, with the sum of the players' handicaps being added together to make sure that teams are broadly similar in skill. So a four-goal competition is one in which the players' combined handicaps must not exceed four. Every time a goal is scored the teams effectively change ends and have to try to score in the opposite goal. A player following in the line behind the ball he or she has just hit has the 'Right of Way' over everyone else on the field. It is the most important rule of polo and is there to prevent serious injury to both players and ponies. You can of course ride people off the line. Got it? I hope so.

Anyhow, the practice chukkas were designed to bring me in slowly to the game and, more importantly, to teach me the theory of who should be where and what not to do in order to avoid dangerous play. When you're galloping around a pitch at forty miles an hour with only a helmet to protect you, it's all too easy to seriously injure yourself or other players if you're not vigilant and careful.

The more I practised the less nervous I became around the ponies. I really began to feel affection for these gracious animals, finding myself able to get closer and enjoy them more. They seemed to be able to sense my growing confidence but I knew that if I wanted to play seriously I needed to buy my own ponies, and that riding them regularly would give me the extra level of confidence I needed to move forward with my game.

I spent hours watching, picking up hints just from seeing the professionals play. I wanted to play more but I couldn't since renting ponies was an expensive business and I had very limited funds. I knew that I would have to wait until the time was right for me to buy my first polo pony.

I spoke about it at great length many times with Jackie, who could see that it was something I was passionate about, even after my limited experience. We had a little bit of money in the bank left over from the advance I'd received for *The Kid* and she agreed to let me use it to purchase my first polo pony. We knew that you actually need a minimum of four ponies in order to play seriously, but one was enough for now and at least I knew it would get me started.

I'd heard through friends of a couple who were in the game and might be able to help me, so I went to meet them. They told me they knew of some good ponies in Argentina, the international home of polo. Since I had no other contacts in the polo world and wouldn't have known how to start going about buying a pony on my own in England, I agreed to let them buy one on my behalf. They knew the sort of thing I needed, something for a beginner with the ability to grow with me as my skills improved, and so made the buying decision for me.

Just before the start of the season, which runs from the end of April to the end of September, I took delivery of Mistico, a delicate and agile pony, jet black with a white stripe on the crown of its head. Mistico gradually lightened in colour through the summer like a chameleon. I'd acquired my first animal and I must say he looked magnificent. It felt brilliant. I was now looking forward to the season ahead, knowing that if I was going to improve at any reasonable rate I needed to find somewhere where I could go to play as often as possible. With that in mind I joined Knepp Castle Polo Club in West Sussex, about thirty minutes' drive from the house. I couldn't wait to get started.

11. A Bit of Pampering

The Kid was due to be published. Even though I was busily getting on with my new life, I once again found myself becoming apprehensive as memories and visions of my past began to reappear as publication day drew closer and closer. Before publication day I thought it would be a good idea for Jackie and me to spend some quality time together in order to calm us down. We were both tense with a mixture of excitement and nerves. Jackie isn't interested in anything to do with adrenalin rushes or fast-moving sports. Her idea of a really good day out is to relax at a health spa, somewhere where she can be a million miles away from the demands of the house and the children. She loves nothing better than to wander around in a luxurious dressing gown being pampered from head to toe. Since she was always so tolerant of my little enthusiasms I thought the least I could do was take her for a weekend at a health farm.

She was keen to show me how great it would be to relax and let go of my inhibitions a bit, and had booked me in for a batch of treatments like a massage and a seaweed wrap. Just the names of the treatments filled me with a strange foreboding. To start with I'm not very good at sitting still. I can't even stay in one room of my own house for more than an hour or two at a time without wanting to get up and move about. I was also unsure how I would feel about being touched by a stranger, even if they were a professional masseur. I dare say it all stems from my childhood.

Anyhow, the massage was the first thing on the weekend itinerary and I ventured cautiously into my allotted candlelit cubicle. I sat in my trunks on the long, funny-looking bed with a hole at one end and, after a while, a lady came in dressed in white. She told me her name, which I was too nervous to remember, and I told her mine and then she asked me to lie face down. She draped a towel over my trunks. Now I realized that the hole was there to stop me from suffocating.

It didn't start well. I couldn't stop chattering through the breathing hole, which was sticking to my cheeks making me sound as if I'd just had my teeth taken out. Then, as the woman put her warm soft hands on me, and started to oil me up with some sweet-smelling lotion, I began to feel deeply uncomfortable. I wanted to overcome the feelings and relax and so I stopped talking, which my cheeks were very happy about, and attempted to enjoy the experience like other people. I tried to force myself, but it was impossible. I lay there completely rigid, very awake and unable to relax. Whatever barriers against being touched by strangers had been built in my brain from my past weren't going to evaporate just because I wanted them to. I could tell I was going to end up feeling far worse at the finish of the session than I had when I first walked in.

'I'm so sorry,' I told the rather shocked woman, sitting up and sliding off the table, 'it's nothing to do with you. I'm sure you're really good at this, but it's my first massage and I'm really not enjoying the experience.'

I escaped from the cubicle as quickly as I could, leaving the poor woman looking puzzled as I hurried to our room to get the gunge off my back.

The next thing Jackie had booked for us was the seaweed wrap. After the massage experience, she told me she thought this one would be right up my street, and was trying to convince me, unable to suppress the odd burst of giggles. What the hell was I about to put myself through? I wondered. We both arrived at the appointed place at the appointed time to be greeted by two people looking like nurses, dressed in all white, who led us into separate cubicles. Jackie smiled at me as I went into my room and I poked my tongue out at her before she was out of sight. I could hear her giggle as the door was closed behind me. Inside was another couch, but this time there was no hole in it. Instead there were layers of some sort of filmy material, which were hanging down from either side. The lady offered to take my dressing gown and handed me a pair of what looked like rubber incontinence pants. I warily placed them over my swimming shorts and was led to the waiting couch for my treatment.

I lay down on the plastic film and prepared myself for the experience, determined to do my best to see this one through to the end and enjoy it. The very polite lady who was going to be administering the treatment then came over with her pot of slimy green seaweed gunk, which absolutely stank. This didn't make me feel any more comfortable than I probably looked. She then smothered me in the foul-smelling paste from the neck downwards.

My skin felt like it was burning off me. My arms were down at my sides and, once she'd thoroughly basted me, she pulled the cling film round me, trussing me up like Tutankhamun's mummy. As the heat built up inside the wrap she spread a layer of towels over it and finally what looked like tin foil on top of that.

I stayed very still and quiet and forced myself to just chill as the temperature inside my cocoon rose to what felt like combustible levels. The sweat was pouring off me as I lay there wondering if I was going to be able to last for the whole thirty-minute session. I knew Jackie was in the next cubicle and would be loving every minute of this, so I gritted my teeth and held on, waiting to feel the benefit.

'I'll be back in thirty minutes,' the lady said, when she'd finished preparing and wrapping me like Christmas dinner.

'But what do I do now?' I squeaked, trying in vain to keep my voice as relaxed as I could.

'Try closing your eyes and enjoying it,' she said, as if it was the most obvious thing in the world. She turned on some kind of rainforest music and quietly closed the door behind her. My eyes were shut and I was suddenly alone, simmering in my own private oven.

The minutes ticked slowly past and it wasn't long before I began to get the fidgets. Beads of sweat were trickling down from my brow, puddling in my eye sockets and then overflowing on to my nose, making it itch. Because I was unable to move my arms to scratch, the intensity of the itching increased and I started contorting my face into strange expressions to try to stop them. It didn't work. I tried to ignore the itching, thinking perhaps I could exert mind over matter, but it was hopeless, the need to scratch merely intensified. It was no good; I was going to have to do something about it.

Terrified of disturbing her careful wrapping, I inched my right hand slowly across my stomach, up over my chest towards the opening for my head. After what seemed like an age my fingers made it into the fresh air and, blessed relief, I was able to scratch my nose, leaving a blob of the smelly gunk on the end of it. Lost in the bliss of the moment I forgot myself and moved too far. I felt the tension of the wrapping go as the left side fell away. 'Oh shit,' I said.

Still moving in slow motion, while at the same time trying to blow the sweaty gunk away from my nose, I slid my other arm across my chest and attempted to pull the wrapping back round me, but the strain was too much, the overall cocoon had been weakened and I felt a blast of cool air as the right side fell away as well. 'Fuck!' I said.

I now had to employ both hands to try to re-wrap myself from

The Kid Moves On

inside the parcel before the woman returned and saw the mess I'd
made of her handiwork, and I was also bloody freezing. Now that
the wrap was off the outside air was getting to my hot skin and I
was beginning to shiver with cold. The green slime was escaping
over everything as I struggled to pull both sides back together. I
must have struggled for fifteen minutes before the lady came in to
check how I was getting on and saw her work strewn around the
room in ruins.

'Get me out of here,' I ranted. 'I bloody hate this.'

'Aren't you enjoying it?' She looked dismayed as I sat up like the
monster from the Black Lagoon, the seaweed falling all around me.

'No, I am not,' I said. 'I just want a shower to get rid of this
smell.'

Once I was showered and fresh-smelling again I went to find
myself a comfy bed by the pool and sat reading a book. Jackie came
to sit with me a short while afterwards. I explained what had
happened, but she'd already heard from the staff and we couldn't
help laughing together. I decided that for the rest of the weekend
I would leave the treatments to Jackie.

12. Published

As the moment of publication drew nearer I became more and more concerned about the path I'd chosen to follow. I kept seeing myself huddled into a corner with Gloria and Dennis hovering over me and I began withdrawing further inside my thoughts. I tried to prepare myself mentally for what was about to happen, but it all felt so personal; having the world reading about things I'd been keeping secret for so many years still left me feeling as naked as on the first visit to the publishers. My recollections of the past seemed as vivid and real today as they had all those years before, mainly because I now understood clearly what was going on, whereas as a child I would just put up with it. Everyone who read the book would now know the kind of degrading, embarrassing things that I went through as a child, as well as the things I'd got up to as a young adult.

The process of putting everything on paper was the first time in my life that I'd ever thought deeply about my early life and attempted to understand what had happened to me, rather than simply blocking it out and trying to fool myself into believing it had never happened. It was as if the truth had been festering unexamined and untreated in my head for years and, as well as worrying about how the public would react to finding out about it, I also had to come to terms with what I had written myself, which I didn't seem to be able to do.

I had to work out a way to handle the truth now that it was coming out into the open. I could no longer stick my head in the sand and hope it would all go away. These things really had happened and I needed to find a way to deal with them. If I didn't then I was afraid I would be going further and further back inside myself, which would affect my family, the three people I loved and felt most protective about.

People like Barbara and the publishers kept telling me that I had nothing to be embarrassed about or ashamed of, and I dare say in their eyes I didn't; but in mine I did because I went through it and now it seemed as though I was reliving the whole nightmare again, day after day. Because I wasn't sleeping well either, this was making me tired during the day and I often felt lethargic. Lying awake in the middle of the night was the worst time for my thoughts. I tried to break the cycle by taking some sleeping pills to help me sleep all through the night but this just made me even more dopey during the day, so I stopped. I knew there was no going back now and that was a frightening prospect as I didn't have control of the childhood thoughts which now seemed to be whirling around my head twenty-four seven. It was as if I'd started the ball rolling and I couldn't do anything to control where it went or when it would stop as it gathered momentum. I was beginning to fear that it might do some damage as it hurtled on its way.

I arrived home from taking one of the kids to school a few weeks before publication to find the post had been. My eyes were instantly drawn to the brown envelope. I just knew what it would contain. It was A4 in size with the Penguin logo shining out on the white address label, giving the game away. I deliberately opened the other post first, leaving the large envelope on the kitchen table while I made myself some toast, my eyes constantly being drawn back to it. In the end I couldn't put the moment off any longer. I sat at the table alone, Jackie having gone out, and I opened it. There it was, my first copy of *The Kid*. I looked all around the book, smelling and feeling it all over. I didn't read any of the words inside as I already knew what was in there. The team at Michael Joseph had obviously invested a lot of effort, and the photographer and designer had produced a stunning cover with a white background and a photograph of the back view of a small, bedraggled boy. My story was printed and published and about to be released to the public. Money had been invested, contracts had been signed and foreign rights were being sold to places as varied as Japan and Denmark. My life had become a product, part of the business cycle and in some respects I thought it would be easier to try to treat it that way.

The cover reminded me of being in that room playing with the train I'd acquired from a jumble sale, the music playing quietly from the Walkman that had been given to me by my teacher, Colin Smith, both of which I hid in my mattress during the day.

As I sat down and stared at it for a while, I wondered what Gloria and Dennis would say when they saw it. Would they deny everything and call me a liar? Would they claim that none of it had ever happened? Only time would tell but, you know what, I really didn't care what they thought. Recent events had hardened me to that. What I did know was that the juggernaut was picking up speed and there was no way I could jump off now. All I could do was hang on tight and hope for the best. I placed the book gently back down on the kitchen table. I got myself a pen and wrote inside, '*To my darling Jackie, I mean every word, all my love, K.*' It instinctively seemed the right thing to do with the first copy.

The publishing team had invited me to London for the odd lunch during the previous few months and I would sit happily in restaurants in the midst of all these enthusiastic young ladies, listening to them talk of serialization deals with newspapers and interviews with the media. I tried not to think or tell them of how I was feeling about suddenly being exposed to the world, or confess that I was finding it hard to come to terms with what I had written, especially with the latest revelations about how Gloria was behaving now.

I received a call late one afternoon to tell me that a serialization deal had been agreed with the *Daily Mail*, which meant they would be printing extracts from the book just before publication. They didn't want to interview me, which I was slightly relieved about, but I was then booked up to do about five interviews with other newspapers and radio programmes after the serialization had appeared. In total the publicity was going to be spread over four weeks.

This was getting scary. I was working myself into a panic and getting annoyed with myself for not being able to think calmly about my past without conjuring up hosts of demons. I tried to remember the good times, like my time at Yarborough children's home where I spent nearly two years away from the house. Then I thought of the day I was sent back home and pictured Uncle David bending down on his knees to say goodbye. I remembered getting out of the social worker's car and walking up the path to the family house once more, knowing that I didn't have any say in my own fate and that nobody would be asking if I wanted to go back. Stepping in front of the media felt as though I was walking out on stage dressed as Worzel Gummidge again. In agreeing to sell the book I'd taken on the responsibility for making it work in any way I could, no matter how apprehensive I might feel at the prospect of talking about my past to a stranger. Sometimes when I thought about it I would start to cry, feeling vulnerable and nervous in a world where everyone would be taking me at face value without knowing me. I was determined to go through with my end of the deal and do everything within my power to make the book a success. The only way I would be able to deal with it was to just keep my head high and not think about all the attention that might be coming my way.

One evening close to publication I looked at myself hard in the mirror. 'I agreed to do this,' I said, staring intensely into my own eyes. 'I was the one who opened the can of worms and I was quick enough to accept the advance money. No one forced me into it. I could always have said "No". Now I have to go through with it and in time I will show everyone that I can move away from my past and prove to them what I am capable of.'

As if that wasn't enough for me to focus on, other things were about to spiral out of control and history was about to repeat itself yet again.

13. Feeling Exposed

The serialization of *The Kid* came out in the *Daily Mail* as expected, just before the book was launched into the shops. The first morning it was out I got up just as the sun was rising, having lain awake thinking about it all through the night. I went to get the paper, not knowing quite what to expect or quite how I felt about it all. Although I understood that they would be printing extracts from the story, and despite the fact that I had posed for their photographer, I was still taken by surprise when I actually opened the paper on that first morning in the car before going home to show Jackie. There it was, the serialization of *The Kid* with a small picture of my adult face staring out at me, and one of the few pictures in existence of me as a child blown up on the opposite page for maximum impact. My eyes quickly scanned over it. My heart was racing. I was, I must admit, excited and nervous, but I knew I didn't want to read beyond lurid headlines:

TORTURED BY HIS OWN PARENTS

It's one of the most shocking stories you will ever read. This boy's parents beat him, bit him, crushed his fingers in a mangle and starved him until he ached with hunger. And the welfare workers who could have saved him just turned their backs.

It's one thing understanding intellectually that something is going to happen, quite another to experience it. I knew the story was coming and I knew they were bound to sensationalize it, but when I saw it there in black and white and realized that the millions of people who bought the paper that day would be seeing the same thing, I felt terrifyingly exposed and worried that people would feel sorry for me. The one reaction I dreaded the most. I could imagine how neighbours, acquaintances and friends who had known nothing about my past would be ringing one another and talking about it when they realized that it was about someone they knew. The only people I'd told were my brothers and sisters. Jackie had told her mother, but that was it. I imagined people who knew my brothers and sisters would be taking the paper to show them, if they hadn't seen it for themselves already. I wondered if anyone would have the courage to show it to Gloria and I imagined her screaming and banging once more against the glass panel, with me just continuing to draw, ignoring her. If she saw it, she would read me describing scenes that she must have hoped no one else would ever know about unless they were in the house at the time. All these questions and feelings were spinning through my mind as I tried to get them into some sort of order.

When I got home I showed Jackie the pages. We both knew what was contained in those columns of words and didn't need to go through it all again. We decided just to put the article away without reading it and get on with everything else we had planned to do with our day. I was determined to stay in control of my emotions, not knowing what sort of reaction I might expect from the outside world.

The day passed without any reaction. The calm was almost spooky. The next day they printed the second instalment with a large picture of me as I look today and another dramatic headline.

My brutal parents beat me. Then I was drawn into a life of guns and violence. All I wanted to do was die . . . until one woman's love brought me hope.

'Bloody hell,' I said when I saw the picture. 'I look like Camp Freddie from *The Italian Job*.'

We laughed and put the paper away with the other one, getting on with our daily life once more. Nothing terrible had happened. The sky hadn't fallen in on us, so maybe this wasn't going to be so difficult after all.

The book might not yet have been launched, but the story certainly had. This picture was easily identifiable as being me and over the following few days I began to notice that strangers were recognizing me in the street. They didn't come up to me, but they would look twice, and maybe nudge someone to point me out. None of it was hostile, but it still made me want to pull back inside myself and hide my face. I was frightened of making eye contact with them in case they were able to see just how vulnerable I felt.

Jackie noticed that I was becoming increasingly jumpy and agitated as the date of the book launch loomed closer.

'Are you OK?' she asked one day, when I was feeling particularly sombre.

'It all feels a little weird,' I replied. She put her arms around me and I hid my face in her chest. She didn't know what to say, but her quiet support and love was enough to comfort me. She could understand now why I would wake early in the morning and come downstairs, unable to sleep, my thoughts driving me insane as I constantly churned over and over the past.

Then late one evening, a few days before publication, Jackie and I were getting ready to go to bed when the phone rang. It was one of those calls that I instinctively knew was wrong. I don't know how I knew that, I just did. I picked it up and it was one of my sisters. Jackie had already gone upstairs. My sister didn't bother to exchange any pleasantries.

'All you all right?' I asked, feeling a little too tired for a long conversation and wanting to get to bed.

She immediately explained that another of my sisters had had her five children taken into care. They had all been placed into a temporary foster home together. My stomach turned over in a horribly familiar way. I was now fully awake, all thoughts of settling down to sleep banished once more. I walked into the lounge and sat down, completely speechless. The news came completely out of the blue. I'd been talking to the sister in question just a few weeks before and she'd been telling me that everything was fine, but obviously it couldn't have been even then.

It was the same family of children who had been smacked by Gloria a few months before and I began to picture exactly what they must have been going through before the Social Services took them to safety. It seemed that it wasn't just Gloria who'd been giving them a hard time. I listened to everything my sister had to tell me and we agreed to speak again soon. I felt as if I was in a daze as I went upstairs and told Jackie what had happened. She was as shocked as me and obviously didn't know what to say or do either. I no longer felt like going to bed, knowing that I wouldn't be able to sleep, so I went back downstairs and sat alone on the sofa feeling numb with shock and sadness.

My mind went back and all I could think about was how long the kids had suffered before the authorities had decided things were so bad they had to step in. I could so easily imagine how frightening and unhappy their lives must have been, and might still be, and it made me feel physically sick. I sat there for over an hour, a thousand thoughts going through my mind. I was angry and confused about what I was feeling. In the end I couldn't fight back the tears any longer. I sat on the sofa and cried more uncontrollably than I ever had before. Jackie must have heard me and came downstairs, shocked by my show of emotion and held me tightly. I'd never cried so much and I felt like screaming the house down with pure frustration just as I had done all those years before.

For the next week my mind turned everything over and over, never finding any answers or any comfort apart from the fact that I could be fairly confident the children were now in a safe place. I couldn't sleep or rest because my thoughts and worries of what might have happened to them were so loud in my head.

I tried so many times to get their mother to talk to me but she didn't answer my calls and eventually the phone number went dead. She must have been too embarrassed to admit what had been going on and, obviously, the authorities wouldn't give me any information beyond the barest facts. It was as if the children had been swallowed up into a huge silence, leaving us to imagine what had been happening to them, but from talking more to my other sisters I began to get a clearer picture about how badly the kids had been treated and how their only hope of a better life would come from being taken into care.

However hard I tried to focus on what was going on in my life now, I kept finding myself being drawn back into the past and remembering how one of my nephews had clung to me when I'd last visited them. Looking back now I realized he must have been starving for some affection. He was a very quiet boy, always ready to please, and the thought of him brought back so many memories of myself at that age. I remembered how desperate I'd been for so long and wondered if it had been the same for him. Questions kept going round and round in my head; they wouldn't stop. I kept winding myself up with the same, constant questions: Could I have done more to help at that stage? Should I be doing more to rescue them now? What should I be doing to help them now? No matter how many times I asked, I couldn't find answers to any of the questions.

One thought I could take some comfort from was that they were safe now, or at least I thought so.

14. Nowhere to Hide

With all this weighing down my thoughts, I had to start doing the publicity for the book. If I'd been nervous about it before, I was dreading it now, knowing that I wouldn't be able to talk about the one thing that was now uppermost in my mind, the plight of my sister's children and how ashamed and useless I felt that such things were still happening in the Lewis family today.

Once the *Daily Mail* story had been printed I was free to talk to the other journalists who the publishers had set up for me. To my surprise and relief it wasn't too bad talking to one person at a time. They were always attentive and didn't seem to want to pry too much into my past since I suppose it had all been written about in the book. They seemed to just want to get an idea of what I was like now, so they could set the stories from the book into context. Jackie was also interviewed and she handled it brilliantly. She was calm, thoughtful and very beautiful and I glowed with pride at the way in which she was able to just take it all in her stride. There were moments when I felt my courage was beginning to build. Maybe, I thought to myself, this isn't going to be such a frightening ordeal after all. But then the enormity of what might be about to happen when I saw *The Kid* in the shops would make me feel mixed emotions, partly excited that people would actually want to read my book and partly nervous because I knew I had not yet dealt with the past.

The book came out on time and I saw stacks of them appearing in the shops as their staff took delivery and set them out. The newspaper interviews began to appear in print and they were very supportive. Everyone seemed to be really laidback about it all and this started to bring a smile back to my face. This once again spurred me on to work harder and in turn suppressed my childhood thoughts. Other journalists I hadn't even met read the book and wrote about it in reviews. There was an article in the London *Evening Standard* in which the journalist called on the newly appointed Minister for Children to read the book and not to 'ignore the harrowing message'.

One of my first radio interviews didn't start as well as expected. Before I went to the studio I was told that a researcher would call to discuss the book. She would then get an idea of the questions to give the DJ for me to answer, which seemed like a good idea. A time was agreed when she would call, so when the phone rang I thought I had prepared myself to answer whatever questions she might have.

'So,' she said, 'tell me about your book.'

No one up to that point had asked me that question and it completely stumped me. How could I explain *The Kid* in a few sentences down the phone if she didn't know anything about me or the story? What was I going to say: 'Ah, yes, I was beaten and tortured by my parents'? I could never be that forthright, as if I was proud about my past.

I couldn't find the words to answer, so all I could say was, 'It's about my life. Do you have any questions for me?'

She was obviously at as much of a loss of what to ask as I was of what to say and we finished the conversation as quickly as we decently could. Afraid that I had messed up I called my publishers and from what I gathered they didn't seem too impressed with the researcher's approach. Apparently she hadn't even seen the book and they agreed I couldn't have been expected to answer such an open-ended question. I could understand her problem. She couldn't possibly read every book that they talked about on the programme, there wouldn't be enough hours in the day. The interview was put on hold and the lady called back a few days later full of apologies, but I told her I was fine about it and was sorry for not being able to answer her first question. By then she had scanned the parts of the book that they wanted to feature on their programme and she asked me some questions that I was able to reply to. The interview itself took place shortly afterwards with the radio DJ and I answered his questions live on air with no problem.

After that I would go into radio stations, wait to be interviewed and if the presenter had a copy of the book on the desk I would ask them politely if they could please turn it over, or better still put it out of sight. Some were a little surprised by the request, believing I would and should be proud of what I had written. I knew I would feel that way eventually, but only when I had proved that I could move away from my past, to myself, my family and everyone who now knew about me. It was hard work talking out loud about my life to strangers, particularly in the artificial surroundings of a radio studio. Being interviewed reminded me of being asked so many questions over the years by social workers, foster parents, doctors and police and never being able to tell them about the things that happened in that house. When things had got so bad that I had managed to say something I was ignored. But now I thought that if I could finally talk about it then it would be like me walking out of that room once and for all and closing the door behind me.

The good thing was that I had been able to control and lock away the bad childhood habits that had reappeared a few months before by thinking of the future, as I always had done before I started writing about the past. This I thought was a start to handling what was going on inside my head. Whenever the interviewers asked me about the future the tone of my voice changed, my face would light up and I could feel my spirits rising, because there were so many things I wanted to do and talk about, so many plans bubbling away in my head that always made me feel good and helped me forget my past. Each time this happened I became more determined to get a grip of what had happened to me and put it away once and for all.

Everyone involved with the publication of the book was thrilled by all the attention but, although I could see it was good for the book and that it was going well, I felt exposed and vulnerable as the publicity spread. The thing I found most difficult was making eye contact with strangers and so I started wearing my sunglasses even when it wasn't that sunny, erecting a barrier between me and everyone else and, more importantly, between me and my past. I took to wearing them whenever I was outside the house. It was as if they gave me a kind of protection, making me feel less naked and hiding my vulnerability. They covered me up from the feeling that I had first experienced when walking through the offices of Michael Joseph all those months before. They allowed me to maintain an illusion of privacy from the public and a screen from the full impact of the truths I had revealed to myself. As the book spread and my children could see copies of it clearly on the shelves in the shops, it wasn't long before they started to ask questions. 'What's the book about? Can I read it?' my daughter would ask. I tried to put off answering but children are naturally inquisitive. Eventually all I could say was that 'Daddy's parents weren't very nice to him when he was small.' She looked at me intently and then asked the inevitable question.

'Why?'

I couldn't answer. Instead I promised that they could read the book when they were a little older. That seemed to satisfy them, for now anyhow.

Shortly after the start of the publicity we were told that the *This Morning* TV programme wanted Jackie and me to go on and be interviewed by Fern Britton and Phillip Schofield. Neither of us was sure we were up to it. When talking to newspaper or radio journalists, we were at least invisible to the rest of the world. People might read or hear my words, but they couldn't actually look at my face as I said them, they couldn't see the emotions in my eyes. It was going to be a big jump to talk on live television and we weren't sure how we would react under such pressure. The publishers told me that this was to be the final interview and would be just what the book needed. I knew I couldn't say no and, in fact, the idea of going into a television studio was very appealing. I was eager to see with my own eyes what went on as I was still trying to get into film school.

The publishers had worked so hard on my behalf and this was a big feather in their caps. If this went well sales of the book were likely to take off very fast, although *The Kid* was already creeping up the bestseller charts, having reached about number six in a matter of weeks. We were told about the programme around a week before we were due to go on. Jackie and I had a long chat that evening in the kitchen and decided we should give it a go. We told ourselves we had nothing to lose and everything to gain.

It was doubly hard to make these sorts of decisions when the one thing that was still going round and round in my mind was the plight of the children who had recently been taken away from my sister. I had been trying to find out what had happened to them, but just couldn't get any information. It was as if they had disappeared into a black hole. So much was going on in such a short time that I didn't know how to deal with it and I was afraid of tripping up or, worse still, showing my true emotions on live television.

'We just have to be ourselves,' Jackie and I agreed, once we'd decided to go ahead. So it was all set and we were booked in for the programme.

The morning of the show we were collected early by car and taken to the studios in London. I guess they wanted to be sure we turned up and didn't back out at the last minute. We arrived on time and were led through what seemed like a warehouse on London's South Bank which was filled with costumes and large stage sets, and then through a labyrinth of offices, until eventually we were shown into a dressing room next to Joan Collins.

We were met there by Jess, our publicity representative from Penguin, and were introduced to the people from the *This Morning* programme who were going to be looking after us during our stay. I think Jess was really there to hold our hands in this strange, new world and I must admit her familiar face was a welcome sight. It wasn't long before we were then escorted to make-up.

'Make-up?' I squawked. 'I'm not having make-up!'

Jackie and Jess chuckled to one another, united by their gender, and took no notice of my protests. I followed begrudgingly behind them into the make-up room. I sat down where I was told to in front of a large mirror with light bulbs all around, just like in the movies. I looked in horror at the table in front of me, which was covered in different types of stuff to put on your face. Jackie and Jess laughed at my expression and warned the make-up lady about my concerns. She just smiled and explained that she would only put a little powder on my face to stop 'the shine', giving me visions of my face looking like a prize egg on live television. As she reached into the make-up pile I was relieved when she just picked up one small pot and brush. As she started brushing the powder stuff on my face I just kept dead still with my eyes closed. As soon as she'd finished powdering and I was wiping my eyes and face, to the continuing amusement of Jackie and Jess, we were then taken back to the dressing room and introduced to some people whose names I couldn't remember because my brain was beginning to seize up with nerves at the prospect of stepping in front of the cameras.

Jackie could tell that I was getting more and more agitated as the moment of exposure approached. This interview was going to be going out live to millions of people. It was different to anything I'd ever attempted before. Until a few months earlier I'd never told anyone about my past and now I was going to be telling millions of complete strangers. They would all be able to see me and I wouldn't be able to see any of them. They would be able to see right into my eyes through the cameras. When you're talking to a newspaper journalist you have time to explain what you're trying to say and to make sure that you're making sense. Here I would have just a few minutes and anything stupid I might say by mistake would be broadcast directly into the homes of millions of viewers. I was wondering what kind of questions they would ask and, more to the point, whether I would have the courage to answer them.

Jackie and I fidgeted the time away nervously exchanging jokes as we waited to be fetched for the final few yards of the walk towards the studio and waiting cameras.

A few minutes before we were due to go into the studio we were escorted to the Green Room, where everyone waited for their turn to step into the spotlight. Jess was still with us as we stepped into the busy room, filled with familiar faces coming and going. Everyone seemed to know one another so Jackie and I sat together at one end of the sofa, quietly waiting our turn.

Above all the buzz of the Green Room the words 'Be yourself, be yourself, be yourself,' kept going round and round in my head. I'd put my sunglasses into my pocket, just in case I couldn't take it and began to get upset and had to hide my eyes at the last minute.

Then a man whose face looked vaguely familiar from the television came in and sat beside me.

'So, what are you on for?' he asked cheerfully, attempting to strike up a conversation.

Again it was the worst question I could have been asked at that moment. I opened my mouth, but no words came out and again I didn't know what to say.

'Kevin's talking about his book,' Jess interjected, seeing that I needed some help.

'What's it about?' he asked.

Just in time a voice interrupted us and we were called to go through to the studio. Jackie went first, I followed and Jess waited in the Green Room for us to return. The heavy doors to the studio opened to let us in. It was dead quiet inside, with Fern and Phillip doing the interview before us. The first thing I noticed was the immense heat that the lights were creating. To the right of me was a black booth with row upon row of monitors all showing different angles from different camera shots. Watching them intently were a line of people who seemed to be whispering directions to the people on the studio floor. I was taken aback by the intense, subdued buzz and heat of the place.

It was at that moment that I finally realized the importance of what I had written and the impact the book would have on the lives contained inside it. I could see just what a big deal this was, something even more out of my experience than I had been imagining. I was feeling desperately out of my depth.

We were escorted across to a set of sofas where we were to wait for Fern and Phillip to come over to sit with us after finishing whatever it was they were doing before our item. I sat as close to Jackie as I could get, every muscle in my body tight with nerves. I could feel tears welling up behind my eyes already, my throat tightening and making swallowing difficult. I could tell Jackie was nervous too, but as always she was completely in control and put her hand on mine to try to steady me down, like you might with a horse before a big race. While I was waiting on the sofa I lifted my head and I could see people all over the studio looking at me. I felt sure they all knew who I was and everything about my life, while I knew nothing about any of them. I tried not to make eye contact with anyone. Even breathing was proving to be a struggle.

Then I realized it was happening. The cameras and lights were shining in our direction. Fern and Phillip were talking about us and at that moment we were visible to all those watching. Fern was walking over to sit on a chair next to me as she talked and Phillip was behind her. The cameras were on us and everything seemed to be closing in.

Both Phillip and Fern greeted us warmly and then Fern began asking questions. I started to talk but I could feel my voice becoming choked as I struggled to answer, desperate to keep my composure. Everything came into sharp focus in my head, right there on that sofa, about what I'd written and what was happening today. I tried to reach into my pocket and get my sunglasses out, but I couldn't get my hand to move. I could feel myself becoming more and more upset as I fought to keep control of my voice and suppress my tears.

I wanted to talk about my sister's children who'd just been taken into care, to say that the things that had happened to me were still happening to other children and that we had to do something to help, but I couldn't do that here. It wasn't the place to say what I wanted to say. I didn't know enough about what had happened and I was ashamed to think that such a thing was still happening in the Lewis family. I had to force my mind back to talking selfishly about myself and what happened to me all those years ago.

When I looked across at Fern I could see tears welling up in her eyes, just as they had in the eyes of the publishers when I first met them. That was still the last thing I wanted. I didn't want people to feel sorry for me or to get upset about my past. I wanted to show them that I was happy today.

'Are you all right?' I asked Fern. 'Would you like a tissue?'

I wanted to get Fern a tissue, but then someone appeared out of shot to hand her one and she dabbed at her eyes as Phillip took over the questioning to give her time to recover. Seeing Fern get upset made me more uneasy. I really needed my sunglasses now, but again I couldn't get my hand into my pocket to get them out. I wanted to escape from all the eyes that were looking at me around the studio, from the glare of the lights and from the cameras, which seemed to be closing in. I wanted to crawl back and hide inside myself, covering my face like I did as a child when I was upset. I didn't want to be seen on television crying, as if I couldn't cope. I kept on trying to get the glasses out at the same time as answering another question, but I couldn't get at them and I felt naked and exposed as I had so many times since putting my life down on paper. I felt a tear roll down my cheek.

Suddenly it was all over and they went to a commercial break. The hustle of the studio staff took over as they prepared for the moment when they went back on air. I stood up straight away, immediately putting my hand into my pocket. The glasses slid easily out, I quickly put them over my eyes as the tears started, thankful for the relief of cutting out the glare and giving me a little privacy. I could feel everyone in the room staring at me, but now they couldn't see my eyes any more.

'Are you OK?' Fern asked, as the glasses covered my eyes. 'Have you got a headache? The lights are very powerful in here.'

'I want to go home,' I said in a quiet voice, my bottom lip trembling.

Fern and I gave each other a hug. I shook Phillip's hand and headed out of the studio unescorted with my head down, leaving Jackie behind to find her own way back to the dressing room. I was met outside and taken back to the dressing room where Jess was waiting for us. Jackie came in shortly afterwards. I'd shot out of the studio so quickly that I still had the microphone clipped on to me. It was removed in the dressing room while I tried to compose myself behind my glasses. I kept them on as we made small talk. I think they all knew how desperately I wanted to go home and so the car was quickly brought round. When I came out of the dressing room I walked past the make-up artist I'd been talking to earlier and she put her arms around me. I said nothing.

They asked if there was anything else we wanted to do while we had the car and driver at our disposal. We just wanted to go. We needed the security of home.

I kept the glasses on all the way home, barely talking, staring out of the window, trying to make sense of what I'd done and what had happened. After a while a smile crept back on to my face as I thought of the first time I had to wear make-up. I began to chuckle. Jackie asked what I was laughing at and I told her. We both started laughing and smiling for the rest of the journey home. It was as if the dark clouds that had been following me were finally lifting.

Later that afternoon the publicity people from Michael Joseph told us they had heard that during the *This Morning* interview everyone in the studio had stopped whatever they were doing to listen and watch the monitors. We were told that the place was completely silent, people's eyes fixed on the screens.

Well, whatever emotions the pressure had unleashed in me must have come across on the screen because the public reacted unbelievably to the interview and the book started to sell beyond even the publisher's wildest expectations. I didn't have to worry about promoting it any more because now people were telling one another about it, recommending it to friends. Reviews were appearing and we shot on up the bestseller charts, even passing Hillary Clinton who had just published her autobiography, arriving at number two beneath Bill Bryson's latest work. The publishers kept telling me it was a fairy tale, that such things only happened occasionally.

Finally my brother Wayne called and said that he had read the book and had rung to wish me luck. He told me he didn't have any arguments with anything I'd written.

'There was one factual mistake,' he said.

'What was that?' I asked.

'You said we went to the hospital after Dennis threw the knife at me, but it was the doctor's surgery. You were too young to have known the difference. Everything else is just as I remember.'

He'd even read parts of it to Gloria.

'What did she say?' I asked.

'She just denied it.'

I didn't care.

15. Given the Chance at Last

By the time summer arrived I was ready to put everything behind me and was eager to move forward in my newly chosen career. In preparation I had read and deconstructed over thirty movie scripts. I had studied their layouts, how they explained their angles, camera shots, internal and external, and every other detail of the film. I tried to compare them to what I had done myself and to what I had in mind with my childhood scribbles on the walls. What amazed me was how the written word could be turned into film, brought to life in each scene, how each shot was explained with such clarity that you could visualize it immediately. Everything I was learning about the medium excited me and drove me on to learn more. It felt as though I was making good use of the past and turning it to my advantage. I had completed my synopses for both my first film script and my first novel. I'd built them up slowly, as I promised myself I would, writing them, then breaking them down again, re-writing over and over until I saw the film and novel with the visual clarity that I'd learnt from the scripts I'd read and studied. But I still needed to learn more about the professions of screenwriting and directing if I wanted to move on to the next stage. I knew in my heart that this was what I truly wanted to do; the question was how to go about it.

I had already approached virtually every film school I could find, mainly in Britain, and with no luck. I'd even tried some in the US, but the answer was always the same: with little or no formal education, and no experience in the industry, I was not the calibre of pupil they were looking for. The rejections were frustrating, but

they didn't discourage me. Every time it happened I would look
back at myself silently playing in that squalid room with my dreams
all around me. I know I don't have what you would call a formal
education, but there can be advantages to that. I was brought up
with no parental boundaries to my thinking and my actions, and
so I've made my own. I know it's that that drives me forward. I
don't question whether I can or cannot do things, I try them
anyway, believing that anything is possible. That is probably the
only good thing to come out of my past and I intend to cling on
to it. Because my parents never taught me where the usual boundaries are, I am often unable to see why other people believe there
are things they can't achieve in life.

Anyone who knew anything about the publishing industry, for
instance, would have known that it was almost impossible for someone with little education to get their autobiography published when
they were still in their early thirties. But I didn't know that, so I
did it anyway. Anyone who knew anything about polo would
believe that it would be virtually impossible for a grown man with
no contacts in that world to take it up if he has only ever ridden a
horse once. But I didn't know that, so I went ahead and did it
anyway.

It was the same when I went into the bar business as a young
man, and set up a telecommunications company. My attitude to
what is possible also helps me with my inventions, leaving me free
of doubt and confident that I will be able to bring things together
if I just try. Everything I have ever wanted has started as a dream,
which I had to make come true. The only way I've ever known how
to do that is by breaking the dream down into manageable pieces
or goals, then tackling them one by one. As each section was
completed I knew I was getting close to the end result. So I wasn't
about to give up on this one, the one I considered the most important in my career and the one that would help me make

constructive use of my past. It was a career I had chosen and was determined to achieve.

I have to admit that for a little while I did consider the possibility of lying about my education just to get a break, but decided against it. I'd gone a lot further in my life than most people my age. I believed completely that I had it in me to move on and achieve whatever else I wanted to achieve. So I kept on searching on the computer and one summer evening I came up with a new name, the Raindance film school. I've tried everyone else, I thought, no harm in trying one more. I sent for their details and a few days later an envelope arrived. I opened it and numerous leaflets slid out on to the kitchen table. There were courses for everything that anyone who wanted to get into the film industry might need; directing, producing, cinematography, 35mm, 16mm, digital sound, lighting, scriptwriting, everything from low-budget movie making to Hollywood blockbusters. It looked very impressive and a tingle of excitement ran through me as I read on.

As I scanned the brochures I could see that they didn't specify anywhere what qualifications or previous experience were needed in order to subscribe to the courses. I was used to phoning and trying to convince those on the other end of the line to take me, so I dialled their number and told the woman who answered what I wanted to do. She explained when the courses started, what they cost and so on. It got to the end of the call and I was going to have to make my usual admission.

'I don't have any educational qualifications or experience,' I confessed, expecting that to be the end of the call as usual.

'If you have the drive, the ambition, and believe you have the ability to write and direct,' she replied, 'then that's fine.'

She had blown the problem away as if it wasn't of any interest to her, saying exactly the words I had been wanting to hear, the ones that I believed with my whole heart were true. I was taken aback, my heart thudding, and said I'd call again soon. I put the phone down and went back through the course literature to work out exactly what I wanted to do, unable to believe my luck. I scooped up all the brochures, which by then had fallen on the floor, and went through them one by one, grinning insanely. I called Jackie, who was out shopping.

'I've found a place that will take me!' I shouted gleefully.

'That's brilliant,' she said. 'When do you start?'

'Haven't booked it yet, call you back,' I said, breathless with excitement.

I was eager to make my choices and ring the film school before they changed their minds. When I got them back on the line we had another long conversation, by the end of which I had booked several different courses to give myself a rounded view of the film industry, with the main emphasis on directing, producing and writing. I put the phone down at the end and punched the air with an excited clench of the fists and a big 'Yes'. It was going to be six months of hard, intensive courses and I was so looking forward to it I could hardly wait. It would start after the summer. Everything was starting to fit into place perfectly.

I was so proud of myself for having kept trying and for not giving up at the first discouragement. Through perseverance I had found somewhere that would take me for who I was, not for what certificates I had. The school had always been there; it hadn't changed its policy just for me, but because I'd searched and searched I had found it. I could have given up the search back in January, when all the rejections were making me ask myself whether I was just dreaming, and whether they were all right and I was wrong. But because of my own ambition and determination I had managed to get a foot on the ladder. I knew there was still a long way to go and I was under no illusion that the really hard work would begin after film school had finished, when I was out in the market, trying to sell my film and to prove what I could do. My eyes were wide open, wider than they had ever been before and I knew problems and difficulties lay ahead, but I was feeling great about the future challenges. In a way it helped me to smooth over my past once more, as if I had turned the clock back two years to a time before I had even thought about tackling my past. Gloria and Dennis were slowly fading away.

I knew for sure now what I wanted to do with my life and how I was going to go about it. I was determined to continue to move slowly, gradually building the blocks of my career. Having got through the launch of the book and having started putting my past firmly behind me, I felt great. I was beginning to hold my head up high with my smile returning once more.

16. Summer Had Finally Arrived

The book had acquired a life of its own now, gaining momentum and going up the charts. Little was required of me by the publishers beyond the odd phone call. My time was my own, for me to do whatever I wanted with. Rarely does someone get a whole free summer, but I did and I was determined to make the most of it.

When I wasn't with Jackie and the kids, I spent most of my spare time on the polo fields at Knepp Castle. I loved the wide-open spaces of the fields stretching out beneath the castle, and the buzz there would be before the game started, with the ponies groomed like princes and princesses neatly lined up at the side of their horseboxes. I must admit it felt a little strange, me and my pony Mistico up against the other players with their string of ponies.

By the time the book promotion work was more or less completed the polo season was well under way and I was itching to join in and play. I had been a little apprehensive about joining a polo club, having heard so many things about it being a snobby game and only for the upper classes and the rich and the famous. So before joining the club Jackie and I were invited to dinner one evening with a few of its members to make sure I wouldn't feel too out of place. It was a great evening and now I'd met some of the people I felt a lot more comfortable about joining. I had bought my boots, kneepads, white jeans and polo stick and Mistico was to be stabled at Knepp. I was ready to go and eager to get out on to the field.

I could also see the funny side of the boy from New Addington playing the sport of maharajas and princes. The first time I put on my outfit I burst out laughing as I looked at myself in the mirror.

I looked like someone auditioning for the Village People. It made me realize how far I had moved away from my past, and I saw it as yet another reason why I should forget about my childhood. I imagined turning up at King Henry's Drive or anywhere during my previous life dressed in white jeans and knee-high boots! I couldn't stop laughing.

Because I was a beginner I was at first put into teams to make up the numbers. If someone needed a minus-two player then I would be able to enter. That was fine by me. I just wanted to play and I needed all the practice and experience I could get.

As well as practising my game, I had to learn basic skills: how to saddle up Mistico, how to groom him and look after the tack. My groom that season was Stacey who helped me with everything. But even at the end of the season I still hadn't got the hang of tacking up Mistico. I was always too excited and eager to get out and play. Luckily Stacey was on hand to help and I was happy to leave it to her. I would arrive early and usually stay to the last game, keen to watch the professionals playing. It was an awesome sight and gave me the same tingle that I had that day when I first stumbled on to the sport. Watching these skilled players on their ponies charging around the field with such control, it seemed effortless, and a great way for me to learn. I would sit studying how they sat into their saddles while taking their shots, how they went from full gallop to a standstill, turning their ponies on the spot and repositioning themselves for the next play. There was so much to learn from just observing, but it was practising and playing that seemed to me to be the best way to improve.

In time I found that I had a good eye for the ball, the problem was I needed to get my pony into the right place at the right moment without falling off. Because I didn't always position Mistico correctly I would often have to lean much further out to reach the ball than gravity could stand and I spent large parts of my early games on the ground looking at his backside. Mistico was getting so used to me falling off that he would stand there, waiting patiently for me to clamber back on. I was pretty sure I could see him laughing at me as he looked down at my prone body on the ground every few minutes. My language was not improving that summer either.

I tried to concentrate on staying in my position on the field, even though I wasn't the best rider in the world. The good riders had such control of their ponies while I was still feeling nervous if mine started to get a bit jumpy. Although I was getting much more confident around him, that confidence was easily unseated! If I took him out a bucket of feed and he cantered up to me I would be hopping behind a fence to get out of the way. I knew I had to overcome this and spent as much time as I could with him, touching him, grooming him, getting comfortable around him. It was so soothing and comfortable as we both got to know one another a little bit more. Sometimes I would just stand there with Mistico by my side and we both seemed equally contented. In those precious moments I would forget all about my past.

Like most people I had preconceived ideas about the polo world before I experienced it for myself, but all I saw during that summer was people from every walk of life coming together for a sport that they were passionate about. There was none of the snobbery that I had first imagined there would be and the social scene was not compulsory – it was there if you wanted it and if you didn't, then so be it. At first I kept myself to myself, just practising and watching, but so many people in the club were so enthusiastic about the sport that you couldn't help but be affected by their love for the game. The professional players could see that I was trying hard to improve and would come up to me and give me advice about how to improve my play. It was a lovely feeling, and something that I was always in awe of because these people did it for no other reason than to help my game so that I would enjoy it more.

I knew that if I really wanted to improve then I had to ride better. I had initially dismissed it as a mere detail but it was now obvious it was the most important skill I needed to acquire. So I began having lessons with Claire, a player who lived not far from me and also played at Knepp. Each morning I would arrive for lessons using her ponies, which I was grateful for, and slowly but surely, with lots of trial and error and determination, my riding began to improve. I was able to position myself correctly and consequently spent less time on the floor and more time in the saddle, which was a great relief to my fellow team players, to Mistico and to my backside. As I improved I began being selected more to play in games because I could always hit the ball and looked out for my position on the field. Consequently I was giving fewer fouls and less advantage to opposing teams. I teamed up with one of the club professionals by the name of Martin and played with him for the rest of the summer. For the last few games I entered my own team. At first I didn't know what to call my team: Kid? No. Kev's Polo Team? Definitely not! Then I came up with Mojo. Mojo Polo Team, I thought, that'll work. The fact that I'd recently been studying the script for *Austin Powers* might have had something to do with it. I looked up the meaning of the word, which is 'magic charm' or 'spell'. It sounded just right – a magical spell to get rid of my past – and so it stuck for the rest of the season.

Even though I didn't win anything that season, I still had a great time in my somewhat limited capacity. I'd made many new friends and towards the end of the season I met up with Martin again. He convinced me that the best way to improve both my riding and play would be to go to Argentina, the home of polo. Jackie knew how passionate I was about the sport and thought it would do me the world of good. I agreed to join him for ten days in Argentina in January. The best thing of all was that now on the odd occasion when Gloria would return to my thoughts I would take a deep breath and imagine the smell of the freshly cut grass and the sight of Mistico playing in the field, happy with his new home, and it seemed that I could just blow the memories of Gloria away.

17. Other People's Stories

A few weeks after the book had been released and people had had a chance to read it, I started to receive letters, forwarded on in batches from the publishers. When I received the first batch I was, to say the least, surprised. In my heart I had known that I wasn't the only person ever to have suffered a bad childhood, and that had been confirmed for me by what was happening to my sister's children, but now I was hearing stories from all over the country which showed that my experience, tragically, was far from unique. The fact that I had been able to find a way to make my voice heard meant that some of the others too were now able to sit down and write letters detailing what had happened to them or to people they knew or loved.

Some of the letters were from people who had been in similar situations to mine and were asking for help or advice on how to deal with the scars and the memories. To begin with I didn't know what to say to them. How could I have answered their letters when I was only just about getting to grips with what I had written? So all I could do was wish them luck for the future. The best letters to receive though were the ones where the writers told me that the book had given them the courage to go out and do something with their own lives after having suffered a bad start. It made me feel good. If I had made just one person realize it was possible to escape from a bad past then the whole project had been worthwhile.

One or two of them were looking back to their own childhoods, in much the same way as I'd done in the book, and I would try to encourage them to look forward instead, like I had with Robert.

There was nothing they could do to change what had happened in the past, but they could make their futures into anything they wanted.

I made sure I replied to absolutely everyone who had given me a return address. I felt that if they'd gone to the trouble of writing to me the least I could do was write back. I replied to their questions as best I could, telling them what I do, and suggesting that they should make a plan for the future, breaking it down bit by bit so that they could actually see how to get to their final goal, but not forgetting that it's OK to change your goal as you move up the ladder. I felt that writing back to them was a constructive thing to do, but also as I kept writing it down it felt as if I was reinforcing my own resolve.

Some letters were disturbing. A number of people wrote to say they knew of children who were having things done to them that were similar to what I'd been through and wondered what they should do. Some of them were neighbours of abused kids, or the parents of their friends; others were relations who didn't know whether they should interfere or not as they were concerned this would bring more trouble to the children from their persecutors. Some wrote of how they weren't able to cope with their past and had tried to take their own lives. Others wrote to say that their brother or sister had ended their lives. There were also letters from parents who believed they had given their children everything, only to see them going off the rails. Some wanted to know why abused children so often cover up for their parents. I knew the answer to that: it was simply fear. Fear of the parents and what they might do if they found out. Fear of what would happen if no one came to help and fear of where they might end up if they were taken away, and also fear of what their friends would think. An abused child nearly always knows they want to get out, but can't see what needs to be done.

The problems of a bad start seemed to travel with many people into their adult lives, a fact which I hadn't accepted until recently.

A grandmother wrote to me about her six-year-old granddaughter and three-year-old grandson. Her daughter was a heroin addict and the children had been taken into care, but now they had been sent back to the derelict house where their mother lived and her granddaughter was having to look after her grandson. The grandmother was afraid to intervene or tell Social Services because every time any officials went round they made matters worse, leaving the children in an even more vulnerable and frightening position. What made it worse was that it was such a horribly familiar story.

Another letter arrived from a mother who knew of a girl who was going through much the same as I went through. She was a friend of her daughter. She told me the child was sleeping on a mattress on the floor with no lightbulb in her room. Her mother hated her just as Gloria hated me. The woman had found out about this when the child was ill and her mother threw her out of the house, not wanting her under her feet all day. The woman had given the girl all the support she could, including hot meals daily, love and encouragement. The girl had told her that she had believed she lived a normal life until she was shown otherwise. The girl didn't want Social Services involved because of her brothers and sisters, who the mother seemed to like. She was planning to leave home at sixteen, which was not far away. The writer said that the child's mother was a loud, overbearing and intimidating woman.

She went on to say that she felt guilty, ashamed and embarrassed for not being able to do more for fear of what would happen to the child behind closed doors. She then asked for my advice. I told her to speak to the NSPCC or Childline and to get the girl to ask their advice, but to continue to support her whenever she could. I assured her that the girl would always remember her acts of kindness and it would at least show her that the world was not always a cruel place to live in. As I read the letter I admired this girl's courage and that of her friend's mother.

I thought about what this woman was saying and it seemed to me she had hit on the biggest problem for children who are being abused by their parents or guardians; everyone is frightened to say anything for fear of retaliation and of making things worse for the children involved. And so we hesitate too long before doing anything. It's the same problem that teachers have with children who are being bullied at school. They can tell the bullies off or punish them, but they can't be with the children every hour of the day, so eventually the bullies are going to get access to their victims again and they are going to be even keener to hurt them as revenge for what they would see as a betrayal. When anyone goes to the rescue of a child in trouble, they have to be able to take them away from the instigator of the trouble there and then if they want to be effective. They can't hope that just by issuing a warning they're going to make anything better. But for that to happen the child in trouble needs to find the courage to speak out, so the situation becomes a stalemate and the most vulnerable people in society, the abused children, are trapped beyond the reach of those who could be in a position to help.

I remember so vividly the social worker asking me, in front of my parents, whether I wanted to stay with them or be taken into care – there was no way I could have found the courage to speak the truth at that moment, and I was anxious to hide my past away, being frightened of the possible repercussions of speaking out. At the same time the authorities can't go round taking children away from their parents every time they hear a rumour about maltreatment. There are certain procedures that have to be gone through, during which the children nearly always have to stay where they are, with their abusers. One thing that was clearly apparent was how long it took for the authorities to intervene on behalf of these vulnerable children. I don't know if we will ever be able to find a solution to this tragic catch-22.

The letters made me cry with frustration. I'd heard so many social workers and politicians saying that the sort of experiences I'd had as a child couldn't happen any more, but it was becoming increasingly obvious to me that there would always be children who would slip through the net of the welfare system and who would be left in the care of inadequate and violent parents or guardians for at least part of their childhood, if not all of it. This fact was being brought home even more forcefully by the problems that my sister's children were having, and it was about to be hammered home harder than I could ever have imagined.

18. Disbelief and Frustration

The last I'd heard about my sister's children was that they had been taken into temporary foster care until their ultimate fate could be decided. I was assured they were all together with a family. Whatever they had been put through in the past, they had reached a safe haven now, or so I believed. I still hadn't spoken to their mother, my sister, who was obviously too ashamed to talk to me, but then I received a call from another sister, the one who had broken the news to me to begin with.

She told me that an official working on behalf of the children in care was asking if there was anyone in the Lewis family who could take on any of the children. She had asked both my sisters and, to my amazement, my sister told me that they were both considering the possibility.

I was horrified. Both of them were struggling with bringing up five and six children each as it was. One had a partner, the other didn't. Money was tight, to say the least. The idea of giving them more children to look after was ridiculous, but they were actually thinking of agreeing, truly believing that it would be better for the kids than having them stay in care, as if being with blood relatives was always better, no matter what the circumstances. I knew that they were doing it out of guilt but that was the wrong motive, especially with the pressures of their already strained and difficult lives.

I pleaded with her to see sense and to realize that the children would be far better off in care, being looked after by people who had the necessary experience and resources, even if they weren't their real family. What astonished me more than anything was that the authorities would even consider burdening a single mum, who had virtually no money or resources, with eight children in total.

Most stunning of all, however, was the news that Gloria had volunteered to take some of the children herself, no doubt seeing them as a potential source of income from the State. You would think such a suggestion would have been dismissed out of hand, but the authorities were actually considering the possibility.

I was appalled. The very idea of it sent a shiver of fear down my spine. It was even worse than what had happened to me. Although they had sent me back to Gloria from the children's home where I was so happy, at least I had had a few years' respite in which to gather my self-esteem and self-confidence before being forced back into the mayhem, but these kids would hardly have had time to unpack before they found themselves shunted back into an abusive household and into the power of a woman who was already known to act violently towards them.

How could such a thing happen? The idea of another generation of innocent children being handed over to someone who was completely unable to stop herself from beating and bullying anyone weaker than herself left me feeling there was no hope of ever improving the situation for any abused children. I found it hard to understand how there could be a bestselling book in all the shops that detailed some of the things Gloria had done to her own children, but the authorities were still able to consider her as a potential guardian for her grandchildren. Pictures of what she'd done to me and my nephews and nieces and what she would be able to do to them in the future if she got hold of them stirred vividly in my mind.

The lady who had been instructed to make the enquiries into the situation also asked my sister to ask me whether Jackie and I would be willing to take any of the children on ourselves. The idea of coping with the pressure of taking on another child from the Lewis family terrified me. I felt awful to have to say no, but I was only just starting to get on top of my own life and there was no way I could face the prospect of jeopardizing my kids' happiness by volunteering for a task I was almost certainly not emotionally capable of handling yet. I was in a state of complete disbelief about the whole situation. It seemed as though the authorities knew nothing of the past, because if they did then why were they considering Gloria after all she had done? That, out of everything, was the most frightening concept. I was absolutely lost for words. Although I was no longer angry about what had happened to me in my past, I was now growing furious about the way in which these children were being dealt with today.

Even if I couldn't give them a home myself, however, I could certainly do something to try to protect them today. I got the number of the woman who was making these enquiries and rang her a few days later, after I had had time to gather my thoughts and calm down. I introduced myself and then kept quiet. I didn't want to say much at first, wanting to hear what she had to say before going on the attack. In my mind I must have been expecting to come up against the same kind of social workers I had as a child, or some bureaucratic monster who would refuse to see why I was making so much of a fuss, but I listened anyway, in order to be sure that my sister had understood the situation correctly.

The lady, whose name was Carol, told me that the children were safe and seemed to be happy now. She was assigned as their legal guardian until their future was decided. Her job was to report back to the courts as to what would be best for the children in the future. She then went on to explain that the children had their own psychologists and independent advisers, including her, who were only interested in what was best for them. As she talked more I realized that she was speaking from her heart, and that she really did have the children's best interests in mind. But then I asked about Gloria and she assured me that it was true Gloria had asked to have some of the children, but that her request had been rejected because she only had a one-bedroom flat. I was so relieved to hear that she wasn't being considered, but I was also amazed that they only dismissed her because her flat was too small, not because she was known to be violent towards children.

I asked Carol if she knew anything about the Lewis family and she admitted to having seen the article in the *Mail*. We spoke for what seemed like ages and I discovered that despite everything that had happened in the past, no one in authority seemed to have any historical information on the Lewis family on file, even though there had been pages of reports written on the children in question while the Social Services pondered whether or not they should intervene.

How could it be that Gloria could be considered for even a second to be a suitable guardian just because she was related to them? How could it be that there was no file on her anywhere?

As we spoke further Carol explained that it was standard procedure to try to find someone in the family who might be suitable to take the children, but in the circumstances of the Lewis family I didn't think it was right. I thought it would put extra pressure on the natural parent to see someone else in the family bringing up their children, especially with as much history as the Lewis family, and this would also put pressure on the children to regularly see their natural parent while not living with them. The calm way in which Carol explained it all to me made me understand why they had to try, but I was adamant that the children should be able to stay where they were, for the time being anyhow, until somewhere permanent and safe was found for them. The children had escaped from the dreadful estate where they lived within damp, filthy walls and played amongst discarded needles, threatened all the time by drunks and violence. They had been taken somewhere safe and they had to be allowed to stay there. Carol then went on to explain that it was her job to report on the way Social Services had handled this case and admitted she was dismayed at how long it had taken for these children to be taken into care when there was clear evidence of abuse. It was towards the end of the conversation that I had to admit to something that I was ashamed to say.

'None of these children should go back to anyone in the Lewis family if they are to have a chance in life,' I said, hating the fact that I had to say something so terrible about my own family. 'Send them my love.'

She agreed and told me she was going to advise that the younger children be sent for adoption and the older ones should be put forward for long-term fostering. At the end of the conversation I gave her my number and said that if she needed anything else then to please give me a call. As I put the phone down I felt relieved that she genuinely had the children's best interests at heart. I just hoped that there were more people like this woman working in the system.

As I calmed down from the idea of Gloria having the children, I began to think again about the question Carol had asked as to whether Jackie and I would consider taking on one of the children. It played on my mind long after I had put the phone down. I couldn't get the picture of my nephew and the way he had clung to me when I visited out of my mind. Jackie and I talked it over that evening, but we could see no way round it. Our life was coming together, our children were happy and settled and if we did take on this child the last thing we could bear was Gloria and my sister turning up at the house, insisting on seeing him. He was a lovely boy and what made it harder was that he reminded me so much of myself, but I also knew that when I was taken into care the one thing I hated the most was going back to visit my mother and father. I missed my brothers and sisters but, after what they had done, Gloria and Dennis were the last people I wanted to see. I would have dreaded being taken to live with any family member if it might have meant Gloria would still be able to get to me.

I was amazed by how the experiences of my little nephew mirrored my own, with no one taking the blame for what was happening to him and to his brothers and sister, but at least there was some comfort and hope for them now that I had been assured they would not be going to Gloria. I know every situation is different and that some children might want to see their parents after being taken away even if they were their abusers, but unfortunately I can only judge from my own experiences of how I felt in a similar situation. In the end we decided that we couldn't take on any of them because of our own children, who will always come first in our consideration. We also knew that it would bring back to the surface too many damaging emotions and that would be unfair to everyone involved, especially these vulnerable children. We decided that if we took any of them on it would be out of guilt and that would not be the right thing for any child.

Once again I tried to put it all behind me, safe in the knowledge that they were protected. The summer was now over. The polo season had finished and Mistico was resting on a friend's farm over the winter. He was with Claire, the young lady who lived nearby and who had helped me to ride, and I knew I could visit him whenever I needed to. It was now time for me to start film school. After all that had gone on over the previous two years I was looking forward to finally turning my past to good use. It would turn out to be a very productive and enjoyable winter.

19. Film School

The research I'd done into the film industry so far had made me realize that if I wanted to make my dream of becoming a scriptwriter and film director come true I would need to learn a lot and apply myself to my studies with an open mind. Just as I'd had to find someone to help me when I started writing the book, and someone to teach me how to play polo, I needed to find someone who could help me understand how to make movies.

All through the summer I had continued studying scripts and the film business in general, so that I would be as prepared as I could possibly be when it was time to start the course. I remembered clearly that in my childhood, when I was trapped in that dark and dirty room, I would scribble my dreams and could let my imagination go free, scribbling my escape routes on the walls. Now I was planning on making use of the past in a positive way.

I wasn't rushing into it with my eyes shut trying to just get on, as I might have done in the past. My eyes were wide open and I was under no illusion just how hard it would be to break into the industry. I had to start somewhere and Raindance film school seemed to be the best place.

By this time I had eleven different ideas and treatments for films, working them out scene by scene in my large black book that I took with me everywhere I went. But I was horribly aware that nine of them were rubbish. That left me with two that I believed in wholeheartedly. I loved putting them together and I knew I ultimately wanted to create big commercial Hollywood films. I found the easiest way to write the scripts was to picture specific stars in the various roles and then build the characters and dialogue around them. Both my stories were full of action, with the sort of heroes I'd loved as a child, great car chases and finales where good triumphs over evil. I just needed to learn the proper language of how to turn the scenes that I'd mapped out in my head and outlined in a synopsis into real words on the page, so that they could be seen clearly on the screen, just as I had read in the scripts I had studied.

It was an early Saturday morning when I set off to London on the first day of the course. I felt just as I had all those years before when I started a new school, nervous and apprehensive of what lay ahead. I put on my rucksack, which I had filled with notepads, pens, pencils, even a pencil sharpener. All that was missing was a lunch box and crayons! With my bag on my back I set off for my new school. I took the train to Victoria and walked in the fresh morning air across the city to Euston, where I was to enrol on the course. When I arrived the first thing I noticed was that the other students were a wide mixture of ages and types. They weren't all budding young film directors straight out of university as I had first imagined. They came from all walks of life and were carrying similar ambitions as me. My first class was about to start as I arrived and so I settled into a seat in the corner of the classroom, notebook in hand, feeling invigorated by the walk and eager to learn.

Throughout the day I kept myself to myself, unsure how to interact with everyone else to start with, not wanting to get too deep into any conversation in case people started asking me questions about myself, just taking in everything that went on around me. I asked plenty of questions of the teachers, determined to make the most of their knowledge. I didn't tell anyone about my scripts or my plans. I was sure they had plenty of plans of their own and they didn't need to know about mine. I just kept my head down and listened to everything the teachers said. The more I learned over the coming months the more certain I was that movie-making was the industry for me.

As the months went on I found I became comfortable about my abilities and the teaching gave me the confidence to put my scripts into my own style, rather than worrying whether they fitted someone else's criteria, and so in the evenings, once I got back home, I would shut myself away until late, writing my first film script, thinking about how I would write and finding my own style.

As well as having the stories on paper and the pictures in my head of how I wanted those stories to come out on the screen, I was also beginning to realize that my background in the business world would be as valuable to me in filmmaking as any other creative skill. I could see that the people who backed directors needed to be convinced that the directors knew how to use the money they were given effectively, and be sure that they didn't see a budget as something that could just be increased if it proved impossible to manage on what had been allotted. I knew from my experience that if there is a limited amount of money available for a project, then that is what you have to work with.

I believed I could see the secret that lay at the heart of the film business and that differentiated the really successful directors from the rest, allowing them to keep on going in an incredibly cut-throat and competitive industry. They possessed an ability, in simple terms, to put bums on seats, attracting people to go to the cinema and then to buy the resulting DVDs. The key to their success was the quality of the scripts and the actors who played the major roles. It was these two factors that I believed attracted people to the cinemas. One wasn't good enough on its own – a good script could be badly acted and therefore wasted, or a good actor could be wasted on a poor script. But there was one final element that I hadn't thought about, but which was crucial to a film's success, and that was marketing. Getting out to the public and letting them know that your film is coming is vital if you want to get people in front of the screen. If you had an 'A'-list celebrity, a good script, and you marketed it successfully, then the result could be spectacular. So I began to look at these three factors in relation to my own ideas.

While writing I thought about the actors and actresses I wanted to play in the film, growing the characters around them. I could choose who I wanted to use, the best people working in the movies today. I didn't need to care about whether they would actually star in it or not, or whether the budget would support them, because there was nothing to stop me writing with them in mind. It helped a great deal, allowing me once again to work without boundaries. If I didn't think enough of my movies to picture them with a big star in, why would anyone else? And so I let my imagination run wild and it was a great feeling.

I would be writing late into the night, typing through certain scenes faster and faster, my heart racing at the same pace as the action. I could clearly visualize what I was writing and even hear the music that would be in the background as the action unravelled. It was like having a private cinema in my head, just like I'd had as a child when trying to escape from the real world around me. I became as consumed in my fantasy world as I had done when I was in that house. The scenes would give me goosebumps as they unfolded in front of me and I would write for so long that sometimes I was forced to stop because my right hand had swollen painfully from all the typing I was doing. My knuckles have never really recovered from the bare-knuckle fighting I did as a young man, when the skin had become so badly split. I would just have to rest it for a day or so, soaking my hand in warm water, movement slowly returning to my fingers, frustrated at my inability to get back to work again and by the thought that it was scars from my previous life that were holding me back.

I learned so much during that winter. I'm always glad to learn and develop skills, but this was different. I really believed that I was making the best possible use of the past. Whereas I had recently been embarrassed by the revelations in *The Kid*, I now felt I could finally prove that I was not going to let the past get the better of me. What made me even happier was that I had the full support of my family and that I was going to show them and everyone else that it was possible to reach the top through sheer hard work and determination, that you didn't have to let a bad start in life hold you back. In fact I saw it as an advantage.

When it came to the end of the course we had to film a sequence that we would direct, which was based on the television series, *The Bill*, in order to experience the sort of pressures we would have to cope with in the real world. I watched a couple of the other people on the course first and I could see that they were spending too much time talking to the actors who'd been hired for the day and generally fussing about. It really annoyed me. I sat in my chair shaking my head, seeing the other directors wasting what I saw was precious time and money. They did not finish their scenes in the allotted time, which they seemed bewildered at, believing, as they did, that they were trying to make an artistic statement. Try doing that on a professional set, I thought, when each day of filming can cost hundreds of thousands of pounds.

The teacher then asked for another volunteer. Everyone else put their hand up to be chosen, by which time I had stood up and was already on my way to the set, ready and eager to show that I could do it. The other hands quickly went down, assuming that I had been chosen. The fact that even the teacher looked surprised as I entered the set didn't put me off one bit. I clapped my hands together, ready to get the scene in the can. Although I loved the solitude and freedom of creating, I also loved the feeling of being under pressure to produce results in a limited time. Pressure that I missed and was beginning to realize I couldn't live without for long.

I was given the scene that I had to shoot. The clock was ticking and I was off. Firstly I gave the actors their lines and sent them away to learn them. That then left me with time to go through the shots with the camera lighting and sound man. I got hold of some tape and started laying strips on the floor, each one marking the positions of the actors and cameras. Everything was in place and I was making good progress. It was time to bring on the actors who had by then learnt their lines and we were ready to shoot.

'Roll sound.'

'Sound ready.'

'Roll camera.'

'Camera ready.'

'Action!'

The camera was rolling and the adrenalin raced through my body. As each shot was completed we moved swiftly on to the next scene, trying not to lose momentum, but making sure everything was in focus and looking right as we went along.

I did everything I could to get the film in the can, and was the only one to finish within the time constraints, which was pleasing. Even with all my efficiency, however, I'd still forgotten to do the necessary close-ups for the scene. I was learning from my mistakes, as I have always done, and I was certain that it wouldn't happen again. The more I learned the more I realized there was to learn.

I thoroughly enjoyed my time at Raindance. It was hard work, but what worthwhile project isn't? By the end of the winter I had completed the first draft of my first film script and over the coming months it would be rewritten two or three more times just to fine-tune it.

I was nearly ready to move on to the next stage.

20. Helpers from the Past

I was still getting letters from the public and, as ever, I tried to answer them as best I knew how. Often I had little idea what to say to the writers, but usually I would tell them what I had done, advising them to keep looking to the future and not to remain tied up in their pasts because that would only hold them back. Then I got a letter from Ginni, the woman who befriended me through her son when I was in Yarborough children's home in East Grinstead and badly in need of an adult role model. I hadn't seen or heard from her for more than fifteen years, but I had written about her in *The Kid*, explaining the enormous help that she had been for me. She congratulated me on the book and said she wished she'd done more at the time. How could she have done more, I thought to myself, when she never realized the extent of what was going on? It seems to be a common regret amongst people that they wish they had done more in the past, and the ones who wish it the hardest always seem to be the ones who did the most in the first place.

Another letter came from Colin Smith, a teacher who I'd talked about a lot in the book because he'd done so much to help me and encourage me during the most difficult times in my life. It was Colin who had introduced me to music, which became a lifeline for me, and who had been instrumental in getting the Social Services to finally put me into a place of safety. If any one person saved me from ending up dead, he was the one. At first I didn't want to read what he had to say. I just stared at the folded letter with his name and address showing through the paper. During the writing of *The Kid* I had come to appreciate just how much this man had done for me. I knew it wasn't easy standing up to protect a child when everyone else preferred to look away, but he had. Knowing that he had read the book meant that I felt he had seen inside my head. I was apprehensive about what he might say or think about the things I had done after leaving school, the things I was less than proud of, but which I believed I had to do to get away from my past. He was someone I have an enormous amount of respect for and I did not want to feel he was disappointed in me.

Eventually I plucked up the courage and sat down to read. His letter congratulated me on the book and said how pleased he was that I'd managed to get something positive from what had happened. He also said, like Ginni, that he felt guilty he hadn't done more to follow up what happened to me after his initial intervention. I suppose everyone always regrets that they didn't do more than they did in any situation, but Colin, more than anyone, will always stand out in my memory, as he was unwilling to turn a blind eye to what he knew was going on, even when he had to tell me that things 'had to get worse before they can get better'. He stuck to his belief that something should be done, even though he was never in full possession of the facts because I kept them hidden.

It was good to know that both Colin and Ginni had read the book and seen the results of their kindness. Being a teacher in the sort of school that families like the Lewises go to must be immensely hard and usually thankless, so I hope that Colin knows how much he has achieved. I'm sure I was not the only one he has made a difference to in his career. After reading his letter I picked up the phone and called him. Even though many years had passed I imme- diately recognized his voice. I remembered him just as I had last seen him as a child. We spoke briefly and I suspect my voice sounded a little quiet and reserved, like a child showing respect to a teacher. We agreed to meet soon. After putting down the phone I told Jackie that I was planning to meet up with Colin again and she was encouraging. Having had time to gather my thoughts, I phoned again and invited him to the house. The day he was due to arrive I remembered the times he had helped me, refusing to give up, even after the disaster when I was asked by the social worker in front of Gloria and Dennis if I wanted to be taken into care and was too frightened to say yes.

I saw him arriving from the window and, as he got out of the car, I was amazed by how little he had changed. He had always reminded me of the actor Alan Rickman, and he still did as he walked up to the front door. He might have been a little greyer, but he was as smartly dressed as I remembered, and everything about him was co-ordinated and orderly. I'd been nervous about whether we would find anything to talk about after so long, but we sat down and immediately fell into relaxed conversation. He asked me how hard it had been to write the book, and I admitted that I had found it hard and that it had made me feel very naked, but that was the only time we mentioned it. We went out to lunch with Jackie and just chatted like old friends. I guess it must be nice for a teacher to know that he has made a difference in a pupil's life. Most of us, I imagine, leave school and don't look back, and teachers never find out how much or how little we appreciated what they did for us. I hope that we will stay in touch for ever now, as friends.

A few weeks later I received an email from the daughters of my final foster parents, Margaret and Alan, who did so much for me when I was a teenager. They had found the book in Australia and even though I'd changed their parents' names, and they were grown up and away from home by the time I was fostered, they'd still recognized their parents in the stories I told and remembered meeting me on their visits home. Alan had been the nearest thing I had to a father, but I had said some angry things in the book about the way Margaret had let me down when I was a young adult. Her daughters told me they shared my love of their father, and that they were sorry for the way Margaret had treated me after Alan had died. They also told me that Margaret had died from cancer a few months before the book was released and they advised me not to regret anything that had happened in the past, but to look to the future. I knew they were right because it was a philosophy I wholeheartedly believe in and am always saying to other people when I reply to their letters. Despite anything Margaret might have done at the end of our relationship, I felt sad that this lady who had helped so many children had passed away with such a terrible disease. I thought it appropriate to think of all the good times we had together and that is how I now and always will remember her.

Another teacher who made contact was Mrs Larkin, who was very kind to me when I was in the junior school. Firstly she pointed out that at the time she was 'Miss' Larkin, a mistake for which I apologize. She then went on to tell me that the only information she was given about me when I joined her class was that Gloria had tried to kill me with a carving knife. Although she kept an eye on me whenever I was changing for PE, she admitted, 'Gloria and Dennis were clever at hiding the bruises they inflicted.' She also admitted that I was not the only child in her class who had a difficult home life, but that she never at any stage received a visit or a call from any social workers about any of us.

'You certainly were a challenging pupil,' she went on, reminding me of one or two incidents between me and other children who had given me a hard time.

It was nice to hear back from so many people and I tried to respond as best I knew how, but I still couldn't admit to them how much my past was haunting me and how hard it was to cope with.

*   *   *

Christmas was just around the corner and I was upstairs with the kids one evening when my mobile went off and a young man introduced himself as working on behalf of the Social Services. At first I was taken aback because I was unsure what he wanted, and then I remembered my sister's children. I had put them to the back of my mind, having thought that everything had been sorted out after my discussion with their legal guardian, Carol. He was calling, he told me, with regard to those children. I wondered what had happened now as I listened, feeling a familiar and unpleasant anxiety as to what I might be about to hear.

'I've been asked to arrange a meeting with your family to see about the possibilities of you or any member of your family fostering your sister's children,' he said.

I was stunned. 'Who will be in the meeting?' I wanted to know.

'Your sister's children.'

'You mean the ones in care?' I had to confirm I'd understood him because I was having trouble believing what I was hearing.

'Yes,' he said, as if this was the most normal and sensible thing in the world.

'Who else?' I asked.

'Your sister, your mother and another sister, and I was wondering if you would come as well?'

Now I was stunned into total disbelief. After all I had been through with Carol, and having explained the situation and ensured that she understood what had happened in the past, and having been assured by her that the children would be safe and that Gloria would not be involved, we seemed to be back to square one. There I was listening to a complete stranger who was now starting the whole business again as if Carol and I had never had our conversation. Not only was he suggesting that the children should be brought into the same room with their mother and Gloria with a view to sharing them out amongst the family, he was also suggesting they went to Gloria for weekend visits. I was stunned into momentary silence and walked downstairs with the phone to my ear to listen to this guy alone, away from the children.

When I felt he had said all he had to say, which he did in the most matter-of-fact way, as if nothing unusual was being suggested, I calmly asked him what he knew of our family history. It turned out he knew nothing. The children's file had just come to the surface on his desk and he was dealing with it in complete ignorance of any of the circumstances. He knew nothing about any of us. He had only been given very limited information with which to make his decision as to how to proceed, which was why he was about to make such a colossal error of judgement. But even with such limited information I couldn't believe that he would put these young children in the same room as their abusers. He told me that he had only been given two pieces of paper with the outline of the case.

It seemed impossible to believe that in a time which is frequently referred to as the 'information age' there were still no central computer files on a family which had as bad a history as ours, that social workers would be left to stumble on in the dark, repeating the mistakes of the past over and over again. It seemed that no lessons had been learned at all. But what was most astounding about this was that the social worker who had been dealing with the case did know about our family history and had still only given this guy these few details.

I asked him if he knew anything about Gloria and he said he knew she had been hitting the children. So much frustration had been building up about this woman that I then lost it.

'Are you out of your fucking mind? Are you actually proposing to bring the children into a room with the perpetrators of their misery? What experience do you have?'

'I have a family of my own,' was his only reply.

I said I would call him back, knowing that I needed to speak with Carol, the lady who supposedly was instructed to act on behalf of the children and in their best interests. I managed to get hold of her almost immediately and explained to her my complete dismay at what was happening. She was just as flabbergasted as I was, not having been told anything about this new meeting. By the end of the call she had promised faithfully to deal with it and, true to her word, she intervened and the meeting did not take place.

For days after that I kept thinking about how disorganized the whole welfare system seems to be. Each section seems to work independently of every other one, never pulling together. What is to stop some other social worker being given the file again in a few months and being asked to sort it out without being given any more information? What security will those children ever have if they are for ever in danger of being dragged into a room with their mother and grandmother, with all the emotional strains that would put them under? The prospect of Gloria having them for weekend visits once more filled me with despair and anger. A system that was supposed to protect children was obviously filled with cracks but those in authority seemed to think everything was OK and getting better.

Carol called me back later that week and told me in no uncertain terms that Gloria would not be involved in any meeting to do with the children and assured me that the children would not be put through any such ordeal.

'That's good,' I said, 'but what about other children?'

'I can only help the ones that are assigned to me.'

It sounded as if she was as frustrated as I was. If they hadn't called me to attend the meeting; if I hadn't spoken to Carol and she hadn't got involved there would have been nothing to stop that meeting taking place. Gloria was still a potential danger to those children and I was beginning to think she might always be, until they were old enough to look after themselves.

Despite all Carol's best efforts, I couldn't rely on the fact that the system wouldn't mess up again. I knew that I had to go and see Gloria personally to tell her to stay away from children once and for all. There would now be no more imaginary glass barriers between us and I knew I had to confront her face to face for the first and final time. I was ashamed to even think that I was related to her. But I kept putting the day off. Every time I'd made up my mind to do it, I would find some pressing reason why I had to be somewhere else. I kept postponing the evil moment, again and again.

21. Travelling Back

During my time at film school we had been talking about the possibility of making a documentary about *The Kid*. I wasn't sure how I felt about the idea of going back to all the places that held such bad childhood memories, especially with the recent problems with my sister's children so raw in my mind. I'd found talking about the past to the media very difficult and so the thought of bringing it all up again made me apprehensive. The difference was I was now beginning to rebuild the barriers I had lost and, to be honest, when the idea came up there was a part of me that was curious about what it would feel like to return. I also began to wonder if physically going back to my past could help me finally put it to rest in my mind. In a slightly sick way I wanted to find out how I would react to going back, although the thought of doing it in front of a camera made me nervous.

Because we had a few people interested I was able to choose a company I felt comfortable with. I didn't want to do anything that was just about the past and wallow in how miserable it all was; I wanted the documentary to look to the future and be hopeful and encouraging to anyone who was watching, just as I had hoped the book had been.

We looked at the various proposals and the best option came from the BBC, who wanted to talk to me and some of my brothers and sisters and also to people like Ginni and Colin Smith. What amazed me was that during the BBC's research for the documentary I found out that Colin had kept detailed records on me when I was a child, noting occasions when I collapsed in the playground after having had a beating at home and other events which I'd thought nobody had noticed. It felt strange to discover that someone else had been watching over me so closely without me realizing and that he still had those records of what he saw. He declined to appear in front of the cameras, being a very private man, but gave them access to the information he had gathered.

I agreed to go ahead with the programme and one of the things that the director wanted to do was go back to the pink tin house in New Addington. The idea of going back made me feel physically sick with anxiety, a mixture of thoughts and feelings that made me very uncomfortable and worried about what I might see. It was obvious that they would ask me to go back to the house as it was a major part of my childhood and I tried to prepare myself mentally. Jackie noticed that I was extremely agitated once more and when they gave me the date of the trip about a week before, I began to get nightmares again. I don't remember what they were about, but I would wake at around one or two o'clock in the morning in a pool of sweat, unable to get back to sleep because all my senses were alert. I would go downstairs and work until morning.

It wasn't the first time I'd been back to New Addington since escaping from home. I had walked around the area when I was writing *The Kid*, to remind myself of the layout and the atmosphere, but I hadn't felt brave enough to knock on the door of the house and ask to see inside. The best I could do was to drive past with it just in sight, unable to actually turn into the Horseshoe. I'd been up to the market where I'd worked as a young boy and bought a packet of chips and some fruit and vegetables, which had brought back some pleasant memories of my first tentative steps towards independence. Then I drove away again, back to the safety of my new life. I tried really hard to prepare myself, wanting to prove I was strong and no longer fearful of the past, but deep down I wasn't sure how I would react to crossing the threshold of the house that held so many terrible memories.

As always seems to happen when I am about to do something related to my past, I didn't sleep at all the night before we were due to go filming. It was a long night, my mind running around in circles about what I would see when I got there. Even though I was now a grown man with the security of a loving family, I knew I still felt as vulnerable as a small boy at the thought of stepping back inside that house later that day. As the night dragged on it angered me that I could still be made to feel like this after so long. I told myself that this would be the last time I would ever have to go back inside the house and once I'd got through this day I would never have to think about it again and I tried to convince myself that I would have gained some sort of closure on my past by making this final trip.

The director and producer wanted to film me inside the tin house on the first day, which we all agreed was best because it would then be out the way. I didn't want to have to do all the other filming with that hanging over me.

It was a cold, rainy winter's day as we set off slowly from my new life to my previous life. As we got closer, I grew more nervous. To break me in gently on the day of filming, I was first taken to the woods at the end of the road, which I used to run away to when I was tiny. They hadn't changed at all. People might come and go, the children of the area might grow up and leave home, but the landscape evolved at its own slow pace, bringing back a hundred memories of me as a small boy running as far away from Gloria and Dennis as possible. I could even find the slope that I used to slide down to get into the cover of the undergrowth quickly when I was in a hurry to disappear, and I wondered if other children used it in the same way as I had, keeping it smooth and well-worn. I remembered the times when I went back home, too scared to stay in the woods any longer, but still terrified to step into the house. As I walked slowly back across the grass in the middle of the Horseshoe I would know that she would be watching me from the window. Before I even reached the garden path the door would be thrown open and Gloria would be standing there, staring down, fag in mouth, ordering me to get inside in a tone that told me what was going to happen as soon as the door was closed against prying eyes. The moment it shut behind me chaos would ensue and everything I had been imagining on the long walk home would happen. The pain of those beatings would stay with me for days afterwards.

At the end of King Henry's Drive, opposite the woods, the tower blocks that I used to run past in my desperate bids for freedom had had a facelift since I'd last been there. The grey pebble-dash walls were now beige, and the window frames had been painted red, making the tower blocks look slightly less forbidding. The goal posts stood in the same place as they had twenty years earlier on the open grass area leading into the woods. As I walked through the woods I noticed that they didn't seem as big now as I remembered. I suppose things all look much larger when you are a small child. But one thing only was on my mind as we strolled around, and that was the pink tin house.

As we drove down from the woods in our wet clothes to the Horseshoe, the crescent where the house stood back from King Henry's Drive, my pulse began to quicken and the butterflies started their familiar war dance in my stomach. The road looked exactly the same as I remembered apart from the red telephone box that had once stood in the centre and had now disappeared. The cars parked in front of the houses were more modern, but otherwise time had stood still. It seemed strange that when so much had changed in my life, so little had changed here.

The family who now live in the pink tin house had read the book and were happy to let us come in and film. I wondered how many other people in the neighbourhood had read what I had written.

I drove past at a virtual snail's pace, my eyes glued to the house.

I parked the car and sat in full sight of the pink tin walls, just staring at it. The net curtains were blocking anyone from looking inside, just as they had when I lived there. Before I got out of the car I tried to compose myself. It was time to confront my demons, I said to myself. I got out and approached the front door, and as I slowly walked up to the house I felt that each step was making me smaller. All my senses were on alert like a wild animal treading cautiously for fear of walking into a trap. I could feel the blood pumping round my body. As my eyes flickered around I noticed that the paint was flaking on top of the metal porch, just as it was all those years before.

As I was getting closer, I was having difficulty rationalizing everything that was going on around me. I tried to keep my breathing steady and not panic and for some reason my mind was blank. I couldn't think of anything. The front door was wide open, but I wasn't ready to go in yet. Instead I stayed at the side of the porch unable to face the entrance directly, peering round the corner, like a frightened rabbit on the edge of a road. All my muscles were shaking with nerves now, my instincts telling me I should turn and run. I tried to consciously calm them down, but there was nothing I could do. All I could do was tell myself not to run away.

I kept dipping my toe into the waters; poking my head round for a few seconds to look and then pulling it back out and taking a deep breath, as if trying to convince myself it was all right to venture the final few steps out of a safe hiding place. Suddenly I burst out crying, my shoulders heaving, unable to control the feelings of what had gone on inside those tin walls as the memories rushed over me. I tried to stand up straight and get control, telling myself that I was better than this, that I could do it.

I could feel that I wasn't ready yet to take the plunge; that I needed a little longer to get used to the idea. I went back to the car to get my sunglasses, wanting to have something to hide behind, something to cover my nakedness. My legs were shaking uncontrollably and threatening to buckle under me at any moment as I attempted to enter the house once again. I was trying to focus my thoughts, but my whole mind was taken up with the task of overcoming my fears so that I could at least step through the door. I felt physically sick.

Eventually, mustering all my courage, my sunglasses giving me the barrier I needed, I cautiously put one leg through the door and then stopped again before following with the other one, taking my reluctant body into the house. As I came into the hallway I couldn't stop the tears from coming and I was grateful to have the protection of the glasses. I still felt physically sick, but at least I was inside. I'd taken the plunge. Someone went to close the door behind me, but I told them to leave it open, feeling a surge of panic. I had to know that I could get out at any moment. I couldn't take the chance of feeling trapped inside the house ever again. I was trying not to breathe too deeply, frightened that if I did I might catch a whiff of some smell that would bring back pictures of my childhood even more vividly. I had to be able to filter the memories that I allowed through, for fear that I would be overwhelmed by them.

The first thing I noticed as I stood in the hallway was that the kitchen door had been blocked off. I could picture how it had been to look through and see the sink full of dirty dishes and me being washed in full view of the school that we backed on to. I could still recall the smoky, greasy smell that would always linger on my body after being strip-washed in the sink water.

It took me almost as long to get from the doorway into the first room as it had taken to get through the front door. I kept bobbing my head round the corner, as if wanting to be absolutely sure there was nobody waiting to pounce before I would go any deeper into the house. Even though my body didn't want to go any further, my mind was curious to see what the rooms looked like now. As I went into the front room I noticed that the door between the room I stood in and the dining room was no longer there, which gave a clear view to the garden at the back. I noticed it was clean and well tended with a new decking area and a familiar view of Wolsey Junior School. I could hear the sound of children playing in the playground and as I walked closer to the window I could see them happily running around in their break. My eyes scanned the garden more closely. It was no longer the overgrown rubbish tip of my youth, but a family garden full of children's toys.

As I started to focus through my tears I could see that the inside of the house was also a hundred times cleaner and neater than when we lived there. I saw the corner I used to hide in while watching TV with filth surrounding me on the floor and clothes piled high against the wall like a jumble sale. I would hide amongst the clothes to keep out of the way of Gloria and Dennis and they also helped keep me warm.

As I walked from the dining room into the kitchen I remembered how my feet would stick to the floor and how when I got up from sitting on the floor my legs would be covered in filth and my feet were permanently black. The hardest time to get used to it was after having returned from the clean environment of Yarborough children's home. I could picture the time when Dennis threw the carving knife at Wayne and the feeling of nausea grew stronger as other images crowded in behind it. The worktop behind the kitchen door where Dennis used to stand, hour after hour, drinking and listening to Elvis songs, was still in the same place it had always been, the sink was still beneath the window where passers-by used to be able to see us being strip-washed in the most humiliating fashion, but the outside toilet had been converted into something else.

Although I managed to force myself to look round the downstairs, I couldn't bring myself to go upstairs and risk meeting all the ghosts that would be lying in wait for me. The visions of Gloria in the room and what she would do to me were just too painful. I knew that once up in those rooms, I would be too far from the open front door and I was sure I would panic. I stayed inside for as long as I could bear it.

'I want to go home now,' I said.

I'd had enough. My brain was racing at a hundred miles an hour. I felt as if I wanted to smash my head against the tin wall just to get rid of all the visions that had been in there for so long. Instead, I tasted blood in my mouth from where I had been biting my lip too hard. Once outside I took a deep lungful of fresh air. That was it, I thought to myself as I headed for the car. I'd done it and there was no way I was ever going to be going back in there.

The owners of the house had tactfully gone out to give the film crew freedom to move about, but the three adult daughters had stayed upstairs out of the way. I went back to meet them at the front of the house not long after, my sunglasses still on to hide my swollen eyes. I thanked them for letting me back into the house. I realized that they were lovely people and that no matter what happened when I lived there they had a different life in that house, a life that seemed a million miles away from mine. They said that if I ever wanted to go back inside they wouldn't have a problem. I kindly thanked them for their offer and said that I could never do that. They seemed to understand. Finally they gave me a bottle of wine, which I thought was a lovely gesture. We said our goodbyes and as I drove away, leaving the house behind me, I knew I would never return. It was a past life and I had finally buried it.

One of the girls from the pink tin house was a cleaner at Wolsey Junior and she very kindly took me around to the school so I could see what had changed. Apart from the entrance hall it all looked completely different, unlike the house. Although Wolsey Junior didn't hold any happy memories, it didn't have the same dramatic effect on me as the house had done.

I found out afterwards that in their research the film crew had found a number of neighbours and people in the area who knew what was going on in that house. They all said they wished they had done more, but were too frightened to help for fear of retaliation from Gloria and Dennis. One was an elderly lady, in one of the other houses on the Horseshoe, called Iris. I didn't remember her, but she remembered me and also said she had realized what had been going on. She thought I had got the worst of it because I had often been the one to stick up for myself and for the others. Iris was a nice woman and she told me she was still in touch with one of my sisters. The day was over and that night I slept more peacefully than I had for ages, safe in the knowledge that I would never have to return.

The following day we went back to Yarborough children's home, which had been converted into a nursery school and flats. As I stood outside I felt much more relaxed than I had done when I visited the pink tin house and even began joking around in front of the camera. These had been relatively happy times for me. I could see the window through which we tried to run away after watching *Huckleberry Finn*. I could see the big white door where I was first greeted by Uncle David, a giant of a man, and where he later got on his knees to say goodbye as I was taken back to the tin house.

The documentary makers wanted to interview me further, but I wasn't keen on the idea of putting myself through the whole thing again as I felt uneasy showing my vulnerability on camera. But then I agreed to go ahead, deciding that as each part of the filming was finished I would be able to put that part of my life behind me. I felt as if I was building a wall bit by bit, adding layer after layer of cement so that it wouldn't come down again if anything else happened in the Lewis family.

I didn't want to do the interview at home, I wanted to feel more detached, and so I asked if we could film it in a neutral place. As they asked their questions I began to describe things that had happened in the tin house, both to me and in front of me. For the first time I spoke out loud about some of the things that happened and I actually felt better after it; but I knew I didn't want to talk about it ever again.

After that the director thought it would be nice to have a section with me and Wayne hanging out together at the pub, playing pool together. I wasn't comfortable with the idea since we never did anything like that and it wouldn't be natural.

'Could we do an activity together?' I suggested, thinking that the novelty value of learning something new would take our minds off the more emotional parts of the meeting. 'How about fly fishing?'

I don't know why I suggested that since Wayne had never done fly fishing in his life and I'd only done it twice before, but I thought it would be fun. The director agreed and we all headed off to a nearby lake. Wayne and I got some practice in while the camera crew were setting themselves up and he immediately caught a huge fish, but the cameras weren't ready and missed the whole event. Once they were up and running we didn't get a single bite all afternoon. In the end the owner of the fish farm allowed us to go to the feeding pond, where it's almost impossible not to catch something. Wayne managed another triumph and couldn't help but take the mickey out of me for my failure to catch a single fish.

Later that evening Wayne was interviewed; I stayed in the room next door just in case he needed me for support. After his interview, which I could see had upset him, we put our arms around each other and held on tightly. It was something we had both wanted to do for a long time. Later that evening we went out together, just the two of us, for the first time since we were children. While we were out I saw some friends and felt so proud to be able to introduce my brother to them.

Talking about the past with Wayne was emotional. He told me that since reading the book he had managed to get better control of his temper and wasn't as defensive towards people as he had been and he felt that as a result of this he had been promoted at work. I felt so pleased for him and was so proud of his achievement that it was almost as though it was me getting the promotion, until he told me to calm down.

On the last day of filming Jackie was interviewed and the kids were filmed playing with us. The smiles on our faces were real that day because it was all behind us and I was now in my new life with a wonderful caring wife and two fantastic children who meant the world to both of us.

All that was left was to confront Gloria in order to tell her to leave the children alone, but now I also wanted to see Dennis, not for the same reason, but because I wanted to know that I was no longer afraid of the past.

Just before the programme was aired the BBC wrote to Gloria and Dennis explaining what they were doing and asking whether they would like to comment. There was no response from Dennis and we didn't expect one from Gloria either, as Wayne had already asked if she would be interviewed, an invitation she had declined. After receiving the letter, however, she contacted the producer and agreed to be interviewed. When I heard of her decision I felt nothing. She knew what went on all those years ago and I felt curious as to how she would justify it and what she would say.

At the end of the filming I was due to go to Argentina. The producer told me that upon my return I would receive a copy of the documentary before it was aired to the public. I was going to have to wait until then to find out what Gloria said. Even though I knew in my heart that I had to confront her – to tell her to stay away from the children once and for all – I still wanted to put the moment of the meeting off. Having just relived my past so painfully, I decided to leave that task until my return, when I would feel more relaxed emotionally and ready to face anything.

22. Argentina

Martin, my first polo coach, had suggested that if I really wanted to improve my game, particularly my riding style, then I should spend some time in Argentina where he also spends part of his year. I was to stay at La Esperanza Polo Club in the town of Coronel Suarez, which is known as the world capital of polo and is where some of the best players in the world have come from. Having never had any proper training I knew that if I wanted to progress I needed to work on my riding skills, so I booked to go over to La Esperanza for ten days at the end of January.

This would be the longest period I had ever been away from Jackie or the kids, and the first time I had ever travelled abroad on my own. I didn't like the idea of being apart from them but I thought this was too good an opportunity to miss. Jackie and I had spent so much time together over the previous year and had so much fun that I felt I could justify it.

As the day of departure drew closer, however, I became increasingly unhappy at the thought of leaving them behind for such a long time. I kept telling myself that it was only for ten days, but the feeling of sadness just wouldn't go away, partly because as a family we are so close and have so much quality time together and partly because I was nervous about how I would fit in to the life of the family who ran the club and who would be my hosts for the stay. I am always completely comfortable with my own loving family around me and the idea of leaving them behind made me feel both guilty and anxious.

Eventually the day of departure came round and the taxi turned up at the house on a cold, drizzly Saturday evening to take me to Heathrow for the night flight. By this time I really didn't want to leave the warmth and comfort of a family weekend together and it wouldn't have taken much for me to stay. But Jackie thought that after all that had happened recently it would do me the world of good. She had packed my bag and made sure I had all the necessary travel documents. There was no turning back. As I left I felt so bad as a father to be leaving them all, especially on such a dreary night.

I hadn't wanted Jackie to come to the airport with me because I thought the goodbyes would be too difficult, especially with the children and with this being our first time apart. When I got to the terminal I realized how much I had grown to rely on Jackie over the years. Not only would I not have been able to organize myself in time for the departure from home, I knew that I would most probably have forgotten all the documentation. Even when I got to the airport I wasn't able to find where I had to be and ended up in the wrong queue. A British Airways member of staff had to take me and lead me through the departure process, which was a little embarrassing, to say the least, but very appreciated as I handed the lady all my paperwork and she sifted through it to find the necessary bits and pieces for me to fly. I already missed Jackie and the kids desperately as I waited for the flight to be announced.

Once on board, I settled into my seat awaiting take-off. We were up in the air in no time, ploughing through the wet and windy evening as I watched the wings flapping around with some discomfort. Eventually I fell asleep and arrived in Buenos Aires over fifteen hours later, feeling uncomfortable from the flight.

I was met at the airport by Carlitos who was a member of the Bertola family, who owned La Esperanza. The polo club was over five hundred kilometres away, just outside the town of Coronel Suarez, South West towards the mountainous region of Ventana. He greeted me warmly and spoke good English. We soon started making conversation and I realized I should have taken some time to learn a few words of Spanish. I told Carlitos that I spoke no Spanish and apologized for my ignorance. He didn't mind as he was happy to practise his English on me and in return he taught me a few basic phrases so that at least I could greet people and thank them.

As we set off on the four-hour drive to the club the air was already humid and the ground steaming from the night's rainfall. We soon settled in to the long drive ahead of us. The distance seemed like nothing to him as he made the trip to the capital regularly, but it was a hell of a long way for me. What amazed me as we drove at what you might politely call a progressive speed was the sheer scale and beauty of the scenery. It was so flat you could see the open lush farmland for miles in every direction. After three and a half hours of driving on completely flat roads, with not much else to look at except the odd passing vehicle, I noticed a small gradient up ahead and I found myself looking forward to the change. I tried to make a joke about it to Carlitos, which fell flat on its face when I had to explain it to him for the third time. Carlitos smiled politely, probably wondering who the hell he had got sitting in the car next to him. As we reached our destination I could clearly see the spectacular Ventana mountains in the background.

Martin and the whole Bertola family, including the father and mother, their sons, daughters, sons-in-law and grandchildren, all came out to greet me. They were so warm and welcoming that I couldn't help but feel truly comfortable in their home. The accommodation consisted of a number of villas, all very European in style, which housed guests like me and other players who had travelled from all over the world. The villas were divided up into cool, elegant apartments with wooden floors and windows which looked out across the open farmland where over two hundred polo ponies grazed and worked in rotation. The sweet smell of newly mown grass floated on the breeze, filtered by the mosquito nets that guarded each open window. It was a very pleasant and peaceful farm and I couldn't have asked for more. Jose Bertola, a five-goal player, was going to be my instructor during my time there, along with Martin who was going to be helping me improve my riding. They were such genuinely pleasant people, and their willingness to try to communicate with me in English when I had no Spanish to offer in return was a relief, although I did feel a little stupid. All I had were the few words Carlitos had taught me, of which I can now remember only 'Hola' and 'Gracias'. They asked what I wanted to do and I couldn't hold back my eagerness to get out on to the polo pitch. They were more than happy to oblige and I soon settled into a very relaxed and chilled routine.

Breakfast would be served at nine thirty in the morning. After that I would have my riding lessons to try to get myself sitting properly in the saddle, not pulling so much on the ponies' mouths or kicking their bellies so hard, just settling in and being more at one with my mounts and not riding with chicken arms and bicycle legs. The mornings' activities would help me work up a healthy appetite for the mighty family lunches, which would lead to everyone having a siesta during the hottest hours of the day in order, I think, to rest their swollen stomachs. If I couldn't sleep I would sit under the shade of the willow trees that surrounded the swimming pool and write in my black book, read or doze.

Sometimes I would come inside and sit in front of the television in the guest lounge, watching videos of the professional players, trying to take in their techniques. I would wait impatiently for five thirty to arrive, when the heat of the sun would begin to relent and we would play chukkas late into the evening.

I soon began to slow down from the frantic pace of life in England. I took off my watch because I wanted to move at their relaxed, chilled pace, which evaporated as soon as we started to play chukkas. Then the whole place came alive with players arriving from all over the area, all of them very skilled. There I would be playing twenty-goal practice chukkas with these very talented players. It felt great and was like mixing with Premier Division footballers, people at the top of their game. At first I felt completely out of my depth, but they knew I wanted to learn and helped me a great deal. It was tiring work, making my inside legs burn from the effort of staying on the ponies, something the other players seemed to do effortlessly in a style I was keen to learn.

After chukkas we would have another rest before the evening meal, which was served in the big house. This was a time when all the family and anyone else who was staying at the club would come together. The food was fabulous, and we ate a lot of esados, which were various meats that they cooked slowly over hot charcoal for hours, making the meat as soft as jelly in the mouth. They were so hospitable and nothing was too much trouble. It was during the meals, as I watched all the different generations mixing together, laughing and enjoying one another's company, that I missed Jackie and the kids the most. Being slightly on the outside gave me an opportunity to observe and think, and it made me realize what a great family life I had back at home. They would ask me about my family and I would eagerly tell them about Jackie and the children. They would all listen attentively, and I told them how the love I had for my family was just like the love they had for theirs.

As my morning lessons progressed I began learning to control and understand the ponies better. Martin was taking time to ride alongside me and I was becoming less nervous when they threw their heads around, became agitated or behaved differently from one another. I was finding out that they all had different personalities, just like people, and you had to respect them. Some were grumpy while others were eager to please, some were leaders, others followers. Some of them would be able to tell that I wasn't an experienced rider, while others didn't seem to notice. By the end of the ten days I had ridden over forty different ponies and my confidence had grown immeasurably. The Argentinians had shown me how important these ponies were to the sport, and how much respect they deserved. These responsive creatures are the finest sporting animals in the world, having to be as fast as racehorses and as agile and powerful as boxers. I also found that the spectators were just as interested in the ponies as the players, and this made sense to me as the ponies made up over seventy-five per cent of the game. I realized that whereas before I had treated all the ponies the same, as machines, I was now looking at them with far more respect and this gave me an added understanding and more confidence in my riding.

Jose was teaching me to focus more tightly on what was happening all around me on the pitch in order to keep up with the others and anticipate where the game was going, rather than just charging around all the time in an uncontrollable gallop. I had to concentrate hard.

I was learning fast and I began to predict for myself where to aim the ball, rather than just whacking it as hard as I could and it going nowhere. I felt that these new skills were not only helping me to discipline myself in the game but also helping with other things as well. I found that by focusing on the game I was doing the same as I was with my family life. The more I was in control of my vivid childhood visions, the more I seemed to be able to filter out those that were of no use to me now. Jose was teaching me that if I made a mistake or committed a foul in the game I didn't have to worry about it, just try and learn from it and get on with the game. A skill that is true in any walk of life. One of the most frequent errors made by a new player is to worry about not fouling, or making a mistake and letting it get you down – another truth in life as well as in sport. The foul or mistake is in the past, so leave it there. Learn from it and move on, more experienced and wiser because of it. Whereas I had always panicked about every error I made, I realized these professionals also made mistakes, but they never dwelled on them. I now firmly believe that learning a new sport helps to develop you in ways you never imagine both in your mind and in your attitude to life.

I was so fascinated by my new-found sport that some evenings, when the others suggested we go out into the town, I would decline, wanting to get an early night so that I was fresh for the next day. On the nights I did go out we would go to a local bar in the historical town of Coronel Suarez, with its beautiful buildings and cobbled streets and I would find myself mixing with some of the top professional polo players in the world. They were so warm, friendly and happy that I was learning their sport. It felt like having a drink with Michael Owen and David Beckham and once again I felt in awe of the game and of the passion of the people who played it.

One night we all went to visit another family in the area. I was a little apprehensive, knowing that they would all be old friends and I would be the outsider, and painfully aware of the language barrier. I needn't have worried: they were as hospitable as the Bertolas and spoke perfect English, which made me feel even more ashamed at my lack of linguistic abilities. I promised myself that I would learn more for my next trip over, which I was already thinking about, except next time I planned to bring my family. At the end of an evening of wonderful food and hospitality under the stars, they produced a worn old leather visitors' book and asked me if I would sign it. As I rested this worn book on my lap I opened it gently and looked at the pages of comments that went back nearly forty years in every conceivable language, all made by previous visitors to their home. I couldn't think of anything to write apart from thanking them for a wonderful evening in a wonderful home with a wonderful family, which seemed to sum up my views of the whole trip. Unfortunately I spelled 'wonderful' wrong, but I could always blame the wine. It reminded me of our dream home – a traditional farmhouse with timber frames inside, and big open fireplaces giving off a smoky smell. I have always found smoky smells comforting ever since being rescued from the pink house by a fireman. Our dream house will have its own life and character and we will spend the rest of our lives there, settled and happy. I knew that once we got our home I would have a book like the one resting on my lap, a book of sincerity that would last for generations. It made me realize just how much I missed and appreciated my family.

I phoned home regularly and towards the end of the trip Jackie told me that a video of the documentary had arrived and that she had watched it. She said it had made her cry. I didn't ask about the interview with Gloria as I no longer wanted her in my head, obstructing my new life.

After dinner one evening the family asked me what I wrote about when I was sitting by the pool and for the first time ever I agreed to show other people what was in my black book and the storyboards for the film and the novel I was creating, as well as my inventions. As I returned from my room with the black book under my arm they all crowded round, curious to see what I spent hours by the pool doing. It didn't matter that some of them didn't speak any English; they could understand what I was getting at just by looking at the pages. Their eyes would light up as I explained my stories and inventions late into the night, and they listened intently and asked questions through Carlitos, their chosen interpreter. It was the first time I had ever let anyone look at these pages, not even Jackie had seen them, and I must admit I felt proud to show them.

Just as those ten days in Argentina had helped me to focus even more clearly on my life and my ambitions, they had also given me a chance to work out what I should do about my parents. I had already decided I was going to have to go to see them. As I was always the one who had tried to stand up to them it was time for me to stand up to them again, especially Gloria, and tell her that she couldn't have anything more to do with any children; that she simply couldn't be trusted not to hurt them any longer.

On my last night at La Esperanza I had a vivid dream. Jackie, the children and I were all living back in the pink tin house that I had been brought up in. We were there because I was a Lewis and it was the Lewis family home. The authorities had arrived unannounced to take the children away from us and into care. The kids were screaming for us as the social workers hauled them off by their arms, pulling hard and I was being held back as I desperately fought for my children. They were being taken away because we were part of the Lewis family and we had all been tarnished with the same brush as Gloria. Then the dream changed and at the end of the table sat a judge. The children were next to the social workers, their arms being held tightly so they couldn't move. The social workers looked at them and us with arrogant expressions. We were all crying, trying to plead for the children to be with us, saying that we had done nothing wrong. Then the judge looked at the social workers with disgust, ordering them to take their hands off the children. As soon as they were released the kids ran towards us and I was jerked awake, covered in a cold sweat. The sheets were soaked as if I had wet the bed, my heart thumping hard.

I was sure the dream had been brought on by the nerves I was feeling at the prospect of confronting Gloria. I knew I had to do it for the sake of the children and I also knew I needed to find some sort of closure for myself in my relationship with her, but that didn't make the prospect of seeing her any less frightening.

Martin and I left later that day to spend an evening in Buenos Aires before my flight home. I said my goodbyes, vowing to return with my family. I especially thanked Jose for all his help in teaching me about the ponies and the game. Knowing I had learned so much more about myself and about dealing with life, I gave a special thanks to his father whose company I had enjoyed so much. I was sad to leave but eager to return to my own family.

When I arrived home I gave Jackie a huge hug and we clung tightly to each other. We collected the kids from school together and we were all excited to be a family once more.

Later that evening I sat down and watched the documentary. Out of everything the one thing that surprised me the most was that during the course of filming they had filmed upstairs in the old tin house and the current family had shown them some of the original scribbles they had found on those filthy walls, now hidden by a wardrobe. The camera had panned in and clearly made out the words 'Help me'. It didn't bother me so much now as finally I saw myself in that room again with no pane of glass. I could see Gloria walking out the door, not even turning to look at me and I was finally left alone to get on with my dreams.

As the interview of Gloria came on, it was obvious that she still didn't believe she had done anything wrong. But what I hadn't known was that her father had beaten her when she was a child. She said she believed that it was normal back then to do what she did to me. But what about what was happening today, I thought. She told the camera I was 'a little terror' as a child and therefore had needed to be disciplined. Finally she said that if she did it all again she would only have two children. As I sat and watched, the thought of the programme going out to millions of people didn't make me feel as naked as the idea of the book had done. It seemed that I had managed to move on and by the end it looked as though it would be possible to get the closure I wanted if I just faced up to my past once and for all – which meant going to see Gloria and Dennis.

I had to do it for the sake of the children, and I had to do it for myself as well. Over the years I had always concentrated on getting myself as far as possible from the brutality and misery of my childhood, determined to work hard and be the best husband and father I could possibly be. I knew I'd done well and had a wonderful life now, but I still had a few more demons that lurked in my memory and my subconscious. Writing the book had been the only sort of therapy I had ever indulged in and it had stirred up too many memories and realizations for comfort. I now wanted to find some sort of closure to the whole business of that part of my life. I would only find that by going to face my parents.

As I thought about what I had to do next I had no idea how Gloria would react to me when I turned up on the doorstep, whether she would physically attack me for what I'd written in *The Kid* or whether she would pretend there was nothing wrong between us and never had been.

23. Dennis

My decision to go and see Dennis was taken as much out of curiosity than anything else. The last time I'd spoken to him was when
he had ended the conversation by telling me he loved me and I
hadn't known how to react to the one gesture I had been so desperate for as a child. His words had been coming back to me a great
deal since then and I felt I needed to go and see him in order to
work out how I felt about him and about the role he had played
in my childhood and in my life now.

I knew from Robert and the girls that he was poorly, but I had
no idea what to expect. I didn't know if he would be pleased to see
me or not. If I hadn't embarked on writing *The Kid* and unlocked
all the memories, I'm not sure I ever would have seen him again.

A few days after getting back from Argentina I drove up to his
flat in the morning, straight after dropping the children off at
school. I thought he was less likely to have taken a drink at that
time of day and I would be able to avoid all the emotional outpourings that came when his inhibitions were removed by alcohol. I
hadn't actually seen him face to face for over seven years and I knew
that during that time he had changed his lifestyle from visiting the
local pubs, as he had when I was a child, to becoming a virtual
recluse. I remembered those long days in the pubs, where he would
just sit, nursing a drink at the bar, exchanging the odd word or two
with a familiar face, while I sat in the corner, waiting for him to
decide it was time to go home, relieved to be out of the house and
away from Gloria. Now he didn't even have that much company
in his life.

Did he really love me? Or had that just been the drink talking? If he did mean it, how should I respond? I had a feeling that he might now need me more than I needed him. The time when I had really needed him to rescue me was as a child, but so many times he would turn into a raging bull, so full of anger and egged on by Gloria. After so many years of him inflicting horrific punishments on me out of all proportion to any crime I might have committed, part of me could see no reason why I should do anything to help him now. If I was to forgive him, then that would mean I was saying what he did was OK.

The man who had been a real father figure for me was Alan, my foster father in the few years before I was left to my own devices. I wasn't sure that I had room to let Dennis back into my life on a regular basis. I wasn't sure if I should feel any sort of responsibility to look after him if he needed it or not, or how he would react to Jackie and his grandchildren.

I knew that I lived such a different life from Dennis now and I wasn't sure he could be part of it or where he would fit in, especially with his drinking which could trigger his temper and drunken outpourings of self-pitying emotion. I could never let my children be subjected to that. So many terrible things had happened in that house when he was the adult and I was the child, it wasn't possible to just put them all to one side and say everything would be all right between us now. But was I being selfish to the children who might like to see their granddad? All they knew of the past was that Daddy's parents weren't nice to him. They didn't know the extent of how he had behaved towards me. To them he would just be an old man who might love them. He was, after all, my father, and now he was ill. Robert had told me he had suffered from three strokes and his arthritis was getting worse. It seemed likely to me that the drink was killing him. If only he could stop, I said to myself, but then I thought, what has he got to stop for?

I drove to the cream-coloured building in south London that housed his flat and I was surprised to find that I didn't feel that nervous, not like I knew I would feel when I finally got round to confronting Gloria. It was a ground-floor apartment with its own front door at the top of a short flight of steps. I knocked. He wasn't expecting me. I didn't call ahead in case he said he didn't want to see me. He opened the door wearing a white shirt and suit trousers, as if he was halfway through getting dressed for going to work in an office somewhere. His sleeves were rolled up and his arms looked sore and scabby. His hair was a bit greyer than I remembered, but he hadn't changed much apart from that; he was still the stocky man I always remembered.

'Hi,' I said, awkwardly.

'Oh, hello,' he replied, in his usual shy manner, standing back to let me into the clean but musty-smelling rooms. He didn't register any great surprise at seeing me.

The small flat comprised of a kitchen, a lounge and a bedroom. I could imagine how claustrophobic it must have seemed when Robert was staying there too, spending his nights on the sofa. It was no wonder they'd fallen out with one another. There were no family pictures anywhere but the walls were covered with pictures and posters of Elvis. Even the mirror had 'the King's' face printed on it.

Everything was stained yellow from the endless clouds of smoke emitted from Dennis's endlessly lit cigarettes. The air smelled as if it hadn't been changed for a long time and I didn't like having to breathe it. I thought of the years he had spent smoking away while he drank himself into his rages. His kitchen was sparse and it didn't look like there was much food there. Even though he was hobbling along as he had always done it was obvious that he was a lot weaker than I remembered. Every so often he would burst into a coughing fit, keeping his mouth closed so that his face turned bright red, just as it used to when I was a child. I didn't want to sit down, so I hovered uncomfortably, not sure if I was a welcome guest or a trespasser, unable to think of any topics of conversation that didn't sound forced and false.

'I heard you wrote a book,' he said at one moment and I nodded, but he didn't ask any more.

'How are you getting on?' I asked, feeling a heavy weight of depression descending on my chest.

He seemed such a sad figure, to have started life by being taken into care and then to have spent so many years drinking and smoking and trying in vain to think of some way to escape from the stress of his marriage and the endless children under his feet. In a way he had found an escape in this depressing little flat, but it seemed the horrors of being trapped with Gloria had been replaced with the horrors of his own company, with Elvis once again his only means of escape.

I couldn't imagine that he had any memories that he could look back on with fondness, no achievements that he could feel proud of, as he sat smoking listening to the King. It was as if he was simply existing, marking time until the drink finished him off. It all seemed such a terrible waste of a life.

I told him that the kids were growing up and going to school and he nodded, with his cigarette in the corner of his mouth, to show that he had taken in the information, but he didn't ask anything about them.

'Are you going to sit down then?' he enquired, with the hint of a mocking smile. I sat, even though I would have preferred to remain standing.

Once or twice, amongst the uncomfortable pauses, he tried to smile at me but it seemed as if living on his own, not going to the pub any more and having little interaction with others had made him even less able to communicate with his fellow man. I couldn't think of anything to say to ease the tension between us.

'Do you need any help?' I asked eventually and he shook his head.

In the uncomfortable silence I began to tell him what I was up to now. I told him I was writing more. I explained about film school, the inventions and everything else that I was trying to achieve. As I sat next to him I became excited about telling him what I was achieving, like I thought a son should proudly tell his father. I explained what my life was like with Jackie and the children and my arms were waving about as I continued to describe my passions. But then I stopped and looked at him. I just wanted a reaction from him. Deep down I really wanted to know if he did care; that would be a start, I thought, but his head just kept nodding in a lifeless way, the smoke curling upwards towards the stained ceiling. I tried to tell him about his grandchildren, but he didn't seem interested. Before I went into the flat I wasn't sure how he would fit into our lives and now I was there I still didn't know how I felt. He just didn't seem bothered.

I doubt if I was in there for more than twenty minutes. At one point I went to put my hand on his shoulder, but I thought better of it. I had a feeling that even a small physical gesture like that might unleash the most terrible flood of emotions which neither of us would be able to cope with. I knew I had been his favourite from little things he had said and done over the years, sometimes just the odd passing look in the middle of some family battle scene or other. I also knew that some of the stress between him and Gloria had been caused by their very different feelings for me. But if he had loved me, then he should have saved me. The fact that he just didn't seem interested now was very depressing. I was trying my hardest to communicate with him, but it was all in vain. We said our goodbyes, not touching each other, and Dennis closed the door as soon as I had gone down a few steps.

As I came away I felt really down and wondered whether I had done the right thing in writing about this fragile man who had tried to work hard but just hadn't been able to cope with all the pressures around him. Was it his fault if he just wasn't up to the job of having a family?

I didn't cry when I got back into the car, but I was lost in thought all the way home. I tried to think of the times when he would take me to the pub with him as a child. Dennis would be drinking at the bar and I would be sat in the corner on the old leather sofas, out of the way, with an orange squash in front of me, happy at the thought of being out of the house for a while, safely away from Gloria.

I didn't feel like doing much else that day, just sat around, trying to work out how I felt and, more importantly, how he felt. I came to the conclusion that I couldn't do anything for him beyond the occasional visit and support if he needed it, although I didn't think he would ever ask. It had seemed as if we were strangers to each other rather than father and son. I decided I would make a point of calling him now and then, but I doubt if he would ever call me again. I told Jackie later about my visit to Dennis and also told her that I was planning to go to see Gloria. She just nodded, to show me that she understood.

24. Gloria

I knew I had to go and see Gloria to make sure that she understood she could not be involved in the children's lives any more. The thought that she could still be hurting children after so many years horrified me and I had no faith that the Social Services would keep her away from them, since they didn't seem to know anything about our family history or seem able to communicate with one another. I didn't want there to even be a risk that she could get access to any of her grandchildren, even for a meeting.

The night after the television documentary was aired with Gloria appearing, albeit in silhouette, she had rung Wayne, saying how surprised she was by the number of neighbours from New Addington who had apparently known what was happening in the house. She must have wondered why they had never said anything to her at the time, not realizing just what a terrifying figure she had been around the estate and how everyone had tried to avoid having anything to do with her. She didn't seem particularly bothered by the accusations that the programme had made about the state the house was always in and about the way in which she beat and terrorized us. Several of the ex-neighbours had said how the house was filthy, the carpets always wet with urine, and one of them remembered watching one of the children peeing on the floor and no one bothering to clear it up.

I hadn't seen Gloria since she came to our wedding and in the film she still looked like a very big, powerful, domineering woman. I wasn't sure how much of that impression had been created by the camera angles and how much by my own memories of being a small child in her power. To me I guess she will always be a monster, no matter how frail she grows with age.

I'd known that I was going to have to confront her for some months, but I hadn't told anyone of my intention until I told Jackie, because as long as no one else knew, I could wait for the right time to go and face her.

I didn't want to do it on my own and so I decided I wanted to go with Wayne, her favourite son. I asked him to come with me. I wanted there to be someone else around while I talked to her, so that she knew it wasn't just me saying these things. I wanted someone to be a witness to what I was saying and to any response she might have, so she couldn't deny the conversation later. Wayne had been in touch with her over the years and still saw her occasionally. He had some of his stuff stored at her flat, which he wanted to collect so there was a reason for the visit, which would make it seem more natural.

I eventually told him that I wanted to go and see her.

'Why?' he asked.

'I just need to see her about something,' I replied vaguely.

The reason I didn't tell him was that I didn't want Gloria to have any prior warning as to why I was coming so that she would be ready with her arguments and demands. It wasn't that I didn't trust Wayne, it was just that if Gloria asked him what I wanted and he honestly didn't know then there would be no need for him to lie to her. He agreed to come. We made a date for a Wednesday and I said I would pick him up from work in the afternoon and we would drive straight to her flat.

As usual I lay awake the night before, thinking about what I was going to have to say and do the next day. I didn't feel as scared of her now because in my thoughts I was able to control her and put away my memories of what she had done to me for so many years. When I woke up the next morning, after having slept only fitfully

I felt deeply lethargic. I got up, but I couldn't put my mind to doing anything. I just went over and over in my mind what I was planning to say to her but none of it sounded quite right. In the end I had to admit to myself that I just didn't feel up to seeing her. It didn't feel right. I didn't want to stumble over my words when I saw her. I wanted to feel confident and strong and not be vindictive. I just felt it was important to make her realize the seriousness of what she was doing to her grandchildren. I rang Wayne and postponed our plans until the Friday.

When Friday came I still didn't feel that I was ready to do it. Fortunately Wayne rang and asked if we could put it off again, as he wanted to go out after work with his friends. I agreed readily and we decided to go up to see her on Sunday morning, which was going to be 29 February, a leap year day.

I was beginning to get annoyed with myself, because I knew I was putting off the inevitable and that if I just bit the bullet it would all be over within a few hours. It was like having something left on a 'things to do' list. The longer I put it off the more time I was wasting thinking about it. I knew I just needed to get it over and done with.

I woke up early on the Sunday morning, before anyone else got up, feeling ready to confront her. I didn't even bother to shower, just got dressed. The kids got up shortly afterwards and I gave them their breakfast, all the time feeling more and more confident about what I was planning to do. It was a sunny morning as I set off to pick up Wayne. The roads were empty and I was actually getting a buzz from the idea of going to see her at last and finally getting what I had to say off my chest.

Once we were in the car on our way into London Wayne phoned Gloria on her mobile to tell her we were coming up. I was now feeling eager to get the job done. We chatted as brothers usually do.

'The reason I'm going to see her is to tell her to leave children alone,' I confessed as we drove along. 'Because if she doesn't she's going to end up getting into serious trouble.'

I'd already told Wayne, after we'd met to film the documentary, about Gloria smacking her grandchildren, which had shocked him.

'Why didn't anyone tell me?' he asked.

'I suppose I thought you already knew,' I said.

'I never knew anything about it.'

'I guess she wouldn't do it while you were around.' We left it at that, both ashamed that we couldn't have done more to prevent it.

We parked outside her block of flats and I was quite surprised by how clean it was. I suppose I'd been expecting something more like our old house had been, with rubbish piled up everywhere. Wayne pressed the buzzer for her flat but there was no answer. He pressed again and nothing. My heart sank. Just as I'd got my courage up to confront her she'd chickened out and done a runner.

Wayne called her mobile phone again.

'It's OK,' he said as he hung up. 'She was just going to go to the paper shop but she's coming now.'

We walked back to the car to wait for her. A few minutes later she appeared round the corner. She had cheap, bleached blonde hair, almost white but stained with cigarette smoke. She was wearing a pair of trousers and a jumper, her bare feet pushed into her slippers despite the chill February air. She noticed us as we got out the car and we headed towards her, Wayne leading the way and me following on behind. As we walked towards her I realized she was still a big woman, that wasn't a trick of my memory. She was at least as tall as me, possibly taller, but apart from that she just looked like any other old lady. That idea shocked me. I'd expected her to be different in some way, still the ogre of my memory.

'All right?' was all she said by way of a greeting before she started talking about herself, just rattling on as we walked towards the flats together. She saw me, but didn't make any expression or gesture and just carried on as if I wasn't there. I didn't say anything. The last thing she had said to me was that she was going to kill herself and I had replied, 'Why don't you?'

Still talking, she opened the door to the block to let us into the hallway, which smelled strongly of disinfectant. That took me by surprise. I'd been expecting to be greeted by the same stale smells of neglect and dirt that I remembered from my childhood. One window had been broken, but otherwise there was no damage.

'That's where they meet sometimes.' She gestured to some chairs set out at the end of the hall. 'I don't go down that end. I don't get on with some of the others.'

She wasn't exactly communicating with us, more chatting on to cover what might have been an awkward silence. As she let us into her ground-floor flat she talked on about the doorbell and security systems, a steady stream of words that I wasn't really listening to as I gathered my thoughts about what I was going to say to her once we were inside the flat.

As she let us in through her front door I couldn't believe my eyes, or any of my other senses. Not only was it clean and tidy, there were even homely touches like a carpet on the floor, fresh fruit in a bowl on the coffee table and a frozen turkey dinner defrosting on the side in the kitchen. The little kitchen table was laid up with cutlery in preparation for her meal. The place bore no resemblance to the hellhole we'd been forced to live in as children. Here everything was orderly and controlled and civilized. She was still babbling on, showing us the cord that she could pull on in an emergency and someone would come to her assistance if she ever got into trouble. As she talked my eyes were still looking around in wonder. I noticed a large doll standing on the other side of the room beside the sideboard. Its arms were pulled up and its hands were covering its eyes, which seemed appropriate. There was none of the dirty, stale smell that I had expected and which would have reminded me of childhood. Without children, it seemed, she could cope with life. I remembered how, in the documentary, she had said that if she could change anything in her life it would have been the number of children she had, that she would have stopped at two and not six. My sisters, not surprisingly, were very hurt by the comment, but it did suggest that Gloria realized her own limitations and knew why things had gone so badly wrong. She liked cute little things, like the doll or the teddies that surrounded the sideboard, and real things like babies and puppies, just like a child would. But as soon as they got under her feet she would be unable to cope and would turn on them in a rage so fierce that it was hard to comprehend unless you'd actually seen it. It was like asking a child to look after a family when all it wanted was a teddy bear to play with or a baby for a couple of hours a day when it was joyful and undemanding. But whether it was babies or puppies, anything that spent time with her always ended up cringing in the corners of a room, terrified of receiving another beating. Child or animal, it made no difference to her.

As my eyes continued to scan the lounge I noticed that there were five picture frames hanging on the wall, four of which were photos that Jackie had sent her of our wedding. The first was of Jackie and me in our wedding outfits, with Gloria standing next to us in the clothes we had bought for her. The next was of me, Wayne and Jackie, the next of Jackie and me cutting the cake and then a group photo. In the final frame was a collage of different pictures of her grandchildren, including our daughter. I was amazed as I looked around, trying to take it all in as she waffled on.

In the middle of the room on top of a coffee table stood a bowl of fresh fruit and next to it was a little wicker basket, lined with tin foil to keep it clean. Inside were a few pick-and-mix sweets.

'I bet these were full the other day,' I said, completely unable to think of anything else to say.

'Yeah. Have one if you want,' she said, still keeping her eyes away from me.

Wayne disappeared off to get his stuff from a cupboard somewhere and Gloria rolled herself a cigarette while I stayed standing. She did it with a deftness born of long experience. When the operation was complete she stood up and went to the back door, opening it to let the smoke out. Then she sat back down and lit up, pulling a clean ashtray within reach. I couldn't believe my eyes. Never in my life could I remember her opening a door or a window to allow fresh air into our house. There had never been any respite from the smells and the filth when I lived with her.

The fresh cold air drifted into the tidy little flat, carrying the smoke away and she continued talking as if she had done nothing unusual, as if this was how she had always behaved. I couldn't believe I was talking to the same woman who had made my life and everyone else's in the family such hell. Could this seemingly normal old lady really have been the monster of my memory? Wayne had once told me that she was different from how we remembered, but I hadn't been able to believe him.

Then it occurred to me that she could only live like this without the pressure of children. If she got any sort of access to her grandchildren she would instantly revert to her former self, as she must have done on the night that she had attacked my sister's children. With these thoughts I suddenly remembered why I was there and felt my resolve returning.

'I've got to tell you something,' I said. She still didn't look at me. 'You have to leave children alone. You can't go anywhere near them. Do you understand?'

She nodded. She didn't protest or argue or question what I was saying or look as if she didn't know what I was talking about. I looked at her, but she couldn't look back. She just nodded. She knew exactly what I was talking about. Her eyes were staring at the floor as she took another long slow drag of her roll-up.

The next moment she stood up and I moved out of her way as she continued talking as if I'd said nothing. Wayne came back into the room asking for a bin bag to put his things in. She got him a bag and he continued to pack.

'Can you sit down,' I said, unsure if she had taken in what I was saying to her, 'because you really have to understand what I'm saying to you.' My voice sounded anxious but controlled.

She had already finished her cigarette by this time and was rolling herself another one as she sat down.

'Do you understand what I'm telling you? If you do not leave children alone you are going to get into serious, serious trouble. Do you understand?'

She nodded again.

'Do you know what I would do, if I was you?' I went on. 'I would enjoy the rest of your life without children. I wouldn't bother to even try to go near your grandchildren, especially the ones who have been taken into care. We both know what goes on. You have to leave them alone. Do you understand?'

'Yes,' she said, her voice subdued, as if she was a child being told off.

As she sat there with me standing over her I began to wonder if I was being a bully, but the thought quickly went out of my mind when the memories of what she had done to her grandchildren returned. I was just saying it as it was. I really wanted to drive home how serious the situation had become. Wayne heard me and glanced at Gloria. I saw her look at him as he continued to pack his things. Now I'd said what I'd come there for I wanted to go as quickly as possible. Wayne finished packing and we went to leave.

In the hall I repeated my message one more time.

'Do you understand, you have to leave children alone?'

She nodded again, still not making any eye contact.

'I hope for your sake you do, because I am deadly serious.'

She came outside with us, wanting to go to the newsagent as she had intended when we arrived. She was talking again and her voice had become loud, just like I remembered it, perhaps because I had made her nervous. She walked off towards the shop without a goodbye or even a backward glance. As she disappeared around the corner I looked up at the bright winter sun and smiled with relief.

'Fuck me,' I said as we made our way back to the car.

'I told you,' Wayne said. 'It's not the same now.'

'So why does she still do this stuff to the kids?'

He shrugged. 'I don't know. Had I known I would have done something about it.'

As I drove home I found myself looking at people walking past; normal-looking old ladies like Gloria, and tired-looking old men like Dennis, and I wondered what went on behind their closed doors. How did they cope with the pressures of life? Were they violent and unable to control their tempers? How many of them, like Gloria, had been beaten as children and so knew no better than to do it to their own families? If there are no records of what she did, how many others are there who the Social Services know nothing about, who go unchecked until it's too late and more damage is done?

I felt relieved that I had finally managed to face her. There was no love between us, but I had known that before I even got there. I'd never treated her like a mother and she'd never treated me like a son. I'd realized that she wanted to get back into our lives, but now that she knew I could remember everything she did to me through those long years, there was no way we could be anything to each other except strangers, only knowing each other through what we read. Wayne and I made little conversation as I took him home, both of us deep in thoughts that we didn't want to share with each other. After dropping Wayne off I felt a real weight lift off my shoulders. I became excited about my life once again because I knew how to deal with my past at last. I had finally put it all behind me. As I walked into the house I gave my children a huge hug and shot Jackie a loving smile.

25. The Next Move

Shortly after going to see Gloria and Dennis I finally met Carol face to face and the social worker now in charge of some of the children. We discussed my sister's children and she told me how they were coming on in leaps and bounds now that they were settled. I said I thought they had been dealt with in a disgusting manner and the social worker agreed, but then went to great lengths to explain that now they were in the system they were finally protected. Three of them were being suggested for adoption and the two older ones for long-term fostering.

Her words made me think hard about what had happened over the past eighteen months or so. It seems to me from my own experience, the experience of my nephews and nieces and from the letters I receive, that the more vulnerable a person is, whether it be a child, a disabled person or an old-age pensioner, the harder it is to have their abusers convicted of their crimes.

The most potentially vulnerable members of our society, therefore, are the least protected. It's easy to blame Social Services or others in authority when things go wrong, but in most cases they are good people doing their best. Despite this I believe there are still a number of ways in which we can improve the situation for the future. Firstly, Social Services must have our whole-hearted support in order for them to recruit more dedicated staff, and the government must provide sufficient funds for this. We must all stop being so negative about the service. Social workers who are out in the field dealing with dysfunctional families need to be given every possible bit of help and support and not be stifled by bureaucracy.

Secondly, those who work in Social Services need to take total responsibility for their actions. At the moment when anything does go wrong all they seem to do is squabble over whose fault it was and moan about the pressures of the job.

In the end every case comes down to being the responsibility of one individual. These individuals need to find satisfaction from their jobs and feel fulfilled by them if they are going to be effective, just like in any other line of work. Part of that satisfaction should come from accepting the consequences of their actions. The consequences of people doing a bad job, when vulnerable children are at risk, are too serious to contemplate.

Thirdly, the spread of information seems at best clumsy and uncontrolled, and at worst dangerous. The new children's bill seems to bring different agencies and professionals together to share information, which is a good development and hopefully will be an ongoing process, with the information being continuously updated.

Fourthly, but most importantly, we need to make parents and guardians as responsible for their actions as we do teachers, doctors, nurses, the police, Social Services and other bodies. We put so much pressure on all these agencies to act responsibly towards our children, where the first port of call should be those who have the most access to them, that is the parents and guardians.

In my experience many of the abusers in our society genuinely believe they are doing nothing wrong. Others are aware of their wrongdoing but believe they can get away with it because their victim is too scared or unempowered to report them.

It must be made easier for the abused to report their problem and to feel confident that if they do so there will be someone there to help them. There must be a system whereby it is known by everyone that if you abuse vulnerable people you will be punished. For example, if a man walks into a pub and breaks a bottle over another man's head, he knows the likely consequences are that he will be arrested and charged. If a parent hits a child over the head with a saucepan in a fit of temper, the chances are they have no such expectation of being punished.

As a nation we have to decide what punishment we think that sort of parental abuse should receive, but we are all still very unclear about that unless someone is murdered. Even in child-murder cases a lot of the perpetrators seem to get away with their crimes. Once we have decided what the punishment should be we must inform everyone, for example with advertising campaigns, just as we advertise the consequences of drink-driving at Christmas time. It is never a simple matter because there are so many possible mitigating circumstances, so many factors to be taken into consideration and argued about, but all the time we are debating and arguing children continue to be attacked. Potential abusers must know what the minimum punishment would be for systematically abusing a child.

But the responsibility doesn't end with the authorities. It belongs to all of us. So what can we all do as individuals to help all the children whose childhoods go so terribly wrong? The answer seems to be that we all have to try a little bit harder to help those who need it, be more vigilant and not so willing to turn a blind eye, whether the children are our relatives, our neighbours, our friends or our pupils.

We also need to educate our children as to what it means to be a parent. They must be encouraged to create lives for themselves before they go on to produce families of their own, and to be very sure they can cope before they set out on the difficult path of parenthood. Everyone needs to be made fully aware of the responsibility and pressures involved in bringing up children so that they can decide whether they are up to it. All of us probably know of someone with small children who could do with a little help. We must never be shy of offering it.

Also, more good people need to be encouraged to provide foster care, and more people need to be encouraged to adopt children over the age of three. There is always a shortage of safe homes. If you are interested, pick up the phone or go on to the Internet and research all the fostering and adoption agencies. I know now's not the right time for Jackie and me to foster, but one day I hope we will.

None of these measures is going to be enough on its own and I fear there will always be children who fall through the net, like I did for so many years. But the more each one of us does, the less likely it is to happen to a child we know. We all have to be a little bit more determined to help in a society that mainly helps itself.

As the spring approaches Mistico is now fit and ready to play and I am looking forward to the forthcoming polo season. I have completed my film script and am currently having the storyboards drawn out shot by shot, bringing my dream ever closer. After that has happened I plan to find an agent who will put me in touch with producers and financiers to get my movie funded. It won't be easy, I understand that, but I am as determined as ever and, as always, I'll be knocking on that door until it eventually opens and I can continue to follow my dream.

I have started work on my first novel and am continuing to take my inventions forward, constructing models and ensuring they work, and I am finally going through the process of patenting them. I have set up a charity called the Sunflower Children's Trust which raises money and awareness for smaller, less well-known children's charities and organizations, especially focusing on the inner cities and our most deprived areas.

As you know my family mean everything to me and we all work hard to have a good life together. I look forward to showing them what I can achieve and to giving them security through my efforts. As the children grow up and start to become independent they will make mistakes as we all do, but Jackie and I will always be there to guide them and comfort them and support them, which is the best any parent can ever do.

I've always wanted to prove what I can do; now I have the chance and I'm grabbing it with both hands. Because I no longer want to look back I won't be writing any more about my childhood or the Lewis family.

I have thought a great deal about why so many people want to read a story like mine and I think there may be two reasons. One must be that they have endured some sort of similar experience, or at least know of someone else who has, and the other must be that they are trying to find out what happens in a world that they can't imagine, because their childhoods were as happy as they should have been.

I think it is very encouraging that people want to know what happens in dysfunctional families like the Lewises because it means they are more likely to spot the danger signals when they see them in other families, and to believe children when they say they are being mistreated. If I am right in thinking that many others are reading it because they have had similar experiences, then it seems that we still have a very long way to go as a society before we can truly say that we are civilized in the way we treat our children.

When I reach my twilight years I want to be able to look back and say, 'Well, the start wasn't all that good, but I sure as hell made up for it with the rest.'

I still want the farm I was dreaming of at the end of writing *The Kid*, and I still want to travel America, but instead of trying to achieve my dreams a hundred different ways at once, I am now more focused. I dream of a big open room with its own character and life, filled with the smell of a large open fireplace, where I can spend the days with my creations. The walls will be blank so that I can go back to writing on them, in my own world with my family near me. It will take a lifetime to cover those walls, but they will end up filled with my life.

Finally I must thank all of you for your support; the people working in the media, the bookshops and the supermarkets who drew *The Kid* to everyone's attention and you, the readers, who took the time to buy and read it. It was you and *The Kid* that helped me get on my feet and live my dreams. From the bottom of my heart I thank you all.

K.

Acknowledgements

The film edition of this book would never have been possible without the commitment and dedication of a few people whom I will always be indebted to.

Firstly, Stephen May and Peter Horton, whose unwavering support for me and the project, even in the darkest hours, I will never forget.

To Ed Atkinson, Wendy Horton, Holly Bellingham, Simon Turner, Jenny and Guy Rowcliffe; your belief in me and the project has really made a difference to this film. Also to Debbie May for first reading the books and then putting them in front of Stephen.

Finally, the film would never have been made without the vision and dedication of Nick Moran, Judith Hunt, the cast and crew – many of you believed in the project from the moment you read the script. I hope the film has made you proud.

To all of the above, you have made a difference to my family and me for which I will be for ever grateful.

Thank you x